Economic Globalization and Ecological Localization: Socio-legal Perspectives

T0369694

Edited by

Robert Lee and Elen Stokes

Library of Congress Cataloging-in-Publication Data
Economic globalization and ecological localization : socio-legal perspectives /
edited by Robert Lee and Elen Stokes.
     p. cm.
  ISBN 978-1-4051-9293-4
1. Environmental law. 2. Law and globalization. I. Lee, R. G. (Robert Gregory), 1952–.
II. Stokes, Elen.
  K3585.E293 2009
337–dc22   2009000266

A catalogue record for this title is available from the British Library.

Set in the United Kingdom by Godiva Publishing Services Ltd
Printed in Singapore by Fabulous Printers Pte Ltd

Contents

JOURNAL OF LAW AND SOCIETY
VOLUME 36, NUMBER 1, MARCH 2009
ISSN: 0263-323X, pp. 1–10

Environmental Governance:
Reconnecting the Global and Local

ROBERT LEE* AND ELEN STOKES**

GLOBALIZATION: THE IMPORTANCE OF CONTEXT

This volume, reflecting, as it does, on connections between global activity
and local effects, is produced in late 2008 and is set amidst turmoil in global
financial markets. As if further evidence were needed, recent months have
served as a reminder that, notwithstanding its promises, economic integration may come at a price, represented in the present climate by home
repossessions, loss of deposits or business failures. Although the global
integration of markets has allowed many economies to grow far more rapidly
that they would otherwise have done, leading indirectly to benefits such as
increased life expectancy, improved standards of living, and greater access to
foreign aid,[1] those benefits have not been costless nor are they evenly
distributed. In spite of hopes that globalization would promote growth and
stability, and eradicate poverty, there are many instances in which globalization can create *dis*benefits. As Joseph Stiglitz puts it, as well as generating
unprecedented prosperity, global market economies have also brought about
unprecedented poverty.[2] This, he argues, constitutes one of globalization's
many 'broken promises'.[3]

Simultaneously, globalization has positive and negative facets, and as
such, it may be characterized as both a highly desirable process,[4] and an

* ESRC Centre for Business Relationships, Accountability, Sustainability and
Society (BRASS), Cardiff University, 55 Park Place, Cardiff CF10 3AT, Wales.
LeeRG@Cardiff.ac.uk
** Cardiff Law School, Cardiff University, Law Building, Museum Avenue,
Cardiff CF10 3AX, Wales
StokesER@cardiff.ac.uk

1 J. Stiglitz, *Globalization and its Discontents* (2002) 4–5.
2 id., p. 6.
3 id., ch. 2.
4 See, generally, M. Wolf, *Why Globalization Works* (2005); J. Bhagwati, *In Defense of
Globalization* (2007).

1

inherently destructive force.[5] In this respect, there is little that can be described as *universal* about globalization. Whilst it may give rise to benefits in some contexts, it inevitably leads to losses in others. For instance, not only is globalization seen as a vehicle for promoting and protecting various rights, values, and resources internationally, but it is also held responsible for heightened states of conflict, inequality, and resource depletion. Globalization is not, therefore, a one-sided phenomenon.[6] Rather, it manifests in a range of processes and experiences with multiple (often contradictory) consequences.[7]

These so-called paradoxes of globalization are well recognized.[8] The huge literature on globalization explores its emergence, nature, impact, and fate. Although definitions of globalization vary, most take the economy as their starting point, and in so doing distinguish between modern (liberal) and postmodern (neo-liberal or 'globalized') conditions. Globalization has been described, for instance, as 'a phenomenon by which economic agents in any given part of the world are much more affected by events elsewhere in the world'.[9] This shift to global economies is often depicted by comparing the new and the earlier order. In contrast with industrial economies, in which the function of people was to provide labour in a production-oriented model, globalization has generated new world economies in which people are first and foremost consumers in an era of consumption and their choices are collectivized under the dominance of markets. Some notorious features of this market-led model include, for example, worldwide sourcing; trade liberalization, where national economies are open to trade; and flexible systems of production, in which transportation costs are so low that goods can be produced in peripheral markets and exported to core ones.[10] Transnational corporations are key players in each of these instances, subverting those companies operating in a single nation as cogs in the machine of international economic activity. Robert Reich describes this as 'the end of the national champion'.[11]

The fact that globalization redefines economic structures and behaviours is indisputable. It also, however, impacts upon political and social (including

---

5 Stiglitz, op. cit., n. 1.
6 See, generally, Z. Bauman, *Globalization: The Human Consequences* (1998).
7 F. Snyder 'Governing Economic Globalization: Global Legal Pluralism and European Law' (1999) 5 *European Law J.* 334–74, at 335; B. De Sousa Santos, *Toward a New Legal Common Sense: Law, Globalization, and Emancipation* (2002) 177.
8 J. Purdy, 'A World of Passions: How to Think About Globalization Now' (2004) 11 *Indiana J. of Global Legal Studies* 1–49, at 34.
9 A.O. Krueger, 'Trading Phobias: Governments, NGOs and the Multilateral System', John Bonython Lecture, 10 October 2000, available at <http://www.cis.org.au/events/jbl/anne_krueger.html>.
10 De Sousa Santos, op. cit., n. 7, p. 167.
11 R.B. Reich, *The Work of Nations: Preparing Ourselves for 21st Century Capitalism* (1992) ch. 11.

2

legal) configurations, and can be understood much more broadly as the global spread of market-oriented policies.[12] One of the most documented transformations associated with globalism in these contexts is the apparent hollowing out, or retreat, of the nation state.[13] Susan Strange, for instance, argues that '[w]hereas states were once the masters of markets, now it is the markets which, on many crucial issues, are the masters over the governments of states'.[14] Although some scholars have argued that the degree of state powerlessness is often overstated,[15] there are certainly instances in which the political authority of the state is becoming less significant. In respect of regulation, for example, there has been a notable shift from state-oriented to 'decentred' techniques.[16] Marking this transition, we have seen a general reduction in the number of command-and-control regulatory provisions, implemented through the state and enforced using sanctions, and the emergence of techniques which rely increasingly on non-governmental actors in their formulation and operation (Lee and Marsden).[17] This latest trend, resulting in what are described as hybrid forms of regulation, reflects notions of 'new' or 'multi-level' governance which recognize that governance functions may be exercised by those other than the state. Unlike classic command-and-control arrangements, hybrid measures are based on negotiated agreements (Gunningham) between the state and parties subject to regulation.[18] As a result of this blending of public and private spheres, the state can no longer be said to have a monopoly on regulatory intervention.

However, the impact of globalization on the nation state is not uniform,[19] and arguments that the private sector simply replaces governments as the dominant force in political transactions are misleading. As Robert Holton notes, the capacity of nation states to continue to regulate cross-border transactions will depend on a host of factors, including their relative wealth. In contrast with economically successful countries (such as the G7) who wield considerable power over transnational regulatory organizations, poorer nations are less likely to be represented in these structures (Heyvaert) and

12 B. Lindsey, *Against the Dead Hand: The Uncertain Struggle for Global Capitalism* (2002) 275.
13 Bauman, op. cit., n. 6, p. 57.
14 S. Strange, *The Retreat of the State: The Diffusion of Power in the World Economy* (1996) 4.
15 See, for instance, L. Weiss, *The Myth of the Powerless State: Governing in the Global Era* (1998); J. McLean, 'Government to State: Globalization, Regulation, and Government as Legal Persons' (2003) 10 *Indiana J. of Global Legal Studies* 173; Wolf, op. cit., n. 4, pp. 221–6.
16 J. Black, 'Critical Reflections on Regulation' (2002) 27 *Aus. J. of Legal Philosophy* 1, at 2.
17 One major purpose of this opening paper is to introduce the essays elsewhere in this volume; we cite these in the manner above for ease of reference.
18 B. Morgan and K. Yeung *An Introduction to Law and Regulation: Text and Materials* (2007) 109–12.
19 R.J. Holton *Globalization and the Nation-State* (1998) ch. 4, particularly pp. 81–3.

3

less able to pursue their interests in inter-state bargaining.[20] Although the distinction between 'rich' and 'poor' is itself too crude, it suggests that the 'hollowing out' of political, or indeed regulatory, authority may operate more profoundly in poorer states. Variations in the residual role of nation states may also be contingent on whether they are home bases or hosts to transnational corporations.[21]

For nation states in which transnational corporations are *domiciled*, this process of 'hollowing out' will be more difficult to discern (Heyvaert). Such states are likely to retain a considerable degree of political authority because transnational corporations are so dependent on the resources they provide. Holton explains that in these situations 'governments hold some cards, especially if they can deliver high levels of political stability, as well as infrastructure and fiscal support'.[22] By contrast, the hollowing out of the state is more likely to arise in *host* countries to transnational corporations, where corporations are less dependent on the resources they acquire within the national territory (such as cheap labour, which can readily be sourced elsewhere). This disconnect between the exploitation of resources in host countries and repatriation of capital to home countries imposes externalities on the former, which may be difficult to internalize to transnational corporations who are almost unrestrained in their capacity to withdraw from one host nation and migrate to another. In these instances, the state-market balance may well be tipped in favour of the market, resulting in transnational corporations having greater political sway than conventional state bodies.

DESTINATIONS FOR DECENTRED POWER

Where this hollowing out can be seen to occur, the question is to whom is power previously enjoyed by nation states transferred? Perhaps the most obvious, and most commonly alluded to, destination for this decentred power is the private sphere. Transnational corporations now rank alongside nation states in terms of economic power[23] and are increasingly capable of avoiding state attention as the object of regulation, becoming partners in governance enterprises that may serve their economic ends (Lee and Marsden, Gunningham, Heyvaert).

Alongside this there is an obvious shift of power away from nation state to global or regional institutions in a reallocation within another public sphere, including here the European Union (Heyvaert) or multilateral institutions

---

20 id., at p. 82.
21 id.
22 id., at p. 100.
23 J. Elias and R. Lee, 'Ecological Modernisation and Environmental Regulation: Corporate Compliance and Accountability' in *Global Governance and the Quest for Justice: Corporations and Corporate Governance*, ed. S. MacLeod (2006).

4

such as the World Trade Organization (Reid and Steele), the World Bank, or the International Monetary Fund. Such shifts might generate a rift between those subject to institutional rule making and the rule makers (Heyvaert, Lee and Marsden). Remoteness and lack of transparency are not infrequent criticisms of such institutions and their democratic mandate is at best vicarious upon the membership of those states that are parties to the global governance framework. The requirement to rebalance and reconnect such institutions with those whose welfare is often said to be the very purpose of the institutional effort is one of the greatest challenges of the sustainability agenda (Reid and Steele, Ross, Stallworthy).

Alongside these distinct public and private spheres, there may also be a 'moral sphere' in which power formerly exerted by the state is reclaimed by civil society. This argument is compellingly made here (by Gunningham) and by Boaventura de Sousa Santos, who argues that, in apparent contradiction to global trends, 'new regional, national and local identities are emerging that are built around a new prominence of *rights to roots*'.[24] Although the effects of globalization, such as the elimination of national borders and integration of markets, are 'universal' in the sense that they seek to promote inter-state consistency, they simultaneously lead to increased particularity and local diversity.[25] As Hilson demonstrates in this volume, globalization must, therefore, be understood as having both global and local dimensions: 'the global is multi-scalar: it does not take place only at the self-evident global scale, but also at the national and sub-national scales'.[26]

Increasing recognition of these local impacts (Bell and Etherington, Stallworthy), and the potential role of civil society to pursue local interests, may in part be because globalization is accompanied by increasing inequalities and vulnerabilities as the gap between rich and poor widens; the richest 20 per cent possess 86 per cent of the world's GDP and the poorest 20 per cent are left with just 1 per cent.[27] While neo-liberals would argue that this is caused by insufficient market liberalization, critics of economic globalization blame either the pace or the very enterprise of global capitalism. The green movement, in particular, is well represented in the latter category of critics, calling for a rebalancing of global institutional structures by resort to alternative governance models based upon ecological localization and environmental justice.[28]

---

24 De Sousa Santos, op. cit., n. 7, at p. 177.
25 B. De Sousa Santos, 'Globalizations' (2006) 23 *Theory, Culture & Society* 393–9, at 393; for an extended version of his thesis, and for more detailed discussion, see De Sousa Santos, op. cit. n. 7, especially pp. 178–82.
26 S. Sassen, 'The Participation of States and Citizens in Global Governance' (2003) *Indiana J. of Global Legal Studies* 5.
27 A. Amin, 'Regulating Economic Globalization' (2004) 29 *Trans. of the Institute of Brit. Geographers* 217–33, at 233.
28 C. Hines, *Localization: A Global Manifesto* (2000).

5

The origins of such initiatives may lie in attempts to combat global environmental problems such as ozone depletion, biodiversity loss, marine pollution, hazardous waste disposal, and climate change (Bell and Etherington, Ross, Stallworthy). Of late, however, the focus has shifted to wider issues of sustainability, with certain issues at the heart of international economic law such as trade liberalization, privatization, foreign direct investment, and the exploitation of intellectual property rights increasingly held up to scrutiny. As a counterweight to these forces (and their ostensibly universalizing effects), localization, with an emphasis on prioritizing local participation, knowledge, and desires, is gaining ground within political structures – both formally through devolved structures (Reid and Steele, Ross) and (to a lesser extent) through reflexive forms of community action (Hilson, Gunningham). It is a curiosity that the emergence of a pressing global environmental programme has created what Marybeth Long Martello and Sheila Jasanoff have described as the 'rediscovery of the local'.[29] This juxtaposition of the global and the local forms the central theme in this special issue.

GLOBALS AND LOCALS

Our attention in this special issue turns to the interrelationship between the 'global' and the 'local' in debates surrounding issues of sustainability, and its implications in law. Along this global-local axis, it seeks to examine not only the capacity of global forces to defeat local interests in the response to territorially confined (local) threats (Stallworthy), but also the extent to which solutions to global environmental problems may depend on local action (Gunningham, Ross, Bell and Etherington, Hilson). It explores the impact of globalization on legal structures (Heyvaert, Gunningham, Lee and Marsden) and their ability to accommodate local concerns (Reid and Steele, Stallworthy), and considers whether globalization, and the elimination of national borders, actually offers an opportunity to reassert the power of local and regional governance (Ross). Although the global-local nexus has long provided a springboard for academic inquiry into globalization, comparatively less attention has been paid to the role of law in this framework. Part of the task of this special issue, therefore, is to consider the extent to which the law upholds, challenges, or has the capacity to challenge global-local relationships as they are currently defined.

To begin to illustrate its repercussions from both global and local perspectives (and whilst recognizing the potential for considerable variation

---

29 M.L. Martello and S. Jasanoff, 'Introduction: Globalization and Environmental Governance' in *Earthly Politics: Local and Global in Environmental Governance*, eds. S. Jasanoff and M.L. Martello (2004) 1–29, at 4.

6

between these two points), we can think about globalization in terms of three different faculties: mobility, visibility, and audibility. First, global forces may in some instances be characterized as more *mobile* than local. Zygmunt Bauman, for example, argues that the phrase 'flexible labour' has different connotations, depending on one's positioning on the global-local scale and the supply-demand bargain. Global players (such as transnational corporations), who demand flexible labour, are virtually free to 'move wherever greener pastures beckon'.[30] Since they exist independently of any fixed territory, they are free to disregard all considerations of 'place' and except those relating to the economic advantages to be gained from certain locations.[31] This freedom contrasts with the rigidity of conditions imposed on those supplying 'flexible' labour. Unlike the global players in this transaction, local workers have no freedom to choose whether to accept or refuse to provide labour:

> What looks . . . like flexibility on the demand side . . . rebounds on all those cast on the supply side as hard, cruel, impregnable and unassailable fate: jobs come and go, they vanish as soon as they appeared, they are cut in pieces and withdrawn without notice while the rules of the hiring/firing game change without warning.[32]

The substantial freedom enjoyed by the global elite[33] can be attributed to the fact that, for them, globalization removes the constraining qualities of time and space. One consequence of this 'time-space compression'[34] is that distances begin to matter less. Anthony Giddens captures this effect in his definition of globalization, which he describes as 'the intensification of worldwide social relations which link distant localities in such a way that local happenings are shaped by events occurring many miles away'.[35] From a local perspective, however, space may retain its restrictive nature, where those who are locally tied are essentially 'prisoners in their local time-space'[36] since they are 'barred from moving and thus bound passively to whatever change may be visited on the locality they are tied to'.[37] Again we see these features of mobility demonstrated in the essays here which suggest that, while global forces are often detached from local impacts (Bell and Etherington, Heyvaert, Lee and Marsden), the mobility and diffusion of the global leaves those less mobile trapped and deserted (Stallworthy) and looking to reassert a sense of place (Gunningham, Hilson).

---

30 Bauman, op. cit., n. 6, at pp. 104–5.
31 id., p. 105. Also on the point of mobility, but from a different perspective, see J. Bhagwati, 'Why the Critics of Globalization are Mistaken' (2007) 155 *De Economist* 1–21, at 10.
32 id.
33 Bauman, op. cit., n. 6.
34 De Sousa Santos, op. cit., n. 7, at p. 179.
35 A. Giddens, *The Consequences of Modernity* (1990) 64.
36 De Sousa Santos, op. cit., n. 7, at p. 179.
37 Bauman, op. cit. n. 6, at p. 88.

The issue of mobility can also be seen to emerge from the notion of 'rules globalization', which describes a process by which rules originating in one jurisdiction are transplanted into others. This is a major theme of Heyvaert's paper and Lee and Marsden also point in their 'third phase of regulation' to the relocation of authority in international processes of governance. These are shifts that then entail responses as either mechanisms are developed to rebalance the interests and knowledge of the local or people seek to claim rights purportedly part of the global compact (Gunningham and Hilson respectively).

Secondly, global interests may be more or less *visible* than their local counterparts. Global interests can be described as more visible where they have greater formal presence in institutional spaces. In epistemological spaces, for instance, a higher premium is placed on scientific discourse and expertise than local or 'situated' knowledges, politics, and values.[38] Much has been written about the seeming 'universalism' of scientific knowledge; indeed, the very notion of 'the scientific community' suggests an ability to reach beyond national borders.[39] Similar contentions can be made in respect of legal spaces, in which nation state regulation is increasingly influenced by transnational factors (Heyvaert, Lee and Marsden, Ross, Stallworthy).

There are also times and locations in which these global forces engineer invisibility. Much of the work in this volume concerns connecting social and environmental conditions to influences that are difficult to track or even barely observable. Climate change provides but one instance of the external effects of economic integration of the type explored here by Bell and Etherington, where, without the sorts of methodology which they present, responsibility may go without attribution. Even where global forces are less visible (even invisible), they may continue to exert considerable influence over the political arena. Georg Henrik von Wright describes this trait as the 'anonymous forces'[40] of globalization, which resonates with Bell and Etherington's notions of an unseen hand of globalization and Hilson's depiction of protestors reframing global issues to make them more locally visible.

Thirdly, even where ostensibly there are spaces in which local interests can be served, it may transpire that those interests are less *audible* than interests of the 'global elite'. As Jasanoff and Martello note, '[f]or local perspectives to prove effective in global contexts, more is needed than a formal entry ticket for local activists'.[41] Institutional visibility alone is unlikely to guarantee that local values are taken into account in political and legal decision-making. Thus, in addition to formal (sometimes superficial)

---

38 S. Jasanoff and M.L. Martello 'Conclusion: Knowledge and Governance' in Jasanoff and Martello, op. cit., n. 29, pp. at p. 338.
39 De Sousa Santos, op. cit., n. 7, at p. 396.
40 G.H. Von Wright 'The Crisis of Social Science and the Withering Away of the Nation State' (1997) 1 *Associations* 49–52.
41 Jasanoff and Martello, op. cit. n. 29, at p. 340.

spaces, participatory or deliberative mechanisms are required to ensure that local interests are effectively represented in these processes (Reid and Steele).

Roland Robertson's concept of glocalization seeks to capture this.[42] Robertson uses the term 'glocalization' to challenge, among other things, the depiction of globalization as a chiefly homogenizing process and of localization as a particularizing process. First, he argues that often what is deemed to be local is in fact merely a perception of local through a more global lens. In this respect, the global and local cannot be conceived of as exclusive concepts. Secondly, Robertson contends that global expressions of locality should not be interpreted as evidence that all forms of locality are homogenous. He warns that 'we should be careful not to equate the communicative and interactional connecting of such cultures . . . with the notion of homogenization of all cultures'.[43] We may interpret glocalization in the additional sense of recasting local interests to give them a more discernible global identity (Reid and Steele, Hilson).

CONCLUSION

This interpretation of 'glocalization' captures the essence of this special edition. Notwithstanding the fact that the essays in this collection cover a diverse range of issues, and each shows the global-local dynamic in different lights, perhaps the one theme that links them all is *disconnection and reconnection*. The lack of connection between global economic markets and more locally-based concerns centring on issues of social, environmental, and indeed economic sustainability is a theme that transcends every essay in this volume. The concerns that it generates centre on a number of sub-themes. As one might imagine in a volume written by lawyers, these involve matters of legal mechanisms by which some degree of accountability can be written into global frameworks. Similarly, there is a focus on process and, in particular, on rights and opportunities to engage with and participate in the shape of global economic forces to promote ecological and social interests. There is also an emphasis on the type of values that might inform this process, and many of the papers call for transparency, respect for local and lay knowledge, democratic engagement, deliberation, and the building of consensus.

Sustainability and social responsibility have become easy to espouse – in part because of the amorphous nature of these concepts[44] which, as Ross

---

42 Turn of phrase taken from R. Robertson 'Glocalization: Time-Space and Homogeneity-Heterogeneity' in *Global Modernities*, eds. M. Featherstone, S. Lash, and R. Robertson (1995) ch. 2, especially pp. 28–32.
43 id. p. 31.
44 P. Gale and S.M. Cordray, 'Making Sense of Sustainability: Nine Answers to "What Should be Sustained?"' (1994) 59 *Rural Sociology* 311.

9

points out here, are open to differing interpretations. However, a number of the papers here suggest that in whatever way one would wish to present such issues, there is compelling evidence that the carrying capacity of ecological systems are under severe pressure from essentially global forces, which tend to evade responsibility for and attribution of these costs. This and the corresponding calls for some restoration of environmental justice and social welfare is another marked theme of the work that follows. The type of governance that might take us in this direction is signified in much of the work in this volume.

Finally, the writing denotes significance of ideas of space and place, of spatial disorders in which too great a footprint of activity across vast spaces leaves local places depleted. This volume addresses how some of this might be theorized, measured, highlighted, and redressed. It would be wrong to portray the papers here as offering solutions but they do tend to indicate where such solutions might lie. More than in the global ordering of economic activity, there is much here to suggest that if answers are to be found, they are situated in the everyday actions in which we could engage as global citizens in local space.

JOURNAL OF LAW AND SOCIETY
VOLUME 36, NUMBER 1, MARCH 2009
ISSN: 0263-323X, pp. 11–31

Free Trade: What is it Good For?
Globalization, Deregulation, and 'Public Opinion'

EMILY REID* AND JENNY STEELE**

Deliberation is an essential element in legitimate and sound decision making. The deliberative ideal has much resonance with ideas of 'localization', employing the value of local and applied knowledge. Participation is also of particular value under globalization. We argue that the capacity of the World Trade Organization (WTO) to absorb and reflect participatory aspects of decision making is crucial to its future legitimacy and status. Should the WTO be seen as one of the darker forces of globalization? Or as an emerging institution of global accountability? The latter depends upon recognition that the potential deregulatory effect of the WTO is contingent, and that the liberalization of international trade should enhance welfare, rather than be a goal in its own right. Deliberative solutions require a strong public sphere, and we therefore consider whether solutions based on 'empowered consumer choice', rather than public deliberation, are unsatisfactory responses to the deregulatory impact of international trade disputes and their outcomes.

INTRODUCTION: GLOBALIZATION AND THE PARTICIPATORY IDEAL

In this paper, we are chiefly concerned with the fate of the participatory, deliberative ideal in conditions of globalization. In theory, deliberative approaches need not involve participation: they may simply entail broad and open-textured consideration by decision-makers. But as a matter of both principle and practice, deliberative approaches almost inexorably tend

* School of Law, University of Southampton, Southampton SO17 1BJ, England
esr@soton.ac.uk
** York Law School, University of York, Heslington, York YO10 5DD, England
jcs507@york.ac.uk

11

towards public participation to one extent or another.[1] As Fisher explains, the main virtue of deliberative approaches in their own terms is not necessarily that they have democratic legitimacy. The core benefits of deliberative processes, for their proponents, typically lie in their capacity to improve decision-making, whilst at the same time helping to build consensus.[2] Indeed it has been authoritatively proposed that the development of 'sound science' in the regulatory sphere is not only assisted by public consultation and deliberation, but actually *necessitates* such consultation: '[t]he validity of risk assessment is measured, ultimately, only by the confidence and trust it inspires'.[3]

Deliberation in general, and the core participatory variations of deliberation in particular, have a particular resonance with the theme of 'localization'. Equally, since deliberation is an exercise in public reason, it would seem to presuppose a strong public sphere. Can the benefits of deliberation in its participatory form be secured or preserved given the emergence of multiple levels of law and governance? Are such approaches the very antithesis of globalization?

1. *Globalization and the public sphere*

We have already begun to outline some key features of the deliberative ideal itself. In the next section, we will expand a little further on this. Although this is well-trodden ground, it is particularly important to be clear about the supposed benefits or virtues of deliberation, especially in its core participatory form, if we are to assess the challenges posed to the ideal and the changing roles currently being assigned to 'the public' in decision-making. Despite increased rhetoric of citizenship and participation in some post-national contexts – particularly the EU – it still needs to be asked whether the challenges posed by economic globalization are actually an insuperable obstacle to fulfilment of the ideal. Alternatively, have important elements of the practice of public deliberation been displaced beyond the reach of legal frameworks?

1 E. Fisher, *Risk Regulation and Administrative Constitutionalism* (2007), offers an admirable account of a 'Deliberative-Constitutive' (DC) paradigm (in this instance, of public administration), and contrasts this with a 'Rational-Instrumental Paradigm' (at pp. 26–35). The DC paradigm is defined without reference to participation as a component element: the hallmark of its approach to democracy is identified as deliberation rather than participation (p. 33). This suits the author's general purpose of moving beyond the democracy-science debate. Even so, Fisher's discussion of DC processes refers to the importance of dialogue and accepts the likely necessity of involving a 'wide array of actors'.
2 J. Steele, 'Participation and Deliberation in Environmental Law: Exploring a Problem-Solving Approach' (2001) 21 *Oxford J. of Legal Studies* 415–42.
3 L. Busch, R. Grove-White, S. Jasanoff, D. Winickoff, B. Wynne, '*Amicus Curiae* Brief: Submitted to the Dispute Settlement Panel of the World Trade Organisation in the case of EC: Measures Affecting the Approval and Marketing of Biotech Products' (30 April 2004) at 20.

12

The issues here are enormously complex because there are arguments both for and against the possibility of a genuinely public sphere in the global arena, and any such development can only tentatively be traced. Ruggie has argued that since 'there is no govern*ment* at the global level to act on behalf of the common good, as there is at the national level' and since 'international institutions are far too weak to fully compensate', there is a need to focus on the role of social processes and movements in 'triggering the emergence of more inclusive forms of govern*ance*', and setting in motion the beginnings of a genuine global public sphere.[4] Ruggie's focus here was not ecological questions, but the development of socially embedded and responsible corporate activity in order to mitigate the volatility and more general vulnerability associated with globally integrated markets. It is extremely important that Ruggie, whose approach to 'embedded liberalism' has begun to exert significant influence over trade lawyers in recent years,[5] here strongly emphasizes the role of civil society as well as the traditional public sector in working towards the global 'embedding' of liberalism, taking globalization liberal, rather than neo-liberal.[6]

It may indeed be argued that public 'mistrust' of GM technology, spontaneously arising and almost certainly informed by transnational discussion and sharing of knowledge, has been a guiding factor in national resistance to the uncontrolled application of such technology. And just as Ruggie argues that resistance to globalization itself is one of the key factors in spurring 'civil society' into contributing to voluntary initiatives to secure corporate responsibility, so also it may be argued that public resistance to GM products exemplifies resistance to economic globalization, rather than simple concern over food safety in a narrow sense. While Ruggie's concept of 'embedded liberalism' has often been cited by trade lawyers, it is notable that in this more recent updating of his theory, he proposes a *global* public realm rather than simply defending the preservation of national (or one might add regional) regulatory autonomy as a space for localized deliberation.[7]

---

4 J.G. Ruggie, 'Taking Embedded Liberalism Global: the Corporate Connection' in *Taming Globalization: Frontiers of Governance*, eds. D. Held and M. Koenig-Archibugi (2003).

5 A. Lang, 'Reconstructing embedded liberalism: John Gerard Ruggie and constructivist approaches to the study of the international trade regime' (2006) 9 *J. of International Economic Law* 81–116.

6 The cited article updates Ruggie's influential work on embedded liberalism and extends it to the current era of globalization. Embedded liberalism, on Ruggie's account, reconciles markets with 'the stable social communities' that such markets require in order to thrive. The role of the public sector in stabilizing global capital is particularly pertinent given the presently unfolding global credit and financial crisis.

7 Lang argues that consideration of 'embedded liberalism' may tend to lead trade lawyers simply to support a wider range of domestic measures of social protection, rather than more positively generating the ability of governments to take such action (Lang, op. cit., n. 5, pp. 98–9). Lang himself urges consideration of whether the WTO can play such a positive role; Ruggie's focus is on newer institutional developments.

13

2. Considering the WTO

It will be important to identify the form of post-national legal order represented by the WTO. The WTO is often characterized as a key component in
the 'darker forces' of globalization, pushing forward a homogenizing and
deregulatory neo-liberal agenda without regard for questions of equality,
welfare, environmental degradation, or participatory democracy. From this
perspective, the WTO is one of the global organizations 'without democratic
pretensions' which conduct global 'governance' (aside from international
politics): it is also termed the *Nébuleuse*, a word designed to represent the
difficulties that the population might have in grasping – let alone influencing
– its processes.[8] But there are also far more positive and optimistic analyses
of globalization, and of the WTO, at large. Some such positive approaches to
globalization emphasize a constructive relationship between global and
local, and place considerable emphasis on global 'civil society'; local
awareness of global issues; and the potential for development of global
institutions, including the WTO. The role of the WTO as a proponent of
unrestrained neo-liberalism is not beyond disagreement, and perhaps not
inevitable: its neo-liberal effects are argued to be contingent and open to
modification.[9]

Critical questions therefore arise concerning the broader potential and
underlying nature of the WTO, and some of these questions can be explored
with the assistance of traditional legal academic skills: the exploration of
disputes, decisions, structures, and principles, in light of competing
interpretations of the overarching purpose of the legal regimes. For example,
Walker has tentatively explored both the EU and the WTO, as two 'post-
national' legal orders, in terms of seven 'indicia' of constitutionalism.
Although the WTO clearly does not fit traditional notions of what amounts to
a 'constitution', most obviously through absence of democratic participation
and of relevant 'citizens', it nevertheless shows some signs of constitu-
tionalization through the development of its jurisprudence and particularly
through exercise of its 'interpretive autonomy'.[10]

Two particular questions arise here. First, and with regard to interpretation of the purposes of the international trade regime, to what extent
does the legal framework of the WTO allow positive development of
protection for non-economic interests, including the environment, perhaps
through further articulation of the concept of sustainable development? This

---

8 T. Evans, 'International Environmental Law and the Challenge of Globalization' in
   Law in Environmental Decision-Making, eds. T. Jewell and J. Steele (1998).
9 Lang, op. cit., n. 5: Ruggie's work has been influential in making this contingency
   apparent.
10 N. Walker, 'The EU and the WTO: Constitutionalism in a New Key' in *The EU and
   the WTO: Legal and Constitutional Issues*, eds. G. de Búrca and J. Scott (2001) 31–
   57.

14

in itself is important to the argument over the inherent nature of the WTO, and the contingency of its neo-liberalism. It does not, however, necessarily touch on the issue of localization, and of diversity in the assessment of knowledge, which lies behind the deliberative ideal. Therefore, there is a second question to explore: to what extent is the WTO trade regime open to arguments which either amount to a participatory and deliberative engagement, or are themselves the result of a participatory and deliberative engagement?

At one end of the scale, does the legal framework of WTO dispute resolution allow for direct participation? The type of participation in issue here is very different from the proposal made by some neo-liberal trade lawyers, that individuals should have direct access as litigants in order to secure their interests in free trade.[11] Rather, to what extent can public concerns about the effect of free trade be accommodated, and those effects mitigated? The fundamental difference appears to turn on a distinction between a cosmopolitan 'human rights' perspective which incorporates freedom to trade as a significant fundamental human right, and an approach which treats civil society (the non-profit, non-public sector) as an important element in achieving the political control of transnational private organizations. At the other end of the scale, does the legal order of the WTO even render the fruits of democratic, participatory processes at state level illegitimate? As has been pointed out, the WTO Appellate Body increasingly finds itself making judgments about national law.[12] It has been suggested that the Panel has in recent disputes veered too far towards reconsideration of facts, and should recall that its function is review, not assessment of the evidence on the basis of which a state has acted.[13] Again, these discussions raise questions of constitutionalism – the relative scope of authority of the WTO Panel and Appellate Body, and Members.

WHY DELIBERATION?

Participation in its deliberative form can be championed for a number of reasons, all of them familiar at the national or local level but taking on more complicated form in the context of globalization. One of these is that the process of participation may build a sense of citizenship, solidarity, or responsibility. A well-known difficulty here in the context of globalization is the identification of the group or polity in connection with which citizenship or solidarity should operate: some authors urge recognition of global or

11 E.-U. Petersmann, 'European and International Constitutional Law: Time for Promoting "Cosmopolitan Democracy" in the WTO' in de Búrca and Scott, id., pp. 81–110.
12 P. Holmes, 'The EU and the WTO: Some Constitutional Comparisons' in de Búrca and Scott, id., pp. 59–80.
13 Fisher, op. cit., n. 1, at p. 202.

'cosmopolitan' citizenship (and many urge its regional equivalent, for example, within the EU); others argue that all sense of citizenship or solidarity has remained stubbornly national. For the latter group, the fact that there has been a major shift from government to global governance and that this is a multi-level and spatially dispersed activity is not reflected in any change in loyalty and identity.[14] Significantly, despite the development of EU citizenship, and the creation of rights attributed to EU citizens, EU citizenship remains explicitly complementary to national citizenship.[15] Whether or not the shift from government to global governance has impacted upon feelings of identity and loyalty, there is little reason to suspect that *global* institutions currently provide a mechanism by which global solidarity or citizenship may be positively encouraged.

In the EU context, it has been suggested that the practice of deliberation and participation may act as a 'seed-bed' for European citizenship in a fuller sense, making up for the well-known absence of a cultural identity by fostering a political identity.[16] This outlook can undoubtedly slip into a top-down approach to the sources of democracy and political engagement: how to create a public sphere from the top, by planting the 'seeds' of partici-pation.[17] As we have seen, Ruggie suggests that actors of the emerging global civil society interact with other non-state institutions in order to help constitute a global public sphere. Participation and engagement are moti-vated partly by the negative social effects of economic and political globalization. Corporate actors themselves (in partnership or debate with civil society organizations) have also begun to play an important role in trying to bridge 'the gaps between global economy and national com-munities'.[18] This, in turn, helps to create the conditions in which liberalism may be controlled and stabilized or 'embedded'; it is not the creation of a new political elite seeking a group of citizens in order to constitute its own legitimacy. This reason for championing participatory deliberation therefore turns on the importance of the public sphere.

Another reason for championing participation is, as explained above, that it may lead to improved decisions through the input of diverse knowledge. Here, 'knowledge' is a distinct idea from 'information'.[19] Participation in

---

14 W. Wallace, 'The sharing of sovereignty: the European Paradox' (1999) 47 *Political Studies* 21, discussed by D. Held and A. McGrew, *Globalization/Anti-Globalization*, at 121.

15 Article 17 EC. This remains the case under the Lisbon Treaty (Art. 20 (1)).

16 D. Curtin, *Postnational Democracy: The European Union in Search of a Political Philosophy* (1997) 58.

17 This is, however, not Curtin's preferred approach: she clearly emphasizes the need for democracy to be fostered from the bottom up, and goes on to emphasize that the civil society sphere will be active in 'widening and expanding the public debate'.

18 Ruggie, op. cit., n. 4, at p. 95.

19 See the discussion of 'situated knowledge' by S. Jasanoff and M.L. Martello, 'Conclusion, Knowledge and Governance' in *Earthly Politics: Local and Global in*

16

this respect reflects the understanding that a diversity of knowledge and vantage points may have validity and contribute to better resolution of controversy. This is not exactly a question of relativism: it does not amount to an argument that cultural differences or public opinion might legitimately cause a decision that is appropriate in one part of the world to be rejected in another – although it may reflect particular features of local knowledge which, in turn, reflect local conditions. It concerns not opinion and taste but reasons, and understanding. It is a recognition of diversity in providing knowledge rather than preferences.

Associated with this is the 'transformative' potential of the deliberative process: the exercise of reasoned argument can transform the views that people hold, enabling agreement but also allowing for new and better solutions to be discovered. The enormous difficulty with this aspect of the deliberative participatory ideal in conditions of economic globalization is simply that the context of globalization may appear to make such exercises either *impossible* (absence of an effective public sphere that is equal to the task, or over-centralization and harmonization), or even *illegitimate* (the existence of reasoned decisions in one locality makes a contrary decision elsewhere appear purely protectionist).

In one respect, 'participation' becomes more important (and indeed sought-after) given globalization, as it seems to provide a direct connection between the decision-maker (which may be a trans-national organization), and the 'citizen', and hence provide much needed legitimacy.[20] But at the same time, the possibility of participation, and the identification of deliberative space, becomes considerably more elusive. Do the legal structures which have developed in the context of global, or post-national, institutions in any sense operate to create new participatory possibilities? Or do they (rather) compound the problems of democratic deficit, of deregulation, and of the weakening of the democratic sphere?

THE EU AND THE WTO

As noted above, the WTO is often cast as one of the darker forces of globalization, bypassing (even negating) democratic decision making at state level. In its interactions with the WTO, the EC might appear to take on the role of protector of local understanding and democratic public reason. But there is considerable irony in this. Though discussion of politics within the EU has often assumed the language of participation, this is in part a response

---

Environmental Governance, eds. S. Jasanoff and M.L. Martello (2004); and the terminology of 'knowledge society' used by S. Jasanoff in *Designs on Nature: Science and Democracy in Europe and the United States* (2005).

20 See M. Lee, *EU Environmental Law: Challenge, Change and Decision-Making* (2005) at 118.

17

to the very problems of globalization which its creation represents.[21] This is certainly not to deny that there has been a degree of public political mobilization over the GM issue within Europe. Indeed, on Jasanoff's account, mobilization over the issue of GM products has resulted in a possibly unique degree of political engagement within the European institutions.[22] But it can plausibly be argued that the outcome of the protracted dispute between the United States and EC over GM food has been influenced as much by the EU's own inability to find a proper response to public, and national, mistrust of GM technology, as by interpretation of the Agreement on Sanitary and Phyto-Sanitary Measures (SPS Agreement) itself.

The greatest threat to the participatory ideal arises from the narrowing of the public realm's sphere of influence. But in the interaction between the EU and WTO, the risk that issues are removed from the public realm is in no sense uniquely created by the WTO. Indeed is the EU a darker force than the WTO? As a Member of the WTO, the EC takes on some characteristics of a state. But it does not share the character of democratic states. Whereas the WTO can find that local restrictions are illegitimate barriers to trade, it cannot determine applicable standards. The EU by contrast has the power to enact harmonization legislation. On one (primarily functional) view, the EU provides an exemplar for the successful evolution of what was initially an organization of economic integration to incorporate a broader and more balanced set of interests including environmental protection and human rights, and the elaboration of EU citizenship.[23] This can provide important lessons for the WTO, to the extent that it implies the purposes of a free trade regime are best understood in combination with the social impact of such a regime. By contrast, it might also be argued that its decision-making structures remain essentially centralized and bureaucratic despite the rhetoric of participation and citizenship, which in too many instances is confined to mere consultation.[24] As such, recognition of a wider range of *interests* is not in itself a guarantee that broader conceptions of risk and harm will also be understood and accepted.

The GM debate as a globalization debate

Although our analysis is in some respects general, many elements of it draw on accounts of disputes over GM food and GM technology. Discussions of WTO law have reached a wider legal audience through the unfolding of such

---

21 As a consequence of the competence and legal personality of the EC, and lack of legal personality of the EU, EU relations with the WTO are undertaken through the EC.
22 Jasanoff, op. cit., n. 19, ch. 3.
23 See E. Reid, 'Protecting Non-economic Interests in the European Community Legal Order: A Sustainable Development' 24 (2005) *Yearbook of European Law* 385–421.
24 K. Armstrong, 'Rediscovering Civil Society' (2002) 8 *European Law J.* 102–32, at 121.

18

issues. A distinctive feature of the controversy over GM in the trade context is that problems of GM are themselves to some extent problems of globalization (including, as we have noted, the awkwardness of decision-making within the EU as a 'post-national' regime). Indeed it is arguable that resistance to globalization itself, rather than concern over food safety, is key to public resistance to GM at least within some parts of Europe. In concerns over the possible effect of new technologies on plant varieties, and on ownership, distribution of wealth, and justice, protesters against GM are in effect protesters against globalization itself. Potential loss of local democratic control is an essential element in the objections raised.

We now turn to questions about the most appropriate characterization of the WTO in respect of globalization, accountability, and democracy.

THE NATURE OF THE WTO

Negative perceptions of the WTO are unsurprising: the fruits of globalization have not been equally distributed[25] and trade liberalization is seen as being a key contributor to this inequality. The WTO constitutes a far more developed legal order for the promotion of trade liberalization than exists in order to protect other interests, including environmental. This, particularly the existence of binding dispute settlement, presents the possibility that WTO rulings will have a wide-ranging normative effect. That this is the case may simply be taken to reflect the collective will of the Members. The WTO is after all an international organization which operates according to rules negotiated by its Members, unlike the EU which constitutes a new political unit. Were the WTO to prioritize any interests other than trade liberalization, this could raise significant legitimacy questions.

Yet what are the objectives of trade liberalization which the WTO has a mandate legitimately to pursue? The Preamble to the WTO Agreement states that:

> relations in the field of trade and economic endeavor should be conducted with a view to raising standards of living, ensuring full employment . . . while allowing for the optimal use of the world's resources in accordance with the objective of sustainable development.

This suggests that trade liberalization should be seen as a means to an end rather than an end in itself. The end is (primarily but not exclusively economic) welfare gain, and includes environmental and social considerations through direct reference to 'sustainable development'. These objectives have the capacity to come into conflict: national environmental legislation can pose a restriction to trade, the corollary being that trade liberalization impacts upon a state's ability to regulate according to its national policy

---

25 Ruggie, op. cit., n. 4.

choices on matters within the scope of WTO law. International law obligations binding upon Members may also conflict with WTO law. The framework of sustainable development, however, conceptualizes and promotes economic, environmental, and social development as mutually supporting objectives. Ruggie characterized the international trade regime, as manifested in the GATT, as representing a compromise between pursuit of multilateral economic liberalization and the pursuit of domestic stability, reflecting 'the shared legitimacy of a set of social objectives to which the industrial world had moved, unevenly but "as a single entity".'[26] Such perspectives on the objectives of the WTO regime and trade liberalization give rise to a very different answer to the question 'Free Trade: what is it good for?' than might be given if the question is approached from the orthodox liberal (or neo-liberal) perspective.

How much weight can be placed on the Preamble? In dispute settlement proceedings, both the Panel and the Appellate Body (AB) have referred to the WTO objective of sustainable development.[27] Moreover, the AB has recognized that 'the General Agreement is not to be read in clinical isolation from public international law'.[28] Although the jurisdiction of the WTO Dispute Settlement Body (DSB) is limited to the enforcement of WTO rules, this is done 'in accordance with the customary rules of interpretation of public international law'.[29] The DSB has demonstrated that it is not wholly antagonistic towards environmental protection, to the extent that that is representative of international law.[30] Yet, this does not reveal much regarding the capacity of the WTO to respond to individual state choices concerning environmental regulation, nor of the WTO's sensitivity to local 'preferences' – including the varying conclusions that may be reached concerning the proper approach to products which have been produced using GM technology, for example.

---

26 J.G. Ruggie, 'International regimes, transactions, and change: embedded liberalism in the postwar economic order' (1982) 36 *International Organization* 379–415, at 398.

27 *United States – Import Prohibition of Certain Shrimp and Shrimp Products,* WT/DS58, AB Report at 131 and Panel Report at 5.54.

28 *United States – Standards for Reformulated and Conventional Gasoline (US Gasoline)* WT/DS2/AB/R, adopted 20 May 1996, AB Report at 17.

29 Article 3.2 Dispute Settlement Understanding.

30 *US – Shrimp* AB Report, op. cit., n. 27. Furthermore, the WTO Ministerial Decision establishing a Permanent Committee on Trade and the Environment states:
> there should not be, nor need be, any policy contradiction between upholding and safeguarding an open, non-discriminatory and equitable multilateral trading system on the one hand, and acting for the protection of the environment, and the promotion of sustainable development on the other.

In the various WTO Agreements different rules apply with regard to national regulatory autonomy. The GATT regime prohibits protectionist measures, and is essentially based upon the requirement of non-discrimination, manifested in the principle of national treatment: the requirement that Members cannot treat imported products less favourably than domestically produced 'like' products.[31] If a national measure infringes the national treatment requirement, a Member may seek to justify it with reference to the *General Exceptions* provided for in Article XX. Of particular relevance to environmental protection are Article XX (b) measures '*necessary* for the protection of human, animal or plant life or health' and (g) measures '*relating to* the conservation of natural resources'.[32] Exceptions founded on either of these grounds must also comply with the Article XX '*chapeau*': they must not be applied in a manner that is arbitrary or disguised discrimination. Both the necessity test and the application of the *chapeau* have raised questions as to the legitimacy of DSB review of national regulatory choices.

Regarding the impact upon national regulatory autonomy, much hinges upon the definition of 'likeness'. This has proved controversial, particularly for its focus upon the characteristics of the product at issue, excluding consideration of the production process. Aside from this (significant) limitation, Members retain their national regulatory autonomy. Notably, the AB has recognized the relevance of consumer preferences in the determination of 'likeness'.[33] Yet the presumption that products cannot be distinguished on the basis of their process of production or manufacture is one that sits uncomfortably with concern for environmental protection. It also sits uneasily with the diversity of perspectives on the risks that may be associated with the introduction of GM technology.[34]

It is the SPS Agreement which has been central to WTO disputes concerning GM.[35] Article 2.1 provides Members with a 'right to take sanitary and phyto-sanitary measures *necessary* for the protection of human, animal or plant life or health', subject to consistency with the SPS Agreement.[36] Any such measures must be 'based on scientific principles and not maintained without sufficient scientific evidence, except as provided for in paragraph 7 of Article 5.' Although Article 3 promotes the use of international standards in the implementation of SPS measures, Article 3.3 explicitly provides for pursuit of a 'higher level of protection' subject once

---

31 GATT Article III.
32 Emphasis added.
33 *European Communities – Measures Affecting Asbestos and Asbestos Containing Products,* WT/DS135/AB/R, adopted 5 April 2001.
34 Jasanoff, op. cit., n. 19. Note text accompanying n. 64 below.
35 See, generally, J. Scott, *The WTO Agreement on Sanitary and Phytosanitary Measures* (2007).
36 The 'necessity' test has not yet been explored in this context.

again to 'scientific justification', or, 'as a consequence of the levels of sanitary or phyto-sanitary protection a Member determines to be appropriate in accordance with [Article 5 paragraphs 1–8]'.

Articles 5.1–5.3 detail the requirements of risk assessment, which should be based on scientific evidence and take economic considerations into account. There is no indication of any role for deliberation or public opinion. Nor are any other considerations to be taken into account.

The AB has clarified in *EC Hormones* that the requirement in Article 5.1, that measures be 'based on' risk assessment, means that there must be 'a certain *objective relationship* between two elements, that is to say, an *objective situation* that persists and is observable between an SPS measure and a risk assessment.'[37] Article 5.7 has been described by the AB as reflecting the precautionary principle,[38] providing for Members to act even when there is a lack of scientific evidence of harm. The precautionary principle will not, however, justify measures which are otherwise incon- sistent with the SPS Agreement; in particular, it does not override Articles 5.1 and 5.2.[39]

The focus upon science in the SPS might counter some of the legitimacy questions raised concerning DSB review of domestic measures, if it is per- ceived to provide an 'objective' basis of review. But it has only deepened those questions. The interpretation applied to the scientific evidence requirements, particularly with regard to precautionary measures, has been contentious. The WTO approach to sound scientific risk assessment is said to give 'hegemonic' status to scientific discourse, whereas in truth 'sound science' varies in its prescriptions with locality as much as any other expert or non-expert discourse.[40] Perez observes bluntly that 'The Panel's sub- missive approach to science asks from science something it cannot deliver: complete determinacy'.[41]

This understanding of the need for scientific expertise to interact with other sources of knowledge and insight, and indeed to respond to questioning and doubts, is a widespread feature of academic accounts from many different perspectives. Joerges, for example, discussing the European Commission's 2001 White Paper on Governance, captured one of the key challenges for legitimate and effective decision-making in the EU in terms of

---

37 *European Communities – Measures Concerning Meat and Meat Products (Hormones)* WT/DS26/AB/R, WT/DS48/AB/R, adopted 13 February 1998, at para. 189.
38 id., at para. 124.
39 id., at para. 125.
40 A. Gupta, 'When global is local: negotiating safe use of biotechnology' in Jasanoff and Martello, op. cit., n. 19. Gupta focused here on the Cartagena Protocol on Biodiversity (2000), rather than WTO cases.
41 O. Perez, 'Anomalies at the precautionary kingdom: reflections on the GMO Panel's decision' (2007) 6 *World Trade Rev.* 265–80.

22

'the characteristics of knowledge in the "knowledge society"'. That knowledge, he explained, can:

> no longer be understood as 'given' and accessible by the mechanisms of elected representation or by the concentration of specialist expertise; it is more adequately characterized as 'constructed' and renewed in a process of collective learning that draws support from social pluralism.[42]

In other words, the *necessity* for deliberation and exchange in constructing knowledge is one of the key challenges to any kind of legitimate decision making. There is a significant tension between the deregulatory and globalizing effects of the liberalized trade regime, and the understanding that knowledge itself – not just decision making on the basis of knowledge – is constructed through collective processes. If anything, this tension is more acute within the EU than it is under the WTO dispute settlement procedure. While, as we have said, the objective of the AB is or ought to be to review the compatibility of state action with the requirements of the relevant treaty obligations, the EU has autonomous law-making powers. Whereas it is generally therefore assumed that within the WTO, the question is one of legitimacy, in terms of compatibility with WTO agreements, of state decision making, within the EU the search for an adequate deliberative element is directly focused on law making. As we have already suggested though, it is also possible to argue that the focus on national autonomy does not go far enough in the global context: the need is for the development of global (as opposed to international) public institutions. Criticisms of the WTO can be crystallized in this way: its deregulatory effects are truly global, even if these were tempered by understanding of its goals in 'embedded', welfare-orientated terms; but even if it develops its dispute settlement powers with proper regard for national regulatory autonomy, it is far from escaping the limits of its international roots.

In connection with *uncertain* risks, and therefore with issues of precaution, the very question of how to approach the 'evidence' – and how much evidence is sufficient to justify action to control or avoid a potential risk – is in issue. Here, above all areas, different views may be taken over necessary thresholds and who has legitimate authority to determine the very existence of a risk that can legitimately be controlled. However that is not to say that such differences have not been explored; indeed, there is a substantial body of research in this area in the field of social sciences. One question, which came to prominence in the *Biotech* dispute,[43] concerns the extent to which this could be taken into account in the WTO context.

---

42 C. Joerges, '"Deliberative Supranationalism" – Two Defences' (2002) 8 *European Law J.* 133–51, at 147.
43 *European Communities – Measures Affecting the Approval and Marketing of Biotech Products,* WT/DS291/R, WT/292/R, WT/293/R.

Among three *amicus* briefs submitted in the *Biotech* dispute was one on the subject of risk assessment from a group of eminent social scientists.[44] The authors of this brief have characterized *Biotech* as a watershed dispute, the report of which would 'redefine the balance between state and global power in legal, political and epistemic terms'.[45] The central point of their analysis, in the context of a dispute in which the compatibility with international trade law of the regulatory choices at 'state' level was concerned, was that local understanding of risks, contextualized and subjected to local experience, was as valid and as legitimate as the abstract, laboratory-based judgement of traditionally recognized scientific experts. They highlight that GMOs constitute:

> a low certainty-low consensus situation: risk assessment techniques associated with GMOs remain scientifically and politically contested both within and across different national regulatory systems

and therefore application of Article 5.7 SPS is appropriate.[46]

Winickoff et al. emphasize the significance of 'framing': the 'process of selection and characterization' of a problem.[47] Differences in framing give rise to 'systematic transnational variations in the assessment of health, safety and environmental risks'.[48] As they also note, the AB recognized in *Hormones* that decision-makers should consider:

> not only risk ascertainable in a science laboratory operating under strictly controlled conditions, but also risk in human societies as they actually exist, in other words, the actual potential for adverse effects on human health in the real world where people live and work and die.[49]

They conclude that an appropriate judicial approach requires the enhancement of 'the sensitivity of judicial tools for detecting protectionism masquerading as health and environmental values, while preserving cultural autonomy in important societal domains'.[50] A key element of this would be the introduction of public participation in risk-based decision making in the trading system, including consideration of practical expertise[51] as well as broader-based risk assessment. The Panel simply 'accepted the information

---

44 Busch et al., op. cit., n. 3; C. Foster, 'Social Science Experts and *Amicus Curiae* Briefs in International Courts and Tribunals: The WTO *Biotech* Case' (2005) 52 *Netherlands International Law Rev.* 433–59; M. Footer, 'Post-normal science in the multilateral trading system: social science expertise and the *EC-Biotech* Panel' (2007) 6 *World Trade Rev.* 281–97.

45 D. Winickoff, S. Jasanoff, L. Busch, R. Grove-White, B. Wynne, 'Adjudicating the GM Food Wars: Science, Risk and Democracy in World Trade Law' (2005) 30 *Yale J. of International Law* 81–123.

46 id., at p. 118.

47 id., at p. 94. See, also, Busch et al., op. cit., n. 3, at s. III.B.2.

48 id., at pp. 96–7.

49 *EC – Hormones*, op. cit., n. 37, at para. 187.

50 Winickoff et al., op. cit., n. 45, at p. 122.

51 Busch et al., op. cit., n. 3, at ss. III C. and IV.B.4.

24

submitted by the *amici curiae* into the record' but 'did not find it necessary to take the *amicus curiae* briefs into account'.[52]

Foster similarly argues that such requisite sensitivity would be enhanced through the input of social scientists, either through the submission of *amicus* briefs or in the capacity of expert advisors appointed in the context of dispute resolution procedures.[53]

The procedure for the appointment of individual scientific experts was, like the possibility for private parties to submit *amicus* briefs, set up by the AB in *EC Asbestos*.[54] The inclusion of social science experts within this procedure has the potential to strengthen the process, although just as the selection of 'scientific' experts raises questions, so too would the selection of social science experts. Risse has highlighted the possible tensions between deliberation, accountability, and legitimacy in attempts to 'increase the deliberative quality of decision-making'. Such tensions arise concerning the selection of participants and the very framing of the deliberation, for example.[55] Indeed this issue is not confined to appointed experts. All attempts to broaden the sources of deliberation face the issue of who is drawn into the deliberative process. At the global or supra-national level, the question of who represents civil society is particularly difficult. Are the participating groups or individuals simply self-appointing?[56] If emphasis is placed upon the spontaneous efforts of civil society actors in edging towards a global public sphere, then the truth is that participants in deliberative processes are indeed likely to be self-appointing. It may be the participants themselves who have raised consciousness of the issues and ensured that debate is engaged at all.

The narrow approach taken to the interpretation of 'precaution' indicates a failure to appreciate the nature of radical uncertainty and the challenges of governance that it produces. Alternatively it might be taken to accept a framing of the issues which is influenced by the nature of the dispute itself (a trade dispute between parties to the Agreement; concerning product safety not wider issues). The concentration on science understates the importance of law in framing the relevant questions. Perez goes further, seeing the reliance on science not just as understating the potential role of law but:

> by failing to create a proper semi-constitutional framework, which could mediate between science politics and the economy – by controlling, for example the political and disciplinary openness of the risk assessment process

52 *EC – Approval and Marketing of Biotech Products*, op. cit., n. 43, at para. 7.11.
53 Foster, op. cit., n. 44, at p. 449.
54 See M.-C. Cordonier Segger and J. Cabrera, 'Public Participation in Americas Trade and Environmental Regimes' in *Sustainable Justice: Reconciling Economic, Social and Environmental Law*, eds. M.-C. Cordonier Segger and C.G. Weeramantry (2005) 409–11.
55 T. Risse, 'Social Constructivism Meets Globalization' in *Globalization Theory: Approaches and Controversies*, eds. D. Held and A. McGrew (2007) at 140.
56 Joerges, op. cit., n. 42, at p. 150.

– the Panel failed to position law as the system which could govern the triangle of science, politics and the economy. As such it has put in question the legitimacy of the WTO as a whole.[57]

This is not an overstated objection. In the balance between the WTO's potential deregulatory effect on the one hand, and its potential for bringing about the embedding of the trade regime on the other, the approach taken in *Biotech* is consistent with a tendency towards deregulation.

THE NEED FOR ACCOUNTABILITY

As seen above, some of the more contentious issues undermining the legitimacy of the deliberative ideal are consequences of the interpretation applied by the decision-maker, rather than inherent in the rules themselves. In assessing the legitimacy of these interpretations, it is helpful to recall that trade liberalization should properly be conceived of as a means to an end, rather than an end in itself; this highlights the contingency of the current interpretations.

Brown observes that:

> The emergence of a global community served by effective institutions of global governance could only avoid being a tyranny that served the interests of only some parts of the world – most likely those already rich and powerful – if it were based on a genuine sense of 'we-feeling' that was truly global.[58]

This can be related to Ruggie's identification of the significance of a shared social purpose in the creation of the GATT. One problem in the GATT and WTO context has been the dominance of economic liberalism as the prevailing ethos of the international trading regime, in particular since the 1970s.[59] Under this ethos there has been less concern for the shared social purpose and little evidence of solidarity. This is both observable in, and gives rise to, inequity in distribution of the benefits of economic liberalization and the dominance of the economically powerful states. This in turn contributes to the negative popular view of the WTO.

The accountability of the WTO is therefore of paramount importance. Keohane argues that the WTO is internally accountable to its Members,[60] yet since the WTO comprises 153 Members, can there be any means by which to reach consensus to hold the WTO institutions, notably the DSB to account? This accountability gap is particularly significant where the DSB is drawing a balance between trade liberalization and other (WTO) objectives, with

57 Perez, op. cit., n. 41, at p. 279.
58 C. Brown, 'Reimagining International Society and Global Community' in Held and McGrew, op. cit., n. 55, at p. 182.
59 See, further, Ruggie, op. cit., n. 26.
60 R.O. Keohane, 'Global Governance and Democratic Accountability' in Held and Koenig-Archibugi, op. cit., n. 4.

26

respect to a Member's regulatory choices, and can contribute to the emergence of the dominant Members' position as determinative of the organization as a whole.

The EC, like other parties to the Agreement (at least those which are democratic) is concerned with its own internal accountability. Keohane points out that:

> if globalization of public authority occurred, individual citizens would have few incentives to try to monitor governments' behaviour. Indeed, the larger the polity, the more individuals can rationally be ignorant, since each person's actions would have so little effect on policies.

He continues with reference to a lack of incentive to vote and the lack of 'coherent civil society' both of which are, as he observes, all too evident in the EU context.[61] Thus Keohane highlights the challenge for the possibility of the deliberative ideal at EU level. At WTO level the difficulty is heightened as it is not a political unit in any recognizable sense. The individual has no role within WTO law. Thus there is no direct accountability to citizen level within the WTO. In short, WTO Members are in principle accountable internally and externally, that is, to both their citizens and the WTO. In contrast, the WTO is in principle accountable to its Members; however, the possibility for any meaningful exercise of this accountability is limited.

THE ACCOMMODATION OF PUBLIC OPINION WITHIN THE WTO?

Members may choose to bring public opinion to the WTO in a dispute context, for example through the incorporation of an *amicus* brief within their submissions. Similarly, as noted above, there is now a process by which interested parties can directly submit *amicus* briefs to dispute settlement proceedings, although as yet such briefs have had little discernible effect.

Scott assesses the extent to which WTO law accommodates 'Member States' responsiveness to public opinion' and finds that this is considerable,[62] provided that it is objectively evidenced, and encompassed within the 'proportionate' (that is, complying with the necessity requirement and or the *chapeau* to Article XX). Thus, for example, in the GATT, consumers' tastes and habits are relevant to establishing what counts as a 'like' product.[63] However, as seen above, the determination of likeness remains contentious, notably in that there is no consideration of production or process methods. Drawing on Jasanoff's comparative account of the interplay between science and democracy in respect of GM technology, this

---

61 id., at pp. 136–7.
62 J. Scott, 'European Regulation of GMOs: Thinking About Judicial Review in the WTO' in *Current Legal Problems*, eds. J. Holder and M. Freeman (2005) at 140–7.
63 *EC – Asbestos*, op. cit., n. 33.

approach, based on the likeness of products, rather than the process applied, is a hallmark of the national response of the United States to GM, in contrast to the response in the United Kingdom and EU.[64] Discussion in terms of products already therefore makes a substantive choice about the relevant features of the import.

In the context of SPS, Foster observes that 'public opinion' can be taken into consideration (indirectly) in relation to Articles 5.5. and 5.6 (and 3.3) but not in relation to Articles 2.2, 5.1 and 5.7.[65] A significant limitation upon the ability of Member States to ensure the accommodation of public opinion applies in the requirement of the need to establish the potential existence of a risk. In *Biotech*, the compatibility of the EU's effective moratorium was judged according to whether evidence of the existence of a risk could be appropriately established, and the dispute therefore directly concerned the conditions according to which a principle of precaution could be legitimately invoked.

In conclusion, there is little scope to engage the views or expertise of non-state actors directly in the WTO, and what potential there is (through *amicus* briefs) has to date been paid little regard by the DSB, despite the AB's facilitation of this process. There is rather more scope for the indirect engagement of public 'opinion' (including the results of deliberative processes) through the Members. However, this is constrained by the narrow interpretations applied by the DSB, which can reflect particular national approaches. This reinforces the question of whether there is indeed a public sphere capable of delivering any element of the deliberative ideal at global level, at least within the context of the WTO: can the diverse range of national approaches be adequately engaged with and reflected at global level? Or will dominant (latent) national approaches, or even the Panel's own assessment of what is a sound reason, prevent this?

A greater awareness of the limitation of current approaches, and the unspoken national assumptions which underpin some decisions, together with a greater regard for the context of the pursuit of trade liberalization and its wider objectives, would allow (and demand) greater sensitivity to local regulatory preferences. A key question is whether space for such sensitivity can be found within the current WTO structure. In so far as current limitations reflect the interpretative choices and assumptions applied in the GATT and in the SPS, it should be possible to take some action to mitigate the extent of this. However, while Foster suggests that it may be possible to reintegrate the subjective element of risk assessment in the SPS,[66] such an approach will encounter the difficulties of framing, highlighted above.

---

64 Jasanoff, op. cit., n. 19.
65 C.E. Foster, 'Public Opinion and the Interpretation of the World Trade Organisation's Agreement on Sanitary and Phytosanitary Measures' (2008) *J. of International Economic Law* 427–58, at 431.
66 id., at p. 448.

This concern notwithstanding, increased sensitivity to local priorities would be consistent with Ruggie's characterization of the GATT as combining a dual purpose – multilateralism coupled with domestic stability and economic liberalization tempered by social purpose. However, Lang cautions that to reinvent 'embedded liberalism' could indeed constrain attempts to deal with contemporary challenges by retreating to an outdated set of priorities and approaches, limiting the creative process which might facilitate resolution of contemporary challenges, including development, the inequity of distribution of economic growth, and environmental protection itself, which might be rather better suited to a more cooperative approach than is reflected in the 'domestic or international' approach of embedded liberalism.[67] The role of the individual, public opinion or deliberation is similarly one which was not conceived within the original conceptualization of embedded liberalism. Thus, recognition of embedded liberalism serves here to provide a starting point from which to recognize and resolve future challenges rather than itself providing a framework for their resolution.

DELIBERATION FROM CITIZEN TO CONSUMER?

As seen above, Ruggie has proposed the need for a global public domain, to bridge the gap between the global economy, and national communities. Defence of the EU's position in respect of GMO release has generally taken the form of a defence of national regulatory autonomy and, thus, national variation, rather than hinting at any such global public space. Meanwhile, it has been widely noted that the EU's response to its experience of WTO dispute processes would appear to have been the adoption of a narrower and more 'scientific' approach to the precautionary principle and, therefore, to the regulation of risk.[68] Increasingly also, it has been noted that there is a drift towards informational and labelling requirements, supplementing prohibition or refusal to licence, or even potentially coming to replace those strategies.[69]

It is by no means clear that labelling of GM products is compatible with relevant agreements.[70] From the EU's point of view, the advantage presumably is not greater effectiveness, which is generally the reason for urging more market-based strategies, but that the consumer's actions in

---

67 Lang, op. cit., n. 5, at pp. 98–101.
68 See, for example, Fisher, op. cit., n. 1, ch. 6.
69 The EU's new framework for regulation of chemicals involves a heavy emphasis on information: E. Fisher, 'The "perfect storm" of REACH: charting regulatory controversy in the age of information, sustainable development, and globalization' (2008) 11 *J. of Risk Research* 541–63.
70 S. Bernstein and E. Hannah, 'Non-state global standard setting and the WTO: legitimacy and the need for regulatory space' (2008) 11 *J. of International Economic Law* 575–608.

making purchasing decisions are beyond reproach because the consumer is not in any sense accountable before WTO Members. As such, the EU and other food importers adopt the position that labelling is not primarily justified by reference to consumer safety, but by reference to consumer preference and consumer choice.[71] The disadvantage is the mirror image of this. Without deliberative processes, will information and labelling have any coherent effects? And if those effects are in some sense coherent, will they nevertheless be beneficial?

The 'market citizen' of old was considered too 'thin' an idea to reflect the new post-national ambitions of the EU.[72] We find ourselves now with a subtly different rhetoric of 'empowered consumers' which could nevertheless be seen as superficially reminiscent of that earlier, politically disengaged variety.[73] It is true that the exercise of labelling and providing information is by no means without controversy – though as a political matter, to argue that consumers ought not to be provided with information seems in principle a relatively hard position to maintain.[74] Even so, determination of which information should be provided still narrows the concerns of regulatory decision-making from gathering and considering *knowledge* in a dynamic process of problem solving, to providing *information* on which private purchasing decisions may be made. Lee, for example, has identified a series of pertinent reasons why such labelling cannot compete, in terms of effectiveness in integrating public opinion in any way that might influence outcomes, with more direct regulatory approaches.[75]

The provision of information through mandatory requirements, and the consumer's decision whether or not to buy the product, are two stages in a continuing process by which national and, in this instance, supra-national

---

71 P. Sand, 'Labelling Genetically Modified Food: the Right to Know' (2006) 15 *Rev. of European Community & International Environmental Law* 185–92, at 190. This brings such labelling within the terms of the Agreement on Technical Barriers to Trade rather than the SPS agreement, altering the potential arguments that may be used to justify the legislation.

72 M. Everson, 'The Legacy of the Market Citizen' in *New Legal Dynamics of the European Union*, eds. J. Shaw and G. More (1996).

73 M. Everson and C. Joerges, 'Consumer Citizenship in Postnational Constellations', EU Working Papers Law No. 2006/47. The resemblance is superficial, however, to the extent that the market citizen of old was 'individually motivated primarily by self-interest' (Everson, id., at p. 90).

74 Sand, op. cit., n. 71, expresses this position – embraced by the United States – as a 'need to know' rather than 'right to know' position. The obvious question is who decides what the consumer needs to know, and on what basis.

75 For example, aggressive pricing may overcome more diffuse concerns; presence on shelves may lead consumers to conclude that the reality of GM is a foregone conclusion (the battle is lost); there are many exceptions in the labelling requirements; and the 'coexistence' of GM and non-GM crops may lead to cross-contamination of a type which makes such labelling ineffective. Lee, op. cit., n. 20, at p. 259.

30

regulators, consumers, and in some instances retailers, manoeuvre. What is missing from this part of the picture is not deliberation as such, so much as institutionally supported public deliberation. This illustrates the continually shifting relationship between citizens (or more blandly, the purchasing public), and the different levels of governance which have been explored here. The apparently simple provision of information to 'consumers' is the present point of engagement in a complex process in which both citizens and retailers have played an important role.

There seems little doubt that consumer resistance to GM products in Europe is motivated in part by consideration of issues of globalization as such – the absence of regulatory choice and perceived risk of injustice and power imbalance among them. These questions are inherently questions on which deliberation would be beneficial, and which engage questions of global justice and effect, as well as requiring local knowledge for resolution. They are questions of 'glocalicity'. To date, the influence of WTO procedures appears to have been to drive these questions inexorably away from the public sphere. This is antithetical to the deliberative ideal which is so widely recognized to be an essential element of legitimacy and sound decision making, in conditions of globalization above all. The crucial question for trade lawyers is whether this is a contingent state of affairs that may be remedied by interpretation and gradual improvement in the openness of the WTO. Continuation on the current trajectory risks further undermining the legitimacy, and credibility, of the WTO, and increasing its marginalization both from other developments in the international community and from the public.

JOURNAL OF LAW AND SOCIETY
VOLUME 36, NUMBER 1, MARCH 2009
ISSN: 0263-323X, pp. 32–54

Modern Interpretations of Sustainable Development

ANDREA ROSS*

Early interpretations of sustainable development based on weak sustainability address neither the limits to the earth's resilience nor our failure to curb consumption. Given the challenges facing the earth today, especially climate change, a much more meaningful instrument is required and a new ethic based on the ecological carrying capacity of the Earth. The article examines the impact of those early interpretations before exploring the importance of ecological sustainability as the moral and (potentially fundamental) legal principle underpinning the concept of sustainable development. It examines the influence of the climate change agenda before examining the mechanisms available to make this ethic operational. Sustainable development has the capacity to set meaningful objectives, duties and rules, and provide boundaries for decision making, as reflected in recent legislation. Enhancing ecological sustainability through improving supply and impact is relatively easy for governments, businesses, and individuals; reducing consumption is much harder, and will require strong leadership.

INTRODUCTION

> Just as reckless spending is causing recession, so reckless consumption is depleting the world's natural capital to a point where we are endangering our future prosperity.
>
> *Living Planet Report 2008.*[1]

The theme of this volume is economic globalization and ecological localization and the relationship between local and global ecosystems,

* School of Law, University of Dundee, Scrymgeour Building, Dundee DD1 4HN, Scotland
a.p.ross@dundee.ac.uk

1 WWF, *Living Planet Report 2008* (2008) 2. Available at <http://assets.panda.org/downloads/living_planet_report_2008.pdf>.

economies, and social networks. Many of the decisions made in relation to the various dimensions of this theme are taken in the name of sustainable development. Indeed sustainable development has been widely adopted as a policy objective by institutions, governments, businesses, voluntary bodies and others. 'Ensuring environmental sustainability' is one of the UN's Eight Millennium Development Goals to be achieved by 2015.[2] Article 2 of the EC Treaty (Nice consolidated version) provides that:

> The Community shall have as its task ... to promote throughout the Community a harmonious, balanced and sustainable development of economic activities ...

Article 6 provides that:

> Environmental protection requirements must be integrated into the definition and implementation of the Community policies and activities referred to in Article 3, in particular with a view to promoting sustainable development.[3]

Within the private sector, the websites and environmental reports for Walmart, Honda, and countless other multi-national companies all herald their commitment to sustainable development.[4]

The purpose of this article is to examine the value of sustainable development as a policy tool in the twenty-first century. It argues that, given the challenges facing the earth today, especially climate change, the early interpretations of sustainable development as a vague, malleable policy tool based on weak sustainability fail to address either the fact that there are limits to the earth's resilience or our cultural and moral failure to curb our consumption. Instead, the demands of the twenty-first century require a much more meaningful instrument for framing decisions. This article examines more recent interpretations of sustainable development and the influences behind these interpretations to assess whether sustainable development can provide a useful mechanism for delivering truly 'sustainable' development.

The article begins with an examination of the impact to date of early interpretations of sustainable development based on 'weak sustainability' before exploring the importance and more recent emergence of 'ecological sustainability' as the moral and (potentially fundamental) legal principle underpinning the concept of sustainable development. The discussion then moves on to explore the influence of the climate change agenda on this shift towards ecological sustainability and considers the mechanisms available to

---

2 <http://www.un.org/millenniumgoals/>.
3 The Lisbon Treaty makes this commitment stronger. The new Article 3 provides that 'Union shall ... work for the sustainable development of Europe ...', see the consolidated versions of the Treaty on European Union and the Treaty on the Functioning of the European Union, OJ C 115 of 9 May 2008.
4 For Walmart see <http://walmartstores.com/FactsNews/NewsRoom/8696.aspx> . For Honda see: <http://world.honda.com/environment/ecology/2008report/>.

make this ethic operational. It emphasizes the importance of certain tools for establishing the earth's limits and the ecological impact of development, and the need to keep these distinct from broader sustainable development processes. The article argues that, with ecological sustainability at its normative core, sustainable development has the capacity to set meaningful objectives, duties, and rules and provide boundaries for decision making. Moreover, these roles are already present in recent Westminster and Scottish legislation. The article ends with the observation that even with a much more ecologically based role for sustainable development, decisions relating to improving supply and reducing impacts are much easier for governments, businesses, and individuals than moves to reduce consumption. This omission needs to be addressed through strong leadership if we are genuinely going to move to true sustainability.

HISTORY OF SUSTAINABLE DEVELOPMENT SINCE BRUNDTLAND

The exact meaning of sustainable development remains unclear. The most common definition, that 'development that meets the needs of the present without compromising the ability of future generations to meet their own needs'[5] (the Brundtland definition), brings together different and conflicting interests, but is vague and imprecise. Indeed, the popularity and resilience of sustainable development can largely be attributed to its malleability. Most interpretations of sustainable development work within the Brundtland formula but vary in relation to the emphasis placed on each of the three components of sustainable development: economy, environment, and society. Disparities also exist about the nature of human needs now and in the future, and technology's role in meeting those needs. When differing values combine with these different definitions, sustainable development can be construed as legitimizing 'business-as-usual' patterns of economic growth or, at the other extreme, requiring a fundamental reworking of the global socio-economic order.[6]

In the United Kingdom, as in most countries, national and business interpretations and strategies for sustainable development have been underpinned by what is commonly referred to as 'weak sustainability'.[7] Weaker interpretations of sustainable development focus more on development and are indifferent to the form in which capital stock is passed on.[8]

---

5 World Commission on Environment and Development (WCED), *Our Common Future (The Brundtland Report)* (1987).
6 J. Alder and D. Wilkinson, *Environmental Law and Ethics* (1999) 141; A. Dobson, *Green Political Thought* (1995, 2nd edn.) ch. 3.
7 A. Blowers, 'Planning a Sustainable Future: Problems, Principles and Prospects' (1992) 61 *Town and Country Planning* 132.
8 D. Pearce, *Blueprint 3 – Measuring sustainable development* (1993) at 15. Capital comprises the stock of man-made capital: machines and infrastructure together with

© 2009 The Author. Journal Compilation © 2009 Cardiff University Law School

Pearce notes that 'on the weak sustainability interpretation of sustainable development there is no special place for the environment. The environment is simply another form of capital.'[9] This is reflected in the description of sustainable development as a trade-off between the environment and economic development prominent in the early 1990s.[10] Later interpretations consider the three components of economy, environment, and society as interdependent and mutually reinforcing pillars, yet still favour high economic growth.[11]

These approaches are based on the premise that technology and international trade will ensure there are always enough resources to meet cultural or human carrying capacity. People will always find another way of meeting their needs: 'necessity is the mother of invention'. Many of the solutions promoted, sought, and developed have focused on improving the environmental credentials of the products supplied with little attention being paid to the demand side of the equation. The result is that while fewer resources are required per unit of energy, transport, food, and so on, more units are being consumed.[12] Technology is used to justify our erosion of the earth's capital instead of simply living off the interest. As more and more pressure is placed on the ecosystem through the increased consumption of resources by an ever-growing population, there must come a stage where the ecosystem cannot meet all the demand.

Humanity's demand on the planet's living resources, its ecological footprint, exceeded the earth's ecological limits by the 1980s and has continued to rise such that now its ecological footprint exceeds the planet's regenerative capacity by about 30 per cent.[13] The effects of this failure to protect and maintain the earth's resources are numerous. The climate is changing; the annual mean Central England Temperature (CET) increased by about 1°C in the twentieth century. Since 2000, the CET has continued to

---

the stock of knowledge and skills, or human capital as well as the stock of natural capital including natural resources (renewable and non-renewable), biological diversity, habitat, clean air, water, and so on. We can pass on less of the environment so long as we offset this loss by increasing the stock of roads and machinery or other man-made capital.

9 The weak sustainability interpretation of sustainable development still requires that the depletion of natural resources that are in fixed supply – non-renewable resources – should be accompanied by investment in substitute sources (id. at pp. 15–16). For a slightly stronger view, see J. Bowers, *Sustainability and Environmental Economics – An Alternative Text* (1997) at 194.

10 See *Sustainable Development: The UK Strategy,* (1994; Cm. 2426) Principle 4; *Rio Declaration on Environment and Development* UN Doc. A/CONF.151/26 (Vol. I) (1992).

11 DETR, *A better quality of life: A strategy for sustainable development for the United Kingdom* (1999; Cm. 4345); and *Programme of Implementation of the World Summit on Sustainable Development, Johannesburg* UN Doc. A/CONF.199/20(2002).

12 DofT, Scottish Executive, Welsh Assembly Government, *Transport Statistics for Great Britain 2007 33rd edition* (2007) s. 3.9.

13 WWF, op. cit., n. 1, at p. 2.

35

rise steadily and in 2006, had risen to 1.09°C above the average for 1961–1990.[14] The Stern Review states that, even if the annual flow of emissions did not increase beyond today's rate, the stock of greenhouse gases (GHGs) in the atmosphere would reach double pre-industrial levels by 2050 – that is 550 parts per million CO_2 equivalent, and this could be reached as early as 2035. At this level, there is at least a 77 per cent chance of a global average temperature rise exceeding 2°C.[15] Furthermore, the average abundance of species is declining – a 40 per cent loss between 1970 and 2000. The number of species present in rivers, lakes, and marshlands has declined by 50 per cent. Habitats, such as forests and river systems, are becoming fragmented, affecting their ability to maintain biodiversity and deliver ecosystem services.[16]

The dangers of the weak sustainability approach were explained by renowned economist Robert U. Ayres in 1996:

> To those who follow us we are bequeathing a more and more potent technology and significant investment in productive machinery and equipment and infrastructure. But these benefits may not compensate for a depleted natural resource base, a gravely damaged environment and a broken social contract.[17]

Chambers also warns that:

> Our dominant culture continues to celebrate expansion in spite of its heavy toll on people and nature. In fact, we desperately try to ignore that much of today's income stems from liquidating our social and natural assets. We fool ourselves into believing that we can disregard ecological limits indefinitely.[18]

Just as every flood, hurricane, drought, and extinction increases our awareness of the fragility of the earth's ecological capital, so in the autumn of 2008, the effects of high-risk borrowing started to tremble through the global economy. The same moral and cultural failure to show restraint in consumption that led to the overnight destruction of many of the world's oldest and largest banks is also true in the context of global ecological systems. The United States borrowed $700 billion to bail out its investment banks and other governments had to follow suit.[19] The general consensus is

---

14 Defra, Met Office, Hadley Centre for Climate Prediction and Research, from: <http://www.defra.gov.uk/environment/statistics/globatmos/index.htm>.
15 N. Stern, *The Economics of Climate Change (The Stern Review)* (2006), in Executive Summary.
16 Global Biodiversity Outlook (GBO-2) published by the Secretariat of the Convention on Biological Diversity in 2006 from: <http://www.cbd.int/gbo2/main-messages.shtml>.
17 R.U. Ayres, 'Limits to the growth paradigm' (1996) 19 *Ecological Economics* 117–34, at 117.
18 N. Chambers, C. Simmons, and M. Wackernagel, *Sharing Nature's Interest: Ecological Footprints as an Indicator of Sustainability* (2000) 47.
19 'Q&A: $700 billion US bailout plan' *Times*, 25 September 2008, see <http://business.timesonline.co.uk/tol/business/industry_sectors/banking_and_finance/article4821160.ece>.

36

that the privatization of profits and the nationalization of losses is not sustainable but how do we stop borrowing from our children? Clearly, economies need to develop a social and ecological consciousness and a sense of responsibility needs to be returned to the global market.

ECOLOGICAL SUSTAINABILITY AS THE LEGAL PRINCIPLE UNDERPINNING SUSTAINABLE DEVELOPMENT

Sustainability[20] is generally understood to mean doing things that can be continued over long periods without unacceptable consequences. The ecological changes we are experiencing are or will soon be creating unacceptable consequences and the weak version of sustainability popular among governments and business is not working. The Stern Review concludes that:

> The evidence shows that ignoring climate change will eventually damage economic growth. Our actions over the coming few decades could create risks of major disruption to economic and social activity, later in this century and in the next, on a scale similar to those associated with the great wars and the economic depression of the first half of the 20th century.[21]

A decision-making process which legitimates and promulgates 'business-as-usual' patterns of economic growth is unsustainable. The attempt to roll three types of sustainability (ecological, economic, and social) into one overarching concept of sustainability has left it pointing in multiple directions without any central meaning. Definitions which use such a weak sustainability approach invariably end up in a balancing act, trading off one against the other.[22]

Everything we do is constrained by the earth's ecosystem and there is a need to revisit the basic principles that govern our decision making to ensure environmental concerns have a greater influence. Strong sustainability is often described as limiting the extent to which environmental capital may be substituted by man-made capital and defining certain environmental assets that are critical to our well-being and survival as critical natural capital.[23] The difficulty with this particular conceptualization is that it fails to give guidance as to how we should determine what does or does not qualify as critical natural capital.[24] In this respect, expressing the concept as ecological sustainability may be more helpful. Ecological sustainability imposes a duty

---

20 The term, sustainability, is problematic since it is used to describe many different attributes including the success of a particular business or its succession plans and the state of an economy more generally.
21 Stern, op. cit., n. 15, in Summary of Conclusions.
22 K. Bosselmann, *The Principle of Sustainability – Transforming Law and Governance* (2008) 52.
23 Blowers, op. cit., n. 7.
24 Bowers, op. cit., n. 9, p. 194.

37

on everyone to protect and restore the integrity of the earth's ecological systems. It advocates the need to operate within the ecological carrying capacity of the earth.[25] Decision making based around ecological sustainability places the discussion of trade-offs within the ecological limits of the earth.

This is hardly a new idea and respect for nature and the 'need for human activity to respect the requisites for its maintenance and continuance' have been present in the ideologies of many ancient civilizations.[26] While recently ignored by the industrialized world, it should be a fairly obvious observation that development must occur within the confines of the earth's capabilities.

Sound environmental management practices already advocate an ecosystem approach which 'recognises the relationships between healthy and resilient ecosystems, biodiversity conservation and human wellbeing'.[27] That said, to make a significant impact on the way we live, ecological sustainability needs to be more than a policy objective. Clearly, the law has a crucial role here:

> Ecosystems don't obey the rules of private property. What one farmer does – in fencing his land, blocking animal migrations, spraying crops, introducing new crop varieties, hunting and fishing, logging, pumping groundwater or managing livestock diseases – has ramifications far beyond the farm.[28]

Bosselmann notes that 'while a legal system cannot on its own initiate and monitor social change, it can formulate some parameters for the direction and extent of social change.'[29] Current legal systems, preoccupied with private property and individual rights, are failing to respond to our modern needs. To really make a difference, the ecological systems approach needs to be supported by a strong moral and legal normative framework. A new ethic is needed which advocates the need to operate within the ecological carrying capacity of the earth. One way of obtaining the necessary status would be to treat ecological sustainability as a legal principle.[30]

The debates about what exactly is required to qualify as a legal principle and the role and value in law of such principles are beyond the scope of this article.[31] It is clear that both legislators and the courts have shown some acceptance of environmental principles generally. While sustainable development itself is not recognized as a legal principle in United Kingdom,

---

25 See n. 57 below.
26 See Weeramantry, separate Opinion to the ICJ's 1997 Case Concerning the Gabçikovo-Nagymaros Project (*Hungary* v. *Slovakia*).
27 WWF, op. cit., n. 1, at p. 30. See, also, <www.cbd.int/ecosystem/principles.shtml>.
28 WWF, id., quoting J.D. Sachs, Director, The Earth Institute.
29 Bosselmann, op. cit., n. 22, p. 43.
30 id., p. 5.
31 For a full exposition see Bosselmann, id., p. 48; R. Dworkin, *Taking Rights Seriously* (1977) 22; G. Winter, 'The Legal Nature of Environmental Principles in International, EC and German Law' in *Principles of European Environmental Law*, ed. R. Macrory (2004) 13–14.

EU or international law, the EU and several other national states have elevated certain environmental approaches, such the polluter pays, to the status of principle.[32] Moreover, the English courts have accepted sustainability as a material consideration in planning decisions, that it is capable of being a main issue in planning law decisions and may deserve significant weight.[33] The leap to accepting ecological sustainability as a legal principle given the ever-growing pressure on the earth's environment is a natural progression.

As such, this article supports Bosselmann's contention that ecological sustainability meets the criteria of a legal principle. It is reflective of a fundamental morality (respect for ecological integrity). It also requires action (to protect and restore). Therefore it is capable of causing legal effect.[34] Furthermore, unlike other environmental principles such as the polluter pays or the precautionary principles which are directive, ecological sustainability is an approach not unlike justice and equality.[35] As such, it should be considered a fundamental legal principle to be used in the same way as the principles of fairness, freedom, and justice.

More importantly, and regardless of the intricacies of the theoretical debate, the main justification supporting ecological sustainability as a fundamental legal principle used in this article is that our ability to deliver the other fundamental legal principles (freedom, equality, justice) reduces as the earth's resources and resilience reduces. The best way to protect these other fundamental legal principles is to operate within a system based on ecological sustainability.

Significantly, this is not just some ideological whim. There is evidence of a trend towards ecological sustainability in various public and private spheres. The remainder of this article explores this trend and how this ethic can be made operational. The Organisation for Economic Cooperation and Development (OECD) has established five criteria for the effective implementation of sustainable development: a common understanding of sustainable development; clear commitment and leadership; specific institutional mechanisms to steer integration (including enforcement and monitoring); effective stakeholder involvement; and efficient knowledge management.[36] These same criteria will also need to exist for any shift from an approach based on weak sustainability to an approach with ecological sustainability at its core. The next two sections explore the extent to which the ecological sustainability

---

32 See Art. 178 of the EC Treaty. See, also, Weeramantry, op. cit., n. 26; Macrory, id.; A. Ross 'Why legislate for sustainable development? An examination of sustainable development provisions in UK and Scottish statutes' (2008) 20 *J. of Environmental Law* 35–68, at 44.

33 *Horsham DC* v. *First Secretary of State, Devine Homes plc* [2004] EWHC 769.

34 Bosselmann, op. cit., n. 22, p. 53.

35 id., p. 57.

36 OECD, *Improving Policy Coherence and Integration for Sustainable Development: A Checklist* (2002) 2.

39

ethic has been accepted and understood by policy makers and is present in strategic aims. The second section concentrates on the influence of the climate change agenda on any strategic move towards ecological sustainability and the risk of the ecological sustainability ethic becoming subsumed within the very different objectives of the climate change agenda. The article then examines the mechanisms needed to determine the limits of various ecosystems and the impact of proposed action or inaction on those ecosystems. It then considers the various possible roles for sustainable development as the means for getting the information about limits and impacts into the decision-making process and providing the rules which structure the decision-making process. The article ends with a discussion about the need for leadership.

ECOLOGICAL SUSTAINABILITY AND STRATEGIC VISION

There is evidence at various levels of governance that ecological sustainability already has some credence as a guiding ethic. One of the strongest formulations is present in the Earth Charter, which is a declaration of fundamental principles for building a just, sustainable, and peaceful global society for the twenty-first century.[37] The idea of a new charter that would set forth fundamental principles for sustainable development was discussed in the Brundtland Report and later at the United Nations' 1992 Earth Summit in Rio de Janeiro.[38] In 1994, Maurice Strong, the Secretary General of the Earth Summit and chairman of the Earth Council, and Mikhail Gorbachev, president of Green Cross International, launched the Earth Charter Initiative with support from the Dutch government. The Charter is the result of a long period of wide civic engagement and consultation. Its final text was approved by consensus at a meeting at the United Nations Educational Scientific and Cultural Organization (UNESCO) Headquarters in Paris in March 2000. Subsequently the Charter has been formally endorsed by thousands of organizations representing millions of people, including the UNESCO Conference of Member States, the World Conservation Union of IUCN, national government ministries, national and international associations of universities, and hundreds of cities and towns in dozens of countries. It has also been endorsed by tens of thousands of individuals, and publicly supported by numerous heads of state.[39]

In the Earth Charter the environment is presented as the basis of all life. This shift from a narrow human centred to broader life centred perspective is expressed in its overarching principles of governance:

---

37 *The Earth Charter*, available at <http://www.earthcharterinaction.org/assets/pdf/EC.English.pdf>.

38 See the Earth Charter Initative at <http://www.earthcharter.org/>.

39 For example, the Government of Mexico, the City of Munich: see <http://www.earthcharterinaction.org/2007/05/mexican_government_commits_to.html>.

40

1. Respect Earth and life in all its diversity.
2. Care for the community of life with understanding, compassion, and love.
3. Build democratic societies that are just, participatory, sustainable, and peaceful.
4. Secure Earth's bounty and beauty for present and future generations.

It then sets out certain actions required to fulfill these four broad commitments.[40]

Change is also evident at a United Kingdom level. The *Framework for Sustainable Development* published jointly by all the administrations in the United Kingdom in 2005 sets out a new approach to sustainable development based on five principles.[41] The first principle is living within environmental limits:

Respecting the limits of the planet's environment, resources and biodiversity – to improve our environment and ensure that the natural resources needed for life are unimpaired and remain so for future generations.

The third principle is achieving a sustainable economy:

Building a strong, stable and sustainable economy which provides prosperity and opportunities for all, and in which environmental and social costs fall on those who impose them (Polluter Pays) and efficient resource use is incentivised.[42]

The reference to high economic growth is gone and this demonstrates a deeper commitment to ecological sustainability.

In *Choosing our future – Scotland's sustainable development strategy*, four priorities have been set for Scotland.[43] The first priority is:

sustainable consumption and production: achieving more with less and includes reducing the inefficient use of resources, looking at the impact of products and materials across their whole lifecycle, and encouraging people to think about the social and environmental consequences of their purchasing choices.

The third priority is:

natural resource protection and environmental enhancement: protecting our natural resources, building a better understanding of environmental limits, and improving the quality of the environment.

---

40 *Earth Charter*, op. cit., n. 37.
41 HM Government, Scottish Executive, Welsh Assembly Government, Northern Ireland Office, *One future – different paths, The UK's shared framework for sustainable development* (2005) 8.
42 The other three principles are: ensuring a strong, healthy and just society; promoting good governance, and using sound science responsibly.
43 Scottish Executive, *Choosing our future – Scotland's sustainable development strategy* (2005). The other two priorities are: climate change and energy; and sustainable communities (creating communities that embody the principles of sustainable development locally).

Later, the strategy states that:

> [t]he business case for sustainability is simple. Smarter use of resources does not just make good economic sense; it is absolutely essential for our long-term survival.[44]

Throughout the strategy, environmental objectives and actions are listed ahead of the social and economic goals, thus reinforcing a vision based on limits rather than trade-offs.

There are also examples of multinational companies promoting an ecological sustainability ethic. Retailer Marks and Spencer plc, for example, is promoting Plan A:

> a five-year, 100-point 'eco' plan to ... work with our customers and our suppliers to combat climate change, reduce waste, safeguard natural resources, trade ethically and build a healthier nation.

Plan A has ambitious targets such as becoming carbon neutral and sending no waste to landfill by 2012.[45]

ECOLOGICAL SUSTAINABILITY AND THE INFLUENCE OF CLIMATE CHANGE

It would be naïve to ignore the influence of the climate change agenda on any modern approach to sustainable development. Environmental law has always been disaster-driven. Changes in responses to nuclear accidents only came about after the Chernobyl disaster.[46] Air quality measures were only seriously introduced following the London Smog crisis in 1952 which killed almost four thousand people.[47] Climate change is pushing environmental matters back into the forefront of political, economic, and legislative discussions.

One reason climate change is grabbing headlines is that it is actually the largest threat to our continued existence. Indeed the *Living Planet Report 2008* states that:

> [p]otentially the greatest threat to biodiversity over the coming decades is climate change. Early impacts have been felt in polar and montane as well as coastal and marine ecosystems, such as coral reefs.

Thus, if one is genuinely concerned about wildlife and biodiversity, tackling the emissions of GHGs should be a priority.

---

44 id., at para. 3.11.
45 <http://plana.marksandspencer.com/index.php?action=PublicPillarDisplay>.
46 1986 Convention on Notification of a Nuclear Accident (Vienna), Misc. 2 (1989), Cm. 565; 25 ILM (1370) (1986); P.D. Cameron et al. (eds.), *Nuclear Energy Law after Chernobyl* (1988).
47 Clean Air Act 1956.

There is however, another reason. Unlike many other environmental concepts or concerns such as sustainable development or biodiversity, climate change can be explained in layman's terms. There is strong evidence that GHG emissions from human activities are now raising the earth's temperature and causing other changes in climate. Emissions are projected to rise significantly over the next few decades, and quite likely beyond, leading to significant increases in global temperatures with profound risks for the natural environment and human society worldwide. Without action to reduce GHG emissions, global temperatures are expected to rise by between 1.4 and 5.8°C by 2100 and sea level could also rise by between 0.09 and 0.88 metres compared to 1990 levels. The consequences include increased storms, floods, drought, desertification, habitat loss, and melting ice caps.[48]

Thus, the problem is clear in relation to what is actually happening to the earth's climate. Its impact on the inhabitants of various parts of the earth at various periods in the future is also clear. The cause of the harm is known and at least some of the steps to curb and adapt to the change are also known. Action is much more possible since there is a tangible concern and clear areas which can be targeted.

Securing the Future – The UK Government Sustainable Development Strategy provides that:

> [s]ustainable development and climate change are two vitally important and interrelated challenges facing us in the 21st century. Our ability to develop more sustainably will determine the speed and degree of climate change we experience. And as the climate changes the choices available to us to develop sustainably will change.[49]

While the strategy clearly acknowledges that sustainable development and climate change address different challenges and have different objectives, it also treats the agendas as being equal in scope. This perspective arguably increases the importance of mitigating climate change and controlling GHG emissions within the remit of sustainable development which, in turn, focuses on limits and thus promotes ecological sustainability.

There are significant benefits with this approach. First, as climate change is arguably the most significant of the environmental harms facing the earth, this higher status may be warranted. After all, as noted above, climate change itself is the biggest threat to biodiversity.[50] Furthermore, its more comprehensible agenda elevates the ecological sustainability platform, at least in relation to keeping our emissions within the limits which the earth can absorb. It may also reflect the other more development oriented aspects of sustainable development.

---

48 Defra, *Climate Change – The UK Programme 2006* (2006; Cm. 6764) 8.
49 Defra, *Securing the Future – The UK Government Sustainable Development Strategy* (2005; Cm. 6467) 73.
50 WWF, op. cit., n. 1.

The difficulty is that while the climate change agenda takes a limits based approach, this is only in respect of one aspect of the earth's ecosystem – the effect of increased GHG emissions on the climate – and that may not reflect ecological sustainability in relation to other aspects of the earth's ecosystem. Despite the huge threat climate change poses to most parts of the earth's ecosystem, it is still true that action which simply reduces GHG emissions may actually harm other parts of the environment or may have serious negative effects on certain communities or economies. For example, solutions such as carbon capture and storage, whereby carbon is trapped and then injected into receptacles on land, in sand or under the sea in former oil and gas reserves, while potentially very effective at tackling GHG emissions may have its own environmental consequences caused by the transport of the carbon and if any should escape.[51] Similarly, a decision to support nuclear energy projects would clearly reduce our reliance on fossil fuels and, as a result, reduce GHG emissions, but could seriously increase, among other things, risks of radiation and the amount of heavy metals needing disposal.

The danger of the approach in the strategy is that it narrows the scope of sustainable development by increasing the weight afforded to the climate change agenda in any decision-making process, creating the risk of ecological sustainability being submerged in another different agenda.

The development of renewable energy sources contributes to a reduction of GHG emissions and provides increased energy security by offering a local alternative to oil and gas. However, renewables in the wider context of environmental sustainability and sustainable development are not necessarily a panacea without their own environmental consequences. As Li explains, too many cars powered with fuel cells add to the water vapour in the air (humidity) which will affect the climate and both the natural and built environment.[52] The production of biofuels takes away land used for food production and this affects the price of certain foods. The intensification of agriculture can also result in increased run-off of nutrients, thus leading to increased eutrophication of lakes, rivers, and seas. Tidal projects can have biodiversity consequences. Wind power can require a great deal of land and needs to be carefully planned around existing uses to minimize the effects on biodiversity and amenity.[53]

The Sustainable Development Commission (SDC) has expressed some concern about this asymmetric vein of the climate change agenda. In its response to the consultation on the Scottish Climate Change Bill, the Commission emphasizes that:

---

51 Intergovernmental Panel on Climate Change (IPCC), *Carbon Dioxide Capture and Storage* (2006) 11.
52 X. Li, 'Diversification and localization of energy systems for sustainable development and energy security' (2005) 33 *Energy Policy* 2237–43, at 2240.
53 id., p. 2242.

Government will need to ensure that action to tackle climate change will not impact upon wider sustainable development ... In scrutinising action on climate change the SDC will work to ensure that Government action on climate change is not at the unnecessary expense of damage to other parts of the environment, or to social and economic needs.[54]

While this quote can be used to support an argument based on ecological sustainability, it could also be supporting a business-as-usual weak-sustainability approach.

At this stage, it is also comforting to remember that tackling climate change does not only concern mitigating GHG emissions. It also concerns adaptation measures to address the effects of climate change (which many scientists now believe is inevitable) on the various regions and communities of the earth, including the economic, social, environmental, and other effects of rising sea levels, temperatures, desertification, and melting ice caps. The *UK Strategy* reflects this reality: 'Adaptation must be brought in to all aspects of sustainable development and climate change has been considered in relation to each aspect of this strategy.'[55] Moreover, as will be discussed below, despite the danger of ecological sustainability and, in turn, sustainable development becoming subsumed into the climate change agenda, the United Kingdom Climate Change Bill appears to be based around a much more holistic vision of ecological sustainability which uses sustainable development as the framework for climate change decision making. For example, it requires the policies and objectives within adaptation programmes to contribute to sustainable development.[56]

ESTABLISHING LIMITS AND IMPACTS FOR ECOLOGICAL SUSTAINABILITY

Ecological sustainability is highly dependent on science to establish what the carrying capacity of a certain ecosystem is in relation to certain impacts and to compare and prioritize between local, neighbouring, and global limits. These are not easy tasks and the development of tools capable of generating robust data on limits and impacts is currently a major area of research. Various useful tools exist such as ecological foot printing,[57] sustainability wedges,[58] and

---

54 Sustainable Development Commission Scotland (SDC)'s response to the Scottish Government's consultation on a Scottish Climate Change Bill, at <http://www.sd-commission.org.uk/publications/downloads/SDC%20Scotland%20Response%20to%20Scottish%20Climate%20Change%20Bill%20Consultation.pdf>.

55 Defra, op. cit., n. 49, at p. 92.

56 Climate Change Bill (as amended in Public Bill Committee 10 July 2008), clause 56(1).

57 See J. Venetoulis, D. Chazan, and C. Gudet, *Ecological Footprint of Nations 2004* (2004) 7; W.E. Rees, 'Footprint: our impact on the earth is getting heavier' (2002) 420 *Nature* 267–8.

58 See WWF, op. cit., n. 1, at pp. 1, 23, 25: see, also, S. Pacala and R. Socolow, 'Stabilization wedges: solving the climate problem for the next 50 years with current technologies' (2004) 305 *Science* 968–72.

45

environmental assessment, including strategic environmental assessment.[59] To promote ecological sustainability, it is essential that these tools continue to focus on the integrity of the environment and remain separate from any broader sustainability appraisals which include social and economic impacts. These tools are the starting point for decision making by providing the necessary information about the ecological limits or carrying capacity of systems at local, regional, and global levels. Local limits may need to be exceeded for the global good and vice versa. Developing and improving the tools capable of comparing local and global impacts must be a priority. Once a determination has been made about the baseline critical natural capital, further decisions will need to balance local needs and cumulative effects in relation to the other less critical aspects of the environment in addition to the social and economic concerns. This is the role of sustainable development.

DELIVERING ECOLOGICAL SUSTAINABILITY – THE ROLE OF SUSTAINABLE DEVELOPMENT

Humans have a need to improve, ask questions and seek answers; we seek fulfilment and this yearning is encapsulated in the term 'development'. The key measures of development in industrialized countries, such as gross domestic product, have largely focused on economic development, consumption, and wealth.[60] More recently, there has been a recognition that wealth does not necessarily equate to wellbeing or happiness and newer measures of development include mortality rates, employment, and wellbeing.[61] To quote the Earth Charter: '[w]e must realise that when basic needs have been met, human development is primarily about being more, not having more.'[62]

The original purpose of the sustainable development agenda was to bring the economic development and environmental protection agendas together.[63] In so doing, sustainable development can usefully be viewed as either a product or a process. As a product, it is an aim to which every project and action should aspire. For example, a given wind farm or strategic policy can be considered to be a sustainable development in and of itself or it can be viewed as part of the larger project of regional, national or global sustainable

---

59 See, for example, Council Directive 2001/42/EC on the assessment of certain plans and programmes on the environment.
60 A. Grainger, 'Introduction' in *Exploring Sustainable Development – Geographical perspectives*, eds. M. Purvis and A. Grainger (2004) 10.
61 See United Nations Human Development Index (HDI) as set out in UNDP, *Human Development Report 2007/2008* at <http://hdr.undp.org/en/reports/global/hdr2007-2008/>.
62 *Earth Charter*, op. cit., n. 37, Preamble.
63 P. Sands, *Principles of International Environmental Law* (2003, 2nd edn.) 9; WCED, op. cit., n. 5.

development. This article focuses on the use of sustainable development as a process. In this context, as Stallworthy observes:

> sustainable development provides a foundation for integration of environmental and other considerations within the process of decision making and a means whereby environmental impacts of our activities, previously uncosted, can be internalised.[64]

However, the term needs to do more than simply bundle together the economic, environmental, and social policy strands. The conflicts internal to the term sustainable development and its imprecise nature have meant it has been manipulated to support or refute different policy outcomes based on different objectives and the amount of weight attached to them. One decision may be sustainable because it attaches more weight to economic considerations over social or environmental ones; another decision may favour environmental factors, and so on. To be effective, sustainable development needs to provide more guidance as to the way these strands relate to one another.

Elkins claims that 'sustainable development requires the adoption of ecological sustainability as the principal economic objective in place of economic growth'.[65] With ecological sustainability at the core of sustainable development, it is then possible to relate the social and economic components of sustainable development to a central point of reference within defined boundaries.[66] Sustainable development becomes a more meaningful organizational framework for balancing the earth's sustainability with our human need to develop. Thus, 'a development is sustainable if it tends to preserve the integrity and continued existence of ecological systems; it is unsustainable if it tends to do otherwise.'[67] The emphasis is on first determining the ecological limits and then establishing what development is feasible within those limits.[68] Once the limits are agreed, the balancing and trade-offs still occur but not in relation to the earth's natural capital.

Given sustainable development's opaque historical meaning, it is not surprising that translating it into meaningful legal formulations has proven problematic and most instruments have tended to be highly generalized.[69] Indeed, the United Kingdom's initial approach to sustainable development was largely non-legislative relying instead on policy directions from the executive and non-statutory aims and objectives.[70] Early legislative formula-

---

64 M. Stallworthy, *Understanding Environmental Law* (2008) 174.
65 P. Elkins, '"Limits to growth" and "sustainable development": grappling with ecological realities' (1993) 8 *Ecological Economics* 269, at 280.
66 Bosselmann, op. cit., n. 22, at p. 52.
67 id.
68 This is no easy feat as the impacts of any decision need to be considered in the context of the local ecosystems, foreign ecosystems, and that of the earth as a whole. See nn. 57–59 above.
69 Stallworthy, op. cit., n. 64, at p. 174.
70 Ross, op. cit., n. 32, at p. 36.

47

tions were so vague and diluted that they could only be interpreted as symbolic or, at best, aspirational. For example, the Natural Heritage Scotland Act 1991 imposes a duty on Scottish Natural Heritage 'to have regard to the desirability of securing that anything done whether by SNH or any other person, in relation to the natural heritage of Scotland is undertaken in a manner which is sustainable'. The Environment Agency and SEPA under the Environment Protection Act 1995 have even more convoluted duties.[71]

That said, especially since 1999, references to sustainable development in statutes have been on the increase and in much clearer and more powerful legal forms. Sustainable development appears as duties, objectives, and procedural requirements. This reflects an acceptance of sustainable development as a policy tool as the United Kingdom tends to legislate to crystallize environmental policy only after it has been tested and is more widely accepted. It has been encouraged by devolution and the increased status of the concept at EU level.[72] Most of the newer provisions use mandatory language and create much stronger obligations. Probably because of the imprecise and evolutionary nature of sustainable development, the vast majority of the provisions do not attempt to define it and instead rely on government guidance to provide the necessary consistency and flexibility.[73] This flexibility permits the normative core of sustainable development to evolve and shift to become more ecologically based without requiring amendment of the statutory provisions.

The simplest provisions link sustainable development to a procedural requirement. These can be obligations to produce or follow guidance, regulations or directions, strategies, reports or they may require notice, audit or publicity. Probably, the most influential of the reporting obligations are those found in the Government of Wales Act 2006 s. 79(1) which provides that '[t]he Assembly shall make a scheme setting out how it proposes, in the exercise of its functions, to promote sustainable development.' Section 79(7) then provides that:

> [i]n the year following each ordinary election (after the first) the Assembly shall publish a report containing an assessment of how effective its proposals (as set out in the scheme and implemented) have been in promoting sustainable development.

Here, the implied aims are supported by procedural requirements to produce a scheme and then report on it.[74] The provision creates a strong obligation as

---

71 See Environment Act 1995 s. 4(1) and s. 31(2). Arguably, given the importance of these agencies, they should have more modern duties.
72 Ross, op. cit., n. 32, at p. 37.
73 id., p. 44; an exception may be the International Development Act 2002 s. 1(3).
74 Sections 79(1) and 79(7) replace ss. 121(1) and 121(7) of the Government of Wales Act 1998. See Welsh Assembly Government (WAG), *Sustainable Development Annual Report 2004* (2004) and WAG, *Sustainable Development Action Plan 2004–2007* (2004). Pursuant to the 1998 provisions, effectiveness reports were published by

the procedural requirement acts as a legal rule. Dworkin explains that 'rules are applicable in an all or nothing fashion. If the facts a rule stipulates are given, then either the rule is valid . . . or it is not, in which case it contributes nothing to the decision.'[75]

Procedural rules can also be used to reinforce strong substantive obligations. Section 38(1) of the Land Reform (Scotland) Act 2003 provides that:

> (1) Ministers shall not decide that a community interest is to be entered in the Register unless they are satisfied – . . .
> (b) that – . . .
> (ii) the land is sufficiently near to land with which those members of that community have a substantial connection and that its acquisition by the community body is compatible with furthering the achievement of sustainable development;

In this case a failure to meet the strong substantive provisions relating to the main purpose of community bodies and interests is supported by serious procedural implications in company and land law. Fox reports that, as of March 2006, there had been five instances where the Scottish Ministers have refused to register the community interest in the Register of Community Interests in Land Charges because the community body has failed to show that its purpose was for sustainable development or that its Memorandum, Articles, membership or constitution were compatible with the Act. In fact, this has been the most common ground of rejection.[76] This type of accountability and review procedures provide the necessary link between the procedures and substantive compliance. If the approach taken to sustainable development has ecological sustainability at its core, this type of provision has the capacity to deliver truly sustainable outcomes.

Sustainable development most often appears as an objective or duty for a regulatory regime or authority. The Planning and Compulsory Purchase Act 2004 s. 39(2) provides that those bodies involved in development planning in England and Wales must exercise the function with the objective of contributing to sustainable development. In this example sustainable development is the primary duty; however, in most cases, it is one of several duties or objectives. Some statutes include qualifications and mechanisms for prioritizing between duties but in others that is left to the decision maker. In some instances, it is simply one of several competing objectives to be balanced against one another.[77]

---

independent consultants and resulted in improvements being made in Wales's substantive commitment to sustainable development. See CAG Consultants, *How Effectively has the National Assembly for Wales promoted Sustainable Development? Report to the Welsh Assembly Government* (2003).

75 Dworkin, op. cit., n. 31, at p. 24.
76 A Fox, 'Update on the Right to Buy Land', Proceedings from the Rural Law Conference held 23 March 2006 (CLT, Glasgow) at 47.
77 See, for example, the Further and Higher Education (Scotland) Act 2005 s. 20.

49

There are instances where the sustainable development duty or objective appears to be the mechanism for balancing other duties or objectives. In these cases it acts as a legal rule. A common phrase is 'shall exercise its powers *in the way best calculated to contribute* to the achievement of sustainable development'.[78] This formulation sets out the mechanism for decision-making as a legal rule but it is couched in discretionary language which means other factors will influence the decision. This does not prohibit these from being considered legal rules.[79] As a result, rules may be formulated to allow the balancing of opposing concerns within the scope of the rule.[80] In these cases, only the policies and concepts referred to in the rule may be used to influence an agency's decision making generally or a particular type of decision.[81]

The Greater London Authority Act 1999 provides a good example of a duty which creates a policy objective to be balanced with other objectives and another duty which arguably creates a rule. Section 30(1) gives the Authority the power to do anything to further its principal purposes.[82] The Act then creates two different approaches for decision-making and both rely on sustainable development. Under subsection (4), which deals with the determination of whether and how to exercise the power, the duty imposed on the Authority is 'to have regard to the achievement of sustainable development'. Thus, sustainable development is simply an aspirational goal which is deliberately framed to be a material consideration in making the decision. In contrast, subsection (5), which deals with the actual exercise of the powers, imposes a duty on the Authority to act in the way it considers best calculated to contribute to the achievement of sustainable development subject to a reasonableness test. This formulation creates a rule which describes a framework for the decision-making process.

Importantly, this approach is also evident in the recent Climate Change Bill. As discussed earlier, it is essential that decisions taken to address climate change operate in the broad framework of sustainable development and are based on ecological sustainability. Some of the more attractive renewable options available need to be pursued within the context of sustainable development, the limits of the earth, and what action best copes with these changes. The approach taken in the United Kingdom Climate

---

78 See Transport Act s. 207(2)(b); Water Industry (Scotland) Act 2002 s. 51; Water Environment and Water Services (Scotland) Act 2003 s. 2(4).

79 Dworkin, op. cit., n. 31, at p. 28.

80 De Sadeleer describes these as rules of indeterminate content and argues that such a rule may be created so long as it appears in a normative text and is formulated in a sufficiently prescriptive manner. N. De Sadeleer, *Environmental Principles: From Political Slogans to Legal Rules* (2005) at 311.

81 See, for example, Land Reform (Scotland) Act 2003 ss. 34, 51.

82 Principal purposes are (a) promoting economic development and wealth creation in Greater London; (b) promoting social development in Greater London; and (c) promoting the improvement of the environment in Greater London.

Change Bill clearly reflects this view. The Bill amends the Energy Act 2004 to include section 125 A(2) which provides that:

> [i]t is the duty of the Administrator to promote the supply of renewable transport fuel whose production, supply or use –
> (a) causes or contributes to the reduction of carbon emissions, and
> (b) contributes to sustainable development or the protection or enhancement of the environment generally.[83]

Thus, while sustainable development as a material consideration can only at best suggest ecological sustainability as a worthwhile objective, sustainable development as a legal rule providing either some procedural requirement or as a framework for making the ultimate decision can actually impose and deliver ecological sustainability. As a result, these provisions have the capacity to deliver the real change needed to ensure development is kept within the earth's ecological limits; whether they actually will do so largely depends on leadership.

LEADERSHIP, ECOLOGICAL SUSTAINABILITY, AND CURBING CONSUMPTION

Technology makes resource use more efficient, yet technological changes that enhance productivity, instead of reducing consumption, often result in increased exploitation of natural resources.[84] Analogous to a weak sustainability approach, as technology has improved, very little attempt has been made to alter human behaviour so that we consume fewer resources. As evidenced from the discussion above, the solutions presented for dealing with climate change remain focused on technology.

Clearly the most effective way of dealing with climate change and contributing to sustainable development is to reduce our consumption of energy. The Sustainable Development Commission has noted that:

> climate change can be most effectively halted if Government tackles unsustainable policies that encourage unsustainable actions within society. End of pipe interventions alone will not deliver the long term emissions reductions required.[85]

If we use less energy then there will be less demand for energy so that new, safe, and secure sources of energy become less pressured. Also, if we use less energy, then fewer harmful emissions are emitted into the atmosphere. Many environmental, social, and economic concerns can be addressed by tackling consumption. The mechanisms used to reduce energy consumption include a

---

83 Climate Change Bill, op. cit., n. 56, Schedule 7.
84 For a fuller discussion about this observation, see S. Beder, *Environmental Principles and Policies – An Interdisciplinary Introduction* (2006) ch. 1.
85 SDC, op. cit., n. 54.

culture of making things last and then reusing them, reducing what we use, and recycling wherever possible. Some actions, such as improvements in home insulation, are one-off changes. Other actions require a concerted cultural and perhaps moral change which will often need to be motivated by the state using market and other regulatory incentives and penalties. While improvements in the public transport network are necessary to provide the opportunity for people to alter their behaviour, it may not be sufficient, especially if road and air transport continue to be more attractive in relation to comfort, cost, and timing. In these instances, taxes which address the true cost of these transport options do work. Indeed, more generally, mechanisms aimed at reducing consumption, while often unpopular, have proven effective. Experience with the congestion charge for London shows a substantial decrease in the number of individuals taking their cars into central London.[86] In the Republic of Ireland, charging consumers for plastic bags resulted in an immediate 90 per cent drop in their use.[87]

So why has this not happened? Leadership has repeatedly been cited as the most important aspect for sustainable development governance.[88] Yet, the immediate response to concerns about rising energy costs and energy security focused on the development and provision of alternative sources of energy including fossil fuels.[89] Furthermore, the present British government seems to take the view that for every decision made to tackle climate change or promote sustainable development, two are made to counteract any benefit often in the name of economic growth. The day after the new Secretary of State for Climate Change, Ed Miliband MP, announced a legally-binding pledge to cut Britain's GHG emissions by 80 per cent by 2050 covering all sectors of the economy, including shipping and aviation,[90] the Prime Minister Gordon Brown was threatening petrol companies with an inquiry under competition laws if they refused to pass on lower oil prices to

---

86 Transport for London, *Central London Congestion Charging Impacts Monitoring. Sixth Annual Report* (2008); and <http://www.tfl.gov.uk/roadusers/congestioncharging/6723.aspx>.

87 See Department of Environment, Heritage and Local Government at <http://www.environ.ie/en/Environment/Waste/PlasticBags/>.

88 S. Cussons, *Review of Statutory Sustainable Development Duties* (2006) 16; A. Ross, 'Sustainable development in Scotland post-devolution' (2006) 8 *Environmental Law Rev.* 6–32, at 14.

89 For example, previously unviable sources of oil and gas are becoming attractive due to the higher price of energy, and the fact they are in secure locations. Many of these sources, such as the tar sands in Alberta, Canada are not only economically expensive to exploit but also environmentally costly. Oil production in the tar sands requires substantial amounts of natural gas and water, and there are also biodiversity issues related to these sources as well as social considerations relating to health and safety and impacts on the local community. Climate Action Network Canada, *Stuck in the Tar Sands – How the Federal Government's Proposed Climate Change Strategy Lets Oil Companies off the Hook* (2008) at 4.

90 'Britain to pledge legally-binding emissions cut' *Independent*, 16 October 2008.

motorists.[91] The previous week, the government had backed plans to allow the expansion of Stansted Airport to handle an extra 10 million passengers a year and increase the number of flights from 241,000 to 264,000.[92] By continuing to provide secure supplies of cheap oil and gas there is little incentive on anyone to consume less fuel or switch to alternative fuels or alternative transport.

CONCLUSION

The earth's fragility has never been more obvious and we are facing unprecedented levels of environmental harm and, as a result, increasing social and economic hazards. Weak sustainability, whereby environmental factors are traded off against social and economic ones, has meant that today's income comes from liquidating our social and natural assets capital. A new ethic is required which advocates the need to operate within the ecological carrying capacity of the earth. Ecological sustainability imposes a duty on everyone to protect and restore the integrity of the earth's ecological systems. Decision making based around ecological sustainability places the discussion of trade-offs within the ecological limits of the earth. Like justice and equality, ecological sustainability is an approach and should be considered a fundamental legal principle. This status is deserved since our ability to deliver the other fundamental legal principles (freedom, equality, justice) reduces as the earth's resources and resilience reduce, and the best way to protect these other fundamental legal principles is to operate within a system based on ecological sustainability.

Modern strategies such as the Earth Charter and the United Kingdom Framework for Sustainable Development show to a greater or lesser extent that there is a growing shift in favour of more ecologically based interpretations of sustainable development.

Given that the impacts, causes, and solutions of climate change are relatively easy to understand, climate change has the potential to be a champion for all aspects of the earth's ecosystems, not just its ability to absorb GHG emissions. Furthermore, the extent and the seriousness of climate change as the most significant environmental harm facing the earth justifies the additional attention it attracts. If this is the case, however, it is essential that strategies and actions which address climate change are based on the principle of ecological sustainability and contribute to sustainable development more generally.

The mechanisms necessary to establish the carrying capacity of the earth's ecosystems and tools such as stabilization wedges, environmental

---

91 'Brown: Petrol firms must lower fuel prices or face OFT inquiry' *Independent*, 17 October 2008.
92 'Government green light for Stansted expansion' *Independent*, 9 October 2008.

53

assessment, and ecological footprints are constantly being refined and improved. It is essential that these tools stay focused on ecological limits and are kept separate from the broader sustainable development tools.

With ecological sustainability at its core, sustainable development has the capacity to set meaningful objectives, duties, and rules and provide boundaries for decision making, roles which are already present in recent Westminster and Scottish legislation. While sustainable development as a material consideration can only at best suggest ecological sustainability as a worthwhile objective, sustainable development as a legal rule providing either some procedural requirement or as a framework for decision making can deliver ecological sustainability. These provisions are capable of delivering the real changes needed to ensure development is kept within the earth's ecological limits.

Success, however, depends on leadership and a long-term view which addresses consumption as well as supply. At the moment, world and business leaders are preoccupied with the prospect of an imminent global economic recession and trying to develop strategies to keep the global and local economies from stagnating. A favoured approach in the past has been to increase public and consumer spending by, for example, a blanket reduction of value added tax. While increasing our consumption of the earth's resources may have been the solution to recession in the past, it is not the solution of the future. The temptation to continue to borrow even more from our neighbours and children in both economic and ecological terms must be resisted. The more we erode the earth's carrying capacity, the more the ability of leaders to provide answers to economic and social crises diminishes. As Wackneragel and Rees observe, we need to 'shift our emphasis from "managing resources" to managing ourselves so that we learn to live as part of nature'.[93] Alternative solutions are not so far away and with ecological sustainability at its normative core, sustainable development has the capacity to provide the necessary boundaries for the difficult decisions facing the world today.

---

93 M. Wackneragel and W.E. Rees, *Our Ecological Footprint – Reducing Human Impact on the Earth* (1996) at 4.

JOURNAL OF LAW AND SOCIETY
VOLUME 36, NUMBER 1, MARCH 2009
ISSN: 0263-323X, pp. 55–74

Environmental Justice Imperatives for an Era of Climate Change

MARK STALLWORTHY*

This paper is about intra- and inter-generational equity, connecting environmental justice discourse with necessary responses to climate change. It offers a review of the role of globalization in this pervasive context, contrasting the disaggregated nature of localized impacts, and seeks to address the potential for adjusting law-policy frameworks as a key part of the search for solutions. It argues that environmental justice approaches can incorporate values into law-policy processes based upon vital aspects of the integrity and functioning of communities, distributional fairness, and capacities for wider engagement and participation in the search for necessary behavioural change. The conclusion is that the ultimate success of the urgent process of addressing climate-related threats, through a meaningful degree of mitigation and adaptation, and multiple levels of decision-making and response, must be informed by the precepts of environmental justice.

INTRODUCTION

The existential threat from climate change, brought about primarily by human-induced greenhouse gas emissions,[1] will ultimately be played out globally, although local early-onset harms already threaten, in widely differentiated ways.[2] It has been powerfully argued that societies tend to collapse soon after reaching a 'peak' that is marked by impacts outstripping resources alongside loss of core values,[3] and this suggests a justification for

* School of Law, Swansea University, Singleton Park, Swansea SA2 8PP, Wales
m.stallworthy@swansea.ac.uk

1 IPCC, Fourth Assessment Report, *Climate Change 2007 – The Physical Science Basis* (2007). Note that carbon dioxide represents about 85 per cent of United Kingdom greenhouse gas emissions.
2 E. Kolbert, *Field Notes from a Catastrophe* (2006).
3 J. Diamond, *Collapse: How Societies Choose to Fail or Survive* (2006) 433, 509.

the adoption of strongly risk-averse strategies.[4] Meanwhile the commitment to sustainable development, for all its roots in 'same boat' idealism,[5] has failed thus far to challenge those established geopolitical systems and sources of power that globally preside over the carbon energy-intensive growth that continues to fuel climate change.[6] In light of the need for meaningful mitigatory and adaptive responses, it is here argued that environmental justice considerations must inform this urgent process at all levels of decision-making.

Justice-related arguments based upon principles of equity and social solidarity have a problematic place in not only the neo-liberal discourse that has characterized globalization, but perhaps also wider ecological discourse. On the one hand, globalization has depended on maximization of wealth generation as defined and measured through the complex economic valuation mechanisms of global capital markets; on the other, ecological perspectives variously support intrinsic, non-utilitarian valuations of environmental interests in ways that challenge anthropocentric views of a natural world that exists to be exploited. A normative focus on social justice, with an emphasis on distributional effects, whether consequent upon environmental degradation itself or those policies that seek its redress,[7] arguably challenges both positions.[8] That said, environmental justice can be seen as more multi-textured than a preoccupation with equity alone might represent, and is also capable of more fully connecting with objectives of ecological justice.[9]

What follows proceeds therefore from related propositions. If humankind is successfully to address the complexities and dangers inherent in this new generation of ecological risk, then it is crucial, first, to acknowledge the multiple implications of comparative advantage and disadvantage; and secondly, to accord priority to legal paradigms that best advance the ecological needs of communities and maximize the engagement of civil society in the search for solutions. Environmental justice arguments must therefore address, both normatively and instrumentally, the challenge of reworking more traditional claims in the face of the threats that climate

---

4 See N. Stern, *Economic Impacts of Climate Change* (2006).
5 World Commission for Environment and Development (WCED), *Our Common Future* (*The Brundtland Report*) (1987).
6 For a contextual treatment of a national vulnerability within, and responsibility beyond, see K. Dunion and E. Scandreth, 'The Campaign for Environmental Justice in Scotland as a Response to Poverty in a Northern Nation' in *Just Sustainabilities – Development in an Unequal World*, eds. J. Agyeman et al. (2003).
7 R.J. Lazarus, 'Pursuing "Environmental Justice": the Distributional Effects of Environmental Protection' (1993) 87 *Northwestern University Law Rev.* 787, 847.
8 A. Dobson, *Justice and the Environment – Conceptions of Environmental Sustainability and Theories of Distributional Justice* (1998) 13.
9 D. Schlosberg, *Defining Environmental Justice: Theories, Movements, and Nature* (2007) ch. 2.

56

change represents.[10] Taking account of the close connections of climate-related risks with patterns of affluence and poverty, this process can enlighten multi-level institutional reflexive abilities towards securing suitable responses.[11] In pursuit of this task, environmental justice imperatives need to be viewed on both temporal and spatial levels. Thus, with sustainability dependent on protecting the integrity of future generations,[12] the depreciation of future interests across the public sphere, as supported by the application of traditionally high discount levels, requires re-evaluation.[13] Furthermore, a prior expectation for instigating and implementing appropriate action must lie upon the developed world, in light of its preponderant responsibility for past (and continuing) carbon emission levels,[14] alongside its technical capabilities and resource capacities.[15]

PERSPECTIVES ON GLOBALIZATION AND THE RELEVANCE OF LOCAL SOLUTIONS

Arguments for low carbon law/policy transitions generally reflect those generic perspectives that dominate wider environmental discourse. Fundamentally concerned with sustainability/survival, they have roots in the values of, on the one hand, ecologism, broadly preservationist, especially in relation to the maintenance of natural capital,[16] and on the other, variants of ecological modernization, essentially anthropocentric, conservationist, and more pragmatic.[17] The former is generally resistant to the negotiation of incremental improvements over 'acceptable' levels of harm, leading to a rejection

10 For a discussion of such 'next generation' discourse in respect of disadvantaged communities in the face of climate change, see M. Burkett, 'Just Solutions and Climate Change: a Climate Justice Proposal for a Domestic Clean Development Mechanism' (2008) 52 *Buffalo Law Rev* 169.

11 Elaborated in Beck's exposition of reflexive modernization: U. Beck, *World Risk Society* (1998); also, in the present context, *What is Globalization?* (2000) 38–42.

12 B. Barry, 'The Ethics of Resource Depletion' in *Liberty and Justice: Essays in Political Theory*, ed. B. Barry (1991).

13 A key theme of Stern, op. cit., n. 4, who concluded the need for a nominal (0.1 per cent) discount rate; compare more traditional approaches, for example, W. Beckerman and C. Hepburn, 'Ethics of the Discount Rate in the Stern Review of the Economics of Climate Change' (2007) 8 *World Economics* 187, emphasizing the ethics of maximizing of preferences by social institutions.

14 D.A. Farber, 'The Case for Climate Compensation: Justice for Climate Change Victims in a Complex World' (2008) *Utah Law Rev.* 77, 393–7.

15 T. Athanasiou and P. Bayer, *Dead Heat – Global Justice and Global Warming* (2002) 73–5.

16 For example, A. Naess, 'The Shallow and the Deep, Long-range Ecology Movement: a Summary' (1973) 16 *Inquiry* 95; C.D. Stone, *Earth and Other Ethics: The Case for Moral Pluralism* (1987).

17 D.A. Farber, *Eco-Pragmatism: Making Sensible Environmental Decisions in an Uncertain World* (1999).

57

of an instrumental in favour of a 'constitutive' rationality.[18] In contrast, managerialist ideas, essentially more open to accommodation of cost-benefit valuations and conflictual trade-offs, are emerging as the dominant force in asserting environmental interests in wider law-policy debates.[19] Such modernist technical and managerial approaches generally underpin most forms of environmental regulation in the attempt to resolve tensions with other sustainable priorities, and now encompass searches for the elixir of clean growth. As will be seen below, relevant public law responses in the environmental sphere range over a considerable spectrum. They, for instance, encompass wider applications of alternative regulatory approaches, such as emissions trading, as well as recent administrative movements towards more inclusive, proceduralized controls on decision making.[20] A justice-based test in each respect would be concerned with how effectively they can bring about broader engagement and enhanced legitimacy,[21] as well as improved quality of outcomes.

Global-local tensions in the present context partly reflect conflicts between technocratic and democratic decision-making paradigms.[22] Though similar issues can also arise in local contexts,[23] from a law/justice viewpoint the consequences of the more widespread disconnections tend to be the more diffused and severe. For instance, the pursuit of globalized, systemic goals threatens profound spatial and temporal dislocations between large-scale causes and particularized effects.[24] Moreover, the characteristic broad visibility of the rule of law within traditional legal orders is undermined,

---

18 L. Tribe, 'Technology Assessment and the Fourth Discontinuity: the Limits of Instrumental Rationality' (1973) 46 *Southern California Law Rev.* 617.

19 Dividing lines may however be blurring: James Lovelock's Gaia theory posits the earth as an organic functioning self-regulating system, in which all species, whilst they survive, play a part, and is a fundamentally ecological perspective: *Gaia: a New Look at Life on Earth* (1979); he has more recently called for investment in nuclear power, on grounds of urgency and lack of alternative: *The Revenge of Gaia: Why the Earth is Fighting Back – and How We Can Still Save Humanity* (2006).

20 For instance, K. Shrader-Frechette, *Environmental Justice: Creating Equality, Reclaiming Democracy* (2002); note that distinctions with substantive review are not always clear-cut: A. Dan Tarlock, 'Is There a There in Environmental Law?' (2004) 19 *Land Use and Environmental Law Rev.* 213, 239.

21 See T. Prosser, 'Democratisation, Accountability and Institutional Design: Reflections on Public Law' in *Law, Legitimacy and the Constitution*, eds. P. McAuslan and J. McEldowney (1985).

22 For a critique of purportedly 'neutral' processes within environmental policy and rule making, see R. Kuehn, 'The Environmental Justice Implications of Qualitative Risk Assessment' (1996) *University of Illinois Law Rev.* 103.

23 Where public interest outcomes are also not guaranteed: see E. Gauna, 'The Environmental Justice Misfit and the Paradigm Paradox' (1998) 17 *Stanford Environmental Law J.* 3.

24 Such as the effect of sea level rise on vulnerable populations on low-lying territories, such as Bangladesh (Bay of Bengal) and the Tuvalu and other island communities (Southern Pacific and elsewhere): see M. Lynas, *High Tide* (2005) especially ch. 3.

58

with displacement of recognized protective mechanisms that affect activities and relations within civil society.[25] A further incident is a diminution of citizen voice on behalf of those presently alive (and, a fortiori, generations to come), as individual and group roles within traditional socio-legal structures become diluted by a homogenizing identification with the global economic language of preference and (consumer) choice.[26]

Nevertheless, any search for a definition of globalization, in light of its multiple incidences and effects, can be elusive. It is generally located within the wide-ranging ascendancies of market liberalism.[27] This has impacted in contrasting ways on traditional views of political authority and autonomy. Thus globalization represents processes which, whilst validated by multi-lateral governance structures, also serve to undermine the nation state, transnational actors instead operating through a 'local-global axis', and related events no longer truly local.[28] Yet projections therefrom to a resulting hegemony of transnational corporate interests are only partly accurate; for something more akin to anarchy appears to be at work, over-whelming 'the control capacities' of corporate actors as well as the state.[29] Indeed, a similar conclusion is arguably manifested in the 2008 systemic turmoil in global financial markets.[30]

The hallmarks of globalization accordingly lie in the modern complexities of interdependence within global markets,[31] the organization of economic society offering a parody of those ecological notions which recognize that in nature everything is interconnected.[32] Globalization's new linkages distort local identities, as in the wider consequences that follow, especially from resulting (voluntary or involuntary) mass movements of people, capital, and resources. Dominant global trends have two particular implications for competing local rationalities. First, an undermining of local autonomy and identity threatens systemic loss of rootedness to place,[33] fulfilling Aldo Leopold's original forebodings for a disappearing 'land ethic'.[34] This effect can be seen not only in the increasing vulnerability of future generations but also in present globalized economic influences on food supply and the

---

25 For instance under the dispute settlement process of the World Trade Organization: see *EC – Biotech Products* (*DS291/292/293*, 26 September 2006), where questions arose as to the compatibility with WTO rules of localized precautionary approaches to the regulation of genetically modified organisms.

26 M. Sagoff, *The Economy of the Earth: Philosophy, Law and Economics* (1998) 16–17.

27 J.S Dryzeck, *Deliberative Global Politics: Discourse and Democracy in a Divided World* (2006) 96.

28 Beck, op. cit. (2000), n. 11, p. 11.

29 Dryzeck, op. cit., n. 27, p. 101.

30 J. Ford, 'A Greedy Giant out of Control' *Prospect*, November 2008, 22.

31 See D. Held and A. McGrew, *The Global Transformations Reader* (2000) ch. 1.

32 B. Commoner, *The Closing Circle – Nature, Man and Technology* (1971).

33 For instance, T.M. Power, *Lost Landscapes and Failed Economies: the Search for the Value of Place* (1996).

34 A. Leopold, *A Sand County Almanac* (1949).

localized consequences, including food security, biodiversity, and carbon emissions.[35] Secondly, a shifting of power toward remote global elites offers a postmodern take on 'post-enlightenment economic rationality' (of free markets, run on neoliberal lines), characterized by the disempowerment of those who 'bear the worst ecological consequences' alongside the relative insulation of those same elites from the ensuing burdens.[36]

ENVIRONMENTAL JUSTICE AND MULTI-JURISDICTIONAL APPROACHES TO CLIMATE CHANGE

At first sight, environmental justice claims, alongside those relating to human rights more generally,[37] might appear to share an awkward place in the environmental canon. In addressing the consequences of climate-related disaggregation of impacts, the idea of environmental justice adopted here has its roots in the organized responses to inequitable treatment of vulnerable American communities in the face of an early generation of environmental threats, through siting decisions regarding harmful activities and installations. The primary aims were to encourage community empowerment and wider recognition for equitable considerations in decision making,[38] seeking fairer means of reconciling apparent conflicts between risk bearers and assumed beneficiaries.[39] Yet environmental justice discourse can also encompass more expansive calls for fuller community recognition and participation in environmental decision making, with the objective of redressing an ecological profligacy that reinforces 'existing social inequalities while exceeding the limits to growth'.[40] This latter consequence can be said now to be encapsulated in the threats from climate change.

Furthermore, the pervasive nature of ecological inter-reliance suggests that propositions based on decoupling environmental justice goals from those of sustainability amount to a category mistake.[41] In the emphasis upon

---

35 V. Shiva, *Stolen Harvest: the Highjacking of the Global Food Supply* (2000).
36 V. Plumwood, *Environmental Culture – the Ecological Crisis of Reason* (2002) 87.
37 C. Miller, *Environmental Rights: Critical Perspectives* (1998).
38 R.D. Bullard, 'Levelling the Playing Field through Environmental Justice' (1999) 23 *Vermont Law Rev.* 453.
39 S. Foster, 'Justice from the Ground Up: Distributive Inequities, Grassroots Resistance, and the Transformative Politics of the Environmental Justice Movement' (1998) 86 *California Law Rev.* 775, 835.
40 D. Pellow and R.J. Brulle, 'Power, Justice, and the Environment: Toward Critical Environmental Justice Studies' in *Power, Justice, and the Environment: a Critical Appraisal of the Environmental Justice Movement*, eds. D. Pellow and R.J. Brulle (2005) ch. 1.
41 As expressed in the need for ecological communication in seeking sustainable solutions: J. Dryzeck, 'Political and Ecological Communication' (1995) 4 *Environmental Politics* 13; similarly, 'practical engagement with the world we inhabit': T.

equity, there is also a crossover with an approach based on social ecology, which has emphasized a need for the resolution of social conflict as a precondition to the achievement of more ecological lifestyles.[42] This can lead into contested debate, as in Lomborg's linkage of highly valid propositions for prioritized targeting of resources at extreme problems affecting quality of life (such as poverty, famine, AIDS, and other epidemics in the third world) with an apparent scepticism over the present urgency of the risks of climate change.[43] The latter argument has been powerfully countered by Stern, whose 2006 report focused upon the rising economic costs of deferring necessary action.[44]

Issues of benefit and burden distribution, alongside other elements of environmental justice claims in ecological contexts, have been largely marginalized by a neo-liberal economic consensus.[45] This has tended broadly to identify progress with forms of wealth accretion produced through rigid applications of economic cost-benefit efficiencies, the tools which favour those aggregate frameworks offered by a globalized marketplace.[46] Resulting efficiencies have in large measure been delivered by a triangulation of autonomy-based ideas of low regulation and preference. Whilst in consequence there have been significant retreats from regulation of markets, it remains widely acknowledged that welfare promotion is not thereby guaranteed.[47] Thus, in the context of the climate debate and the wide variety of factors that undermine behavioural change,[48] Sunstein suggests a palliative in the form of 'libertarian paternalism'.[49] This remains a fundamentally choice-based response, also reflected in ideas based on attempts to influence the behavioural economic context in which choices are made.[50]

Benton, 'Ecology, Community and Justice' in *Justice, Property and the Environment*, eds. T. Hayward and J. O'Neill (1997).

42 M. Bookchin, *Toward an Ecological Society* (1980).

43 B. Lomborg, *The Skeptical Environmentalist: Measuring the State of the World* (2001).

44 Stern, op. cit., n. 4, p. 211, concluding that immediate, effective action might involve annual global costs at around 1 per cent of GDP, in default of which such figure would shortly rise to 5–20 per cent.

45 D.A. Farber and D. McCarthy, 'Neoliberalism, Globalization, and the Struggle for Ecological Democracy: Linking Sustainability and Environmental Justice' in Agyeman, op. cit., n. 6.

46 D.T. Hornstein, '"Reclaiming" Environmental Law: a Normative Critique of Comparative Risk Analysis' (1992) 92 *Colorado Law Rev.* 562.

47 C. Jolls and C.R. Sunstein, 'Debiasing through Law' (2006) 35 *J. of Legal Studies* 199, 202–03, 234: seeking to limit 'boundedly rational' behaviour without 'aggressive regulation', by altering people's 'perceptions of the world around them'.

48 Such as projection bias (relating future expectations to the here and now), unrealistic optimism (the future will take care of itself) or simple myopia (with judgement on hold).

49 C.R. Sunstein, 'Willingness to Pay versus Welfare' (2007) 1 *Harvard Law & Policy Rev.* 303, 324–30.

50 With reference to 'choice architecture': R.H. Thaler and C.R. Sunstein, *Nudge: Improving Decisions about Health, Wealth, and Happiness* (2008).

Such approaches, without more, by reason of their retained commitments to growth as conceived and advanced through global capital markets, offer little prospect of achieving the urgent progress insisted upon by Stern.

It is against the background of such value conflicts that the UN Framework Convention on Climate Change acknowledged the reality of human-induced impacts and the need for international responses to the potential risks from global warming.[51] A main rationale for the subsequent Kyoto Protocol, and in particular underlying specific commitments to emissions reductions, was that the most serious impacts and hence most grievous injustices afflict communities in non-developed and developing states.[52] The recognition of joint but differentiated responsibility led to the setting up of flexible mechanisms to address problems of both intra- and inter-generational equity.[53] Thus, based upon the principle of additionality, the Clean Development Mechanism (CDM) constitutes an attempt to harness international resources toward redressing emissions whilst supporting necessary development. In addition, a start has subsequently been made towards a commitment to assistance with adaptation, based on a 2 per cent levy on purchase of CDM credit allowances.[54] However, necessary international funding aid and technology-led responses remain in an inchoate state,[55] as parties to the Convention look to negotiate, in a December 2009 meeting of the parties at Copenhagen, a successor agreement effective from 2012.[56] It accordingly becomes essential that suitable mechanisms are formulated as a priority in those legal jurisdictions with greatest capacity to respond.

Nevertheless progress at domestic or regional levels will clearly not be enough. Beck, describing the 'cosmo-politics' of climate change as being 'necessarily inclusive and global', has contrasted 'the illusion' that climate change 'can be addressed by a solo effort. This is merely another way of dodging the key issue of global justice'.[57] This focus on globalized response has led to a further call for 'a cosmopolitan state system' better equipped to

---

51 31 ILM 851 (1992).
52 37 ILM 22 (1998).
53 Based upon commitments to emissions reductions by developed (Annex I) states, these enable markets to generate credits, earned as Emissions Reduction Units under Joint Implementation ('purchasing' emissions reductions in other developed states) and Certified Emission Reductions under the Clean Development Mechanism (in respect of reductions in developing states).
54 Approved at the UN Climate Change Conference, 13th Meeting, Bali: *Action Plan* (2007).
55 For an attempt to address the gap in an international framework, see N. Stern, *Key Elements of a Global Deal on Climate Change* (2008) chs. 6, 7.
56 The first commitment period, mandating specific cuts in emissions on the part of Annex 1 states, runs from 2008–12.
57 U. Beck, 'In the New Anxious World Leaders Must Learn to Think Beyond Borders' *Guardian*, 13 July 2007.

address global problems.[58] Yet whilst in the face of a global imperative localized solutions are not sufficient, they do however remain necessary, and three arguments are offered in response to the above. First, in terms of legal order, the considerable modern growth of international environmental law is often handicapped by a lack of supranational arrangements, as well as continuing questions as to implementation and enforceability. Some comparison may be made with other globalized contexts: such as the banking and finance sectors, where little regulation appears to exist beyond those retained within sovereign jurisdictions.[59] Measures aimed at progress toward global climate change solutions, after a vague, inauspicious start, have led to a putting in place of more effective institutional and functional apparatus. There is potential for more effective development,[60] with a heavy dependence on what can be achieved through a successor to replace Kyoto.

Secondly, for all that there are valid questions as to whether a system of legal order still premised on statehood can address the new dimension of threats to the global commons,[61] the tasks faced are daunting. In order to maintain any hope of holding to a 2°C rise above pre-industrial levels, a minimum of 50 per cent greenhouse gas emissions reductions on Kyoto's 1990 baseline are likely to be necessary globally (involving at least 80 per cent reductions by the developed world) by 2050.[62] Moreover, whilst emissions continue to rise globally, even if a sustained reduction path could be embarked upon immediately (say no later than 2012), then year-on-year cuts in a developed state such as the United Kingdom (where minimal progress in aggregate percentage reductions has been achieved in the past decade) perhaps of the order of 3–6 per cent might be required.[63] Realistic law-policy responses, given the monumental effort required for low-carbonizing fossil-fuel dependent economies, remain reliant upon state and regional initiatives.[64]

---

58 U. Beck, 'Nation-State Politics Can Only Fail the Problems of the Modern World' *Guardian*, 15 January 2008, echoing ideas of cosmopolitan democracy: see, further, N. Low and B. Gleeson, *Justice, Society and Nature: an Exploration of Political Ecology* (1998).

59 A marked exception, especially contentious in environmental contexts, can be found in relation to tariffs and trade, under the World Trade Organization mechanisms.

60 P. Birnie and A. Boyle, *International Law and the Environment* (2002, 2nd edn.) 533.

61 See J.P. Barber and A.K. Dickson, 'Justice and Order in International Relations: the Global Environment' in *Just Environments: Intergenerational, International and Interspecies Issues*, eds. D.E. Cooper and J.A. Palmer (1995) 122–3.

62 See, for example, Stern, op. cit., n. 4.

63 Stern, id., p. 227. Scientific conclusions for emissions pathways in light of cumulated emissions are increasingly pessimistic as to achieving levels of stabilization at (or near) the 2°C sought: see, for example, K. Anderson and A. Bows, 'Reframing the Climate Change Challenge in Light of post-2000 Emission Trends' (2008) 366 *Philosophical Transactions* 3863.

64 For a discussion of the EU's nascent regional steps toward furthering 'international environmental equity', see P.G. Harris, 'The European Union and Environmental Change: Sharing the Burdens of Global Warming' (2006) *Colorado J. of International Environmental Law and Policy* 309.

63

In addition, national structures, especially, afford processes for both legitimizing action, and encouraging justice and accountability,[65] and can be supported by established institutional and regulatory frameworks for the purpose of both elaborating and delivering upon climate-related commitments.[66]

Thirdly, in light of the internationally acknowledged linkage of climate and development needs, in default of action by developed states (including commitments to technology transfer, increased financial flows into developing economies through the CDM, as linked with global emissions trading and compliance with financial aid commitments), it is unrealistic to expect that developing countries will be willing to commit to obligations at all under the Kyoto process (which commitment will become essential from around 2020).[67] Thus, especially with both agreement over and the eventual effectiveness of a successor to Kyoto in the balance, no developed state can seriously anticipate making progress in addressing climate change, or in encouraging progress elsewhere, without delivering appropriate domestic measures.[68] In consequence, in order to maximize the potential effectiveness of Kyoto's replacement,[69] initial reliance must be placed preponderantly on national and regional efforts.[70]

Whilst the analysis above highlights the need to address differential human impacts, there are wider, more systemic implications concerning fundamental features that characterize globalization and its forms of economic activity. It is not possible here to broaden the analysis into a more radical re-evaluation of the tenets underlying economic rationality as manifested in the phenomenon of globalization. Yet, from a justice-based perspective, the character of the global economy, especially as founded on ease of capital movement,[71] has been a systemic tolerance of asymmetric consequences.[72] Even the securing of appropriate policy responses, without a more fundamental reassessment of systemic economic goals, will have

---

65 R. Eckersley, *The Green State: Rethinking Democracy and Sovereignty* (2004).
66 For example, the United Kingdom's Climate Change Act 2008, purporting to impose legally binding domestic targets, supported by transparent budgeting and reporting processes.
67 For a discussion of the role of developing states, see Stern, op. cit, n. 54, ch. 3.
68 Environmental Audit Committee, Sixth Report, *Reaching an International Agreement on Climate Change*, HC (2007–08) 355, paras. 30–31.
69 Kyoto I has been described as merely 'playing for time': Lovelock, op. cit. (2006), n. 19.
70 See, further, UNDP, *Fighting Climate Change: Human Solidarity in a Divided World* (2008).
71 Features have included profitability increasingly identified with maximizing transactions in financial instruments: see, for example, Ford, op. cit., n. 30, pp. 25–6, describing 'momentum trading'.
72 See A. Dobson, 'Social Justice and Environmental Sustainability: Ne'er the Twain Shall Meet' in Agyeman, op. cit., n. 6.

profound effects on those with the greatest vulnerabilities, in view of the need to move through rapid and radical levels of behavioural change.

Although it is arguable that insufficient attention has been devoted to equity discussions in contemporary environmental law discourse,[73] unless attention is given to justice-related arguments in relation to climate mitigation and adaptation, then necessary commitment (buy-in) and investment levels are unlikely to be met. Moreover, with personal consumption levels subject hitherto to mostly residual regulatory controls, it becomes necessary to address how the capacities of civil society to move towards a low-carbon economy can be more effectively engaged.[74] In the next sections the argument turns its focus to the values that might dictate the terms of risk response through policy decisions and accompanying law mechanisms. Discussion for these purposes will be informed variously, with particular illustrations drawn from deliberations in the United Kingdom in relation to questions of adaptation to rising sea levels through coastal realignment, and of mitigation through a potential extension in the tool of emissions trading to include personal carbon allowances.

A JUSTICE-BASED VIEW OF CLIMATE ADAPTATION

Albeit with a broad shared focus on distribution, environmental justice approaches differ from traditional liberal views of justice, reaching further by reason of being motivated by notions of the good life in the context of the environment. In this they can be said to embrace values beyond distributional equity, including what has been termed recognition and integrity, alongside capacities for participation and wider community functioning.[75] The element of ability to function is less immediately acknowledged in legal contexts, perhaps reflecting the latter's close ties with ruling economic paradigms, although there is a mutual recognition of liberty and self-determination.[76] Community functioning directly identifies with ecological values and sustainability, relating to what is required to support those capabilities that nurture and enhance the value of life.[77] Moreover, notions of recognition, and participation in decision making, provide a recognizable base for the interposition of public law in the context of the environment. A range of related shifts in public law processes are gradually emerging,

---

73 Burkett, op. cit., n. 10, p. 239.
74 See discussion of the psychologies surrounding this issue, including bounded 'willpower' as well as the more common bounded 'rationality': A. Green, 'Self Control, Individual Choice, and Climate Change' (2008) 26 *Virginia Environmental Law J.* 77.
75 Schlosberg, op. cit, n. 9.
76 J. Barry, *Green Political Thought* (1999).
77 For example, A. Sen, 'Capacity and Well-Being' in *The Quality of Life*, eds. M. Nussbaum and A. Sen (1992).

especially as to public information, transparency, and review opportunities affecting regulatory systems,[78] together with formalized participatory strategies and enhancements to access to justice.[79] The existence of the Aarhus Convention,[80] despite ambiguities and limitations which reflect an adherence to 'existing distributions of power',[81] offers a normative expression of a fuller processed-based contribution to environmental protection in the public sphere.[82]

A useful illustration of public law's wider application to decisions over adaptation can be seen in debates taking place in the United Kingdom over managed coastal realignment, in the face of sea level rise exacerbated by climate change. A new, long-term strategy for flood and coastal erosion risk management can be justified in terms of sustainability goals.[83] As in the case of sustainable development more generally, cost-benefit analysis is central to the process of determining commitments to physical defences; localized protections are particularly vulnerable in the face of comparative economic formulations.[84] The adoption of a newly sustainable approach appears to impose disproportionate impacts on those in identified locations, in light of a previous lack of a long-term ecological coastal policy.[85] In response, there is an administrative reluctance to recognize any obligations toward affected communities on grounds of equity.[86] This is supported by a

---

78 See *Massachusetts et al.* v. *Environmental Protection Agency*, 127 S.Ct. 1438, U.S. (2007).

79 See, further, J. Holder, *Environmental Assessment – The Regulation of Decision-Making* (2004).

80 UN Economic Commission for Europe, *Convention on Access to Information, Public Participation in Decision-Making and Access to Justice in Environmental Matters,* DOC. ECE-CEP-43 (1998).

81 M. Lee and C. Abbot, 'The Usual Suspects? Public Participation under the Aarhus Convention' (2003) 61 *Modern Law Rev.* 80 who also discern 'little to encourage more general public involvement'.

82 *R (on the application of Greenpeace)* v. *Secretary of State for Trade and Industry* [2007] EWHC 311.

83 See Office for Science and Technology, *Foresight Flood and Coastal Defence Project: Future Flooding* (2004).

84 C. Nadal, 'Pursuing Substantial Environmental Justice: the Aarhus Convention as a Pillar of Empowerment' (2008) 10 *Environmental Law Rev.* 28.

85 Compare an acknowledgement of 'an issue of distributional equity where a few individuals lose their home and all their security whilst others elsewhere are protected': Defra, Flood Management Division, *Background Paper, Payment of Compensation, Relocation, and Other Issues in relation to Flood and Coastal Erosion Risk Management* (2004) para. 35; note that the Chancellor's Autumn 2007 pre-budget statement contained an ex gratia Treasury allocation (£10m) for assisting in adaptation to climate change on the part of vulnerable communities.

86 Stated grounds include, as well as cost, avoiding perverse incentives and distorting insurance provision: Defra, *Managed Realignment: Land Purchase, Compensation, and Payment for Alternative Beneficial Land Use* (2003); also, draft *Protocol for the Withdrawal of Maintenance by the Environment Agency from Flood Defences for Economic Reasons* (2008).

traditional common law default position to the effect that any duty placed on the state to protect against sea encroachment is, at most, one of imperfect obligation.[87]

An environmental justice approach can seek to advance such issues as participation in decision-making processes, alongside related process issues, based upon notions of informed consent, legitimate expectation, and prior notice. This suggests that, in order to engage communities and contribute to defensible outcomes,[88] adjustments must be planned for across reasonable timeframes, and fixed upon in the light of previous policies. Risk-based regulatory approaches are part of an iterative process, and here policy shifts must be set against a background of an informal, managed neglect at many locations over a period of at least half a century.[89] This further raises questions as to the building of trust within local communities,[90] and the balancing of competing interests,[91] including the point at which legitimate regulatory objectives justify redistributory adjustments.[92] Whilst non-compensable regulatory imposts can be justified on grounds of reciprocity (the idea that collectively determined improvements even out over time),[93] without undermining the fundamental principle that regulatory constraints should generally not trigger property-based compensation, it can be argued normatively that entitlements should arise where such subsequent adjustments are 'strategically determined'.[94]

A supplementary, human rights perspective offers further ground for challenge, within the framework of the European Convention on Human Rights, on the basis of positive state obligations to act proportionately to ensure protection from unlawful interference.[95] An initial claim could be based on whether, and in what circumstances, state defence withdrawal

---

87 *A-G* v. *Tomline* (1880) 14 Ch D 58, 67; compare Germany, the Netherlands: EUrosion Project Report, *Living with Coastal Erosion in Europe: Sediment and Space for Sustainability* (2004) 103.

88 J. Steele, 'Participation and Deliberation in Environmental Law – Exploring a Problem-Solving Approach' (2001) 21 *Oxford J. of Legal Studies* 415.

89 M. Stallworthy, 'Sustainability, Coastal Erosion and Climate Change: an Environmental Justice Analysis' (2006) 18 *J. of Environmental Law* 357.

90 R.D. Bullard, *Environmental Justice for All* (1994) ch. 1.

91 J. Steele, *Risks and Legal Theory* (2004) 203, referring to geographical 'hotspots'.

92 In the context of the underlying conflict between control and expropriation (compensable and non-compensable forms of acquisition): see *R (Trailer and Marine (Leven) Ltd)* v. *Secretary of State for the Environment* [2005] 1 WLR 1267.

93 See F.I. Michaelman, 'Property, Utility and Fairness: Comments on the Ethical Foundations of "Just Compensation" Law' (1967) 80 *Harvard Law Rev.* 1165.

94 D.A. Dana, 'National Preservation and the Race to Develop' (1995) 143 *University of Pennsylvania Law Rev.* 655, 670; W. Howarth, *Flood Defence Law* (2002) 512 describes the dilemma of determining 'when, if ever, a failure to provide' defence involves expropriation.

95 In particular, conditional rights to respect for home and private life (Art. 8), a fair and impartial public hearing to determine rights and obligations (Art. 6), and peaceful enjoyment of property (Art. 1 of the First Protocol).

could amount to an expropriation.[96] In an analogous context, a landowner appealed successfully against a regulatory refusal to permit private repair of coastal defences.[97] Whilst the Secretary of State's final determination (based upon conservation and habitat arguments) rendered reference to human rights nugatory, it had earlier been acknowledged that upon a balancing of loss of homes and property it appeared 'clear that the refusal of consent would constitute an unnecessary and disproportionate interference'.[98] These questions require further elaboration, but it is clearly arguable that regulatory actions that interfere with recognized rights may be non-compliant where the state cannot justify on grounds of fairness and proportionality. Indeed, in another context the Court of Human Rights has ruled that the state as regulatory authority may be required to justify failure to prepare infrastructure protections in light of previous events and warnings.[99] Although the circumstances were arguably egregious, this demonstrates that state perceptions of the general interest are not absolute, and that a form of due diligence can be applied judicially in appropriate circumstances. Thus, inadequate state responses to environmental threats can engage human rights claims,[100] even to focus on quality of risk assessment and management.

Beyond human rights claims, a more communitarian justice-based approach suggests that vulnerable communities might argue that altered sustainability priorities, upon inadequate notice in light of previous expectations, amount to state-sanctioned losses.[101] Viewed instrumentally across a timeframe quite enough for reasonable notice purposes, the number of coastal properties likely to be affected by the above remains a tiny fraction of the built stock; by contrast, where more widespread exposure occurs, as in developed flood plains, with no state exploration as yet of inland managed retreat, the timescales for any policy adjustments are potentially adequate. The contrast partly reflects a crucial distinction, in terms of a general availability of private flood insurance,[102] not afforded to properties threat-

---

96 Any such finding could lead to an award of compensation reasonably relating to property value: see *Holy Monasteries* v. *Greece*, judgment of 9 December 2004, Series A no. 301-A, 34–35.

97 *England* v. *English Nature*, decision letter (Defra, March 2008), on file with author.

98 This was the view of the inspector hearing the appeal: id., para. 115, specifically, by reference to Art. 8 and Art. 1 of the First Protocol.

99 *Budayeva* v. *Russia* (Application 15339/02, Judgment 20 March 2008): in the context of the right to life (Art. 2) and deaths and injuries resulting from anticipated mud slides (as well as damage to property).

100 Principles developed under Art. 8 can be relied on for the protection of the right to life: id., para. 133; also, *Öneryildiz* v. *Turkey* (2005) 41 EHRR 20, paras. 90, 160.

101 Absent a claim based on human rights or expropriation, in the light especially of the lack of administrative guarantees, relief under the public law doctrine of legitimate expectation appears unlikely: see S.J. Schonberg, *Legitimate Expectations in Administrative Law* (2000).

102 The basis for which is a voluntary agreement: Association of British Insurers/ Government Joint Statement on Flooding and Insurance, July 2008.

ened by erosion, and its consequent impacts on state economic commitments to flooding and coastal defence.[103]

Accordingly, it is fair to expect that should widespread sustainability retrenchments become necessary then reasonable timeframes should be made available for resulting adjustments in individual expectations and related risk-based decision making. Where climate change adaptation imposes disproportionate burdens, the normative expectations of environmental justice require the adoption of appropriate procedures, based upon fairness,[104] including reasonable and explicit adjustment periods.[105] Due notice would accordingly facilitate opportunities for action to internalize environmental costs in a structured and timely fashion.[106] This would more generally further progress towards policy transformations,[107] in light of modern risk-based regulatory approaches, with clarity as to administrative priorities for addressing identified risks, supported by measures to maximize transparency, participation, and accountability.[108] The adoption of such reflexive strategies would additionally act as a stimulus toward necessary community-wide responses in the face of the threats and uncertainties of climate change.[109]

A JUSTICE-BASED VIEW OF CLIMATE MITIGATION

We now turn to questions of the still wider engagement of civil society, towards countering externalization of harm by a global economy that has continued to meet an 'expectation that greenhouse gas emissions are costless'.[110] The focus is on the potential for securing mitigation through reduced emissions under a system of personal carbon allowances with trade

---

103 In its effective reliance for cover on the commercial insurance sector, the United Kingdom is unusual in comparison which equivalent jurisdictions in Europe: see n. 87 above. In the United States, subsidized premiums are available through a federal funded public scheme.

104 Steele, op. cit., n. 91, p. 113.

105 L.A. St Amand, 'Sea Level Rise and Coastal Wetlands: Opportunities for a Peaceful Migration' (1991) 19 *Boston College Environmental Affairs Law Rev.* 1 points to an aspiration that the public discussion process be complete before threats materialize.

106 A number of eastern seaboard states have adopted a structured approach to equitable discounting of property values, reflecting differential risks, by state legislation placing communities on formal notice as to expectation of realignment: see E.P. Hawes, 'Coastal Natural Hazards Mitigation: the Erosion of Regulatory Retreat in South Carolina' (1998) 7 *South Carolina Environmental Law J.* 55.

107 C. Rose-Ackerman, 'Progressive Law and Economics – and the New Administrative Law' (1988) 98 *Yale Law J.* 341.

108 See E. Fisher, *Risk Regulation and Administrative Constitutionalism* (2007).

109 R.L. Fischman, 'Global Warming and Property Interests: Preserving Coastal Wetlands as Sea Levels Rise' (1991) 19 *Hofstra Law Rev.* 565, 602.

110 J. Purdy, 'Climate Change and the Limits of the Possible' (2008) 18 *Duke Environmental Law & Policy Forum* 289 illustrates by reference to low-density housing and inefficiencies in transport patterns and architecture.

69

in surplus credits. The generation of ideas for alternative, economic mechanisms exemplifies a radical form of environmental modernist approach. Whilst trading-based solutions maintain marketized assumptions and techniques, which cannot alone be described as transformative, they do also both offer opportunities to incentivize lowest-cost solutions, and enable a regulatory rebalancing of market conditions in favour of those acting in environmentally efficient ways.[111]

Viewing schemes generally, this comes at a cost in a number of respects, such as, first, that trading models tend to reflect those same ruling legal principles that underpin the neoliberal economic state, and which tend to be resistant to cost internalizations. Persisting with structures that have fostered traditional perceptions of economic growth could be said to maintain rather than challenge what has been described as 'an oppressive, fossil-centred industrial model'.[112] Thus, the idea of tradable permits attaches an economic value to a right to produce carbon emissions,[113] and expressed in property terms makes only a qualified concession toward ideas of stewardship, whilst carrying the risk that property-based market innovations may undermine substantive change.[114] Secondly, viewing the larger canvas of trade-based emissions solutions, as under Kyoto's flexible mechanisms,[115] schemes enabling purchase of allowances in lieu of reductions, whilst covering allocation shortfalls, also impose risks of opaque and at worst symbolic or even sham claims.[116] Such trading opportunities reflect the notion that emissions impact globally, but tend also to discourage domestic carbon efficiencies, with resulting carbon 'leakage', and emissions relocated into manufacturing and distribution processes elsewhere.

Nevertheless, cap-and-trade applications are capable of meeting key objectives that include delivering on pre-determined aggregate reduction targets and incentivizing behavioural change. Depending on both the rigour

---

111 Elaborated in a seminal article by B.A. Ackerman and R.B. Stewart, 'Reforming Environmental Law' (1985) 37 *Stanford Law Rev.* 1333.
112 L. Lohmann, 'Carry on Polluting' *New Scientist*, 2 December 2006; for similar conclusions applied to a domestic stage, G. Monbiot, 'Don't be Fooled by the Climate Change Bill – Carbon Trading Torpedoes It' *Guardian*, 24 July 2008.
113 For example, Commission Communication, *Bringing Our Needs and Responsibilities Together: Integrating Environmental Issues with Economic Policy*, COM(2000) 576 final, 20 September 2000.
114 Despite recent events in global financial markets, there continues to be an expectation of growth in secondary markets, and related development of securitized instruments and derivatives, in respect of emissions credits (under the EU Emissions Trading Scheme and CDM): see Financial Services Authority, *The Emissions Trading Market: Risks and Challenges* (2008).
115 In relation to CDM, op. cit., n. 53, these may also contribute to emissions allowances under the EU Emissions Trading Scheme: *Linking Directive* 2004/101/ EC [2004] OJ L338/18.
116 Regulatory problems include assuring additionality (and actuality) of purported carbon efficiencies and emissions reductions elsewhere.

applied in setting caps and consistency in application,[117] greater certainty of outcomes is offered as compared with other incentives-based schemes.[118] With incentives based upon carbon pricing, which is in turn dependent on (reducing) levels of availability of excess credits for trade, problems encountered in the early phase of the EU emissions trading scheme (EUETS) included those resulting from widespread over-allocation.[119]

A main rationale for a personal scheme would be to tap into those benefits in ways that are more visible than through trading further upstream. Indeed, arguably the greatest potential advantage in a system of carbon pricing for individuals would lie in the raising of carbon awareness, and hence more direct engagement, both to address gaps between value claims and actual choices,[120] and to inform climate change related decision making more generally. It has been argued that no other initiative could produce the kind of radical behavioural changes required,[121] that is, toward sustainable consumption decisions.

In relation to the 'carbon footprint' of citizens, whilst it is estimated that individual carbon-intensive behaviour accounts for around 42 per cent of United Kingdom emissions,[122] regulation has remained largely problematic. Most formulations for a cap-and-trade scheme based upon personal carbon allowances would be based in principle on equitable access to carbon credit allocations, and thus reflect the equal access entitlements to the global atmospheric commons inherent in the notion of contraction and convergence.[123] In contrast, liberal perspectives that challenge the efficacy of welfare equality, by virtue of such factors as preference fulfilment and cultural and social circumstances, might regard the idea of equal rights as overly simple. Thus, the right to emit carbon has, for instance, been described as a good 'related in complex ways to other goods', although to conclude from this that 'a full theory of climate change justice' needs to be

---

117 Allowable totals should reduce over time.
118 Compare competing ideas based on carbon taxation or subsidy or extending traditional approaches to regulation; indeed a trading scheme is likely also to be less regressive than carbon taxes: S. Roberts and J. Thumim, *A Rough Guide to Individual Carbon Trading: the Ideas, the Issues and the Next Steps* (2006).
119 Directive 2003/87/EC, *Establishing a Scheme for Greenhouse Gas Emissions Allowance Trading within the Community* [2003] L275/32, in force from January 2005; see, further, European Parliament, *The Future Elements of the EUETS* (IP/A/ ITRE/ST/2007-08/PE 400.999) (2008) para. 2.3.
120 M. Vandenbergh and A.C. Steinemann, 'The Carbon Neutral Individual' (2007) 82 *New York University Law Rev.* 1673.
121 Environmental Audit Committee, Fifth Report, *Personal Carbon Trading*, HC (2008–09) 565, paras. 16–24.
122 See Defra, *Assessment of the Potential Effectiveness and Strategic Fit of Personal Carbon Trading* (2008); and Defra, *Synthesis Report on the Findings from Defra's Pre-Feasibility Study into Personal Carbon Trading* (2008) para. 2.1.
123 See A. Meyer, *Contraction and Convergence: the Global Solution to Climate Change* (2000) (Global Commons Institute at <www.gci.org.uk/>).

set 'in the context of a general theory of global justice'[124] hazards the kind of delay that, in light of the scale of present threat, Stern has warned against.

The efficacy of a personal trading system would depend on a rigorous capping policy, along with supplementary decisions concerning extent of activities regulated, range of participants, and the basis for any exceptions on grounds of fairness. Credit allocations would represent a pre-determined aggregate quota for regulated transactions (such as for fuel and transport), surrendered at point of purchase by holders.[125] Whilst it appears that management and technical questions, concerning operational control, monitoring, and enforceability, would not raise insurmountable problems,[126] the United Kingdom government has baulked at the idea on grounds largely of acceptability and cost.[127] Alternatives do exist, and include a trading scheme extended to those larger enterprises and institutions currently outside the EUETS criteria for major emitters.[128] A still broader pricing impact could be achieved by a more fully upstream scheme, applied to those sectors that bring to market and distribute fossil fuels. Increased cost effects, especially in the latter case, would filter down to the citizen-consumer level, dependent on the ability of the scheme to produce a meaningful carbon price. Inequitable downstream impacts (such as fuel poverty, or lack of adaptive capacity) could be alleviated from the proceeds of auctioning allowances; or alternatively, a proportion of upstream credit allocations might be reserved to individuals or representative organizations, in support of downstream carbon-efficient investment.[129] A more private solution suggested in the United States would enable the distribution of revenue from voluntary offset projects (via community groups or suppliers) towards the subsidy of adaptation measures by vulnerable communities. [130] A structured domestic form of CDM has also been proposed (although, given the degree of hypothecation involved, tax might be the more suitable option), to enable

---

124 D.R. Bell, 'The Case against a Universal Right to Equal Carbon Emissions' in *Seeking Environmental Justice*, ed. S. Wilkes (2008) 254–5.

125 Either by surrendering transaction by transaction or in a single transaction, in which latter event regulated purchases would thereafter be subject to the equivalent premium at point of sale.

126 Environmental Audit Committee, op. cit., n. 121, paras. 43–5.

127 Defra *Synthesis Report*, op. cit., n. 122, para. 1.5, suggests £0.7–2 billion to set up, with annual running costs in the order of £1–2 billion. This compares with estimated costs of a fully upstream scheme affecting fuel sources of around £50 million.

128 A new 'carbon reduction commitment' scheme is planned from 2010. The EUETS applies to 11,000 major installations across Europe. Thus far (through stages 1 and 2) the basis of allocation of carbon credits has been generally at no cost, but auctioning is anticipated to be a more significant element post-2012.

129 D. Harrison et al., 'Using Emissions Trading to Combat Climate Change: Programs and Key Issues' (2008) 38 *Environmental Law Reporter* 10367, 10379.

130 M. Vandenbergh and B. Ackerly, 'Climate Change and Individual Behaviour: the Equity Problem' (2008) 26 *Virginia Environmental Law J.* 55.

72

capacity building for those otherwise unable to invest in efficiency measures.[131]

Given that lack of acceptability appears to be a significant ground of governmental cooling in relation to the idea of personal allowances, it is strange that the political challenges involved have not been targeted more squarely. With equitable treatment essential to acceptability, it is quite possible to build in appropriate adjustments to reflect particular needs.[132] These could include those parts of the community with acknowledged socio-economic vulnerabilities (fuel poverty) or with restricted accessibility to services on account of isolation (certain rural communities). The Environmental Audit Committee thus accepted that, in order to achieve public acceptance, it is essential to emphasize commitment to redistribution in respect of excessive burdens.[133] More generally also, it can be argued that individual allocations should encourage personal responsibility in relation to emissions, with opportunities for stimulating more direct engagement in climate change policy-making. This contrasts with the reduced directness offered by the inevitably opaque contributory pricing effects of schemes focused further upstream. A further advantage of a carbon rights framework, based upon a universal form of 'regulated property', is that commitment and buy-in on the part of civil society is encouraged in the field of personal transactions.[134] In this way, a fair structure for restricting rights to access resources, by a matching of individual environmental 'space' to global limits,[135] would serve to further those transparency objectives that are an essential element of social learning and potential for behavioural change.

CONCLUSIONS

It has been argued here that the fundamental challenges around how – and how quickly – we respond to climate change cannot be resolved without an absolute acknowledgement of ecological realities and commitment to environmental justice. Whilst law/policy solutions must ultimately be found globally, attention has been here largely directed at available environmental justice frameworks for addressing localized impacts, typically within traditional legal jurisdictions. Meaningful progress towards acceptable levels of risk limitation and amelioration of impacts depends upon the achievement of systemic, environmental, justice-based behavioural

131 Burkett, op. cit., n. 10.
132 R. Starkey and K. Anderson, *Domestic Tradable Quotas: A Policy Instrument for Reducing Greenhouse Gas Emissions from Energy Use* (2005).
133 Environmental Audit Committee, op. cit, n. 121, paras. 84–89.
134 J.B. Wiener, 'Global Environmental Regulation Investment Choice in Legal Context' (1999) 108 *Yale Law J.* 677.
135 D. McLaren, 'Environmental Space, Equity and the Ecological Debt' in Agyeman, op. cit., n. 6, pp. 22–5.

transformations. Alternative liberal approaches, reliant on a reworking of economic ideas of trickle-down wealth, by encouraging individuals and groups toward gradual rethinking of approaches to rational choice, appear heavily contingent in the face of the fundamental issues at stake: a case of too little too late.

The vital contribution of environmental justice discourse as elaborated here lies in three directions. First, it enables attention to be directed toward holistic approaches across all aspects of the public sphere, rooted in acknowledgement and recognition of the integrity of local communities and their ability to subsist (and hopefully flourish) in the face of the consequences of climate change. Secondly, in pursuit of a policy agenda based upon a meaningful adherence to ecological rationality, it has the capacity to develop, apply, and where necessary reinvent recognized legal concepts. Thirdly, it can offer normative legal frameworks for enabling a broader recognition of such ecological values, as well as for linking these to functional ends. In these latter respects, environmental justice offers a means for encouraging wider engagement and participation within civil society. Through its emphasis on fairness and shared responsibility, alongside public deliberation concerning the nature of threats faced and range of available responses, this can stimulate broad acceptance as to what is, and what is not, sustainable. It can accordingly motivate social learning toward a reassessment of values, assisting in the generation of appropriate, acceptable, and legitimated outcomes.

Issues of fairness are integral to the values underlying environmental justice, as has been seen in discussion of the illustrative applications offered above; instrumentally they also encourage inclusivity and wider social responsibility, towards identifying realistic entitlements and responsibilities in the face of ecological realities. As well as its scientific and technical complexities, the challenge of climate change encompasses a vast potential for conflict both within and across jurisdictions. The multiple instrumental tasks in producing appropriate legal responses are still also beset by contested value-based perspectives by virtue of spill-over from other policy priorities. Here the crucial issue to address is what Stone has identified as a lack of moral clarity surrounding human responses to climate change.[136] Environmental justice discourse can contribute to meaningful responses to this challenge by offering clear, value-based perspectives, alongside a capacity to utilize and transform recognized legal frameworks towards addressing this most fundamental of sustainability questions arising from the quality of our stewardship of the global commons.

136 C.D. Stone, 'Is Environmentalism Dead?' (2008) 38 *Environmental Law* 19.

JOURNAL OF LAW AND SOCIETY
VOLUME 36, NUMBER 1, MARCH 2009
ISSN: 0263-323X, pp. 75–93

(Re)Connecting the Global and Local:
Europe's Regional Seas

STUART BELL* AND LAURENCE ETHERINGTON*

One of the challenges to sustainable development is the disconnection between environmental impacts and their underlying causes. Whilst impacts are often localized and perceptions limited accordingly, sources can often be traced to broader factors, and there is a need for methodologies to establish these linkages between localized effects and global causes. Europe's Regional Seas provide a useful illustration, characterized by a variety of ecological problems influenced by a range of local and wider factors within complex ecosystems. The Driver-Pressure-State-Impact-Response (DPSIR) model is one methodology used to establish connections between ecological conditions and human activity. Whilst there are some significant challenges in developing and using such models, they deepen understanding of ecological systems and the influences of socio-economic forces on them. In particular, they can help in contextualizing the apparent effectiveness of regulatory interventions and understanding the role that the forces of globalization play in creating localized ecosystem degradation.

INTRODUCTION

The environmental problems encountered within Europe's regional seas are emblematic of the tensions between economic globalization and ecological localization. Those problems are often manifested through localized impacts on the environment, but their fundamental sources can often be traced to

* York Law School, University of York, Heslington, York YO10 5DD, England

sb595@york.ac.uk   lme503@york.ac.uk

This paper draws on work undertaken by the authors, together with Dr Philip Cooper of the University of Bath and Dr Julian Williams of the University of Bristol, as part of the European Lifestyles and Marine Ecosystems ('ELME') Project funded by the European Commission under the Sixth Framework Programme.

75

broader, globalized phenomena. Of course, many of those large-scale developments represent the aggregation of individual (and so 'local') preferences as expressed through desires and decisions. These relationships are complex, and in the case of marine ecosystems the consequences of these (aggregated) preferences are often hidden from view, so that there is a 'disconnect' in perceptions of individual decisions and their aggregated outcomes. These (dis)connections between the global and local and between individual preferences and aggregated environmental effects are all characteristics of complex environmental systems where cause and effect are difficult to disentangle. In many of the key environmental challenges of the twenty-first century, this complexity raises significant issues for policy-makers.[1] In the past, policy and regulatory responses to environmental problems have been relatively linear and limited in scope. Thus, put crudely, the earliest responses were characterized by localized 'end-of-pipe' solutions to local issues.[2] With greater understanding of the causal links between activities and environmental degradation, broader, more integrative approaches have been adopted.[3]

In recent years, even these integrated tools have proved to be ineffective against diffuse and multi-faceted problems such as climate change and the degradation of the marine environment. Part of the reason for this is that policy-makers and regulators have reached the limit of their ability to use blunt 'command and control' regulatory instruments to deal with multi-link causal chains. As Dryzek has suggested, one of the great weaknesses of administrative rationalism as a management approach to controlling environmental problems is that once the 'low-hanging fruit' have been picked, there are still the complex problems to solve.[4] Thus, as the law of diminishing returns suggests, with well-established systems of environmental regulation, greater effort is required to improve the effectiveness of future environmental policy. One of the ways in which these more complex issues are being tackled is through the use of frameworks and indicators for the assessment of environmental problems. As Martello and Jasanoff have identified, 'How we understand and represent environmental problems is inescapably linked to the ways in which we choose to ameliorate or solve

---

1 Most obviously seen in the wide-ranging responses to the complexities of climate change both at a transnational and domestic level, see, for example, the range of measures adopted by the United Kingdom government: Defra, *Climate Change: The UK Programme 2006* (2006; Cm. 6764).
2 D. Robinson, 'Regulatory Evolution in Pollution Control' in *Law in Environmental Decision Making*, eds. T. Jewell and J. Steele (1998).
3 N. Gunningham and P. Grabosky, *Smart Regulation: Designing Environmental Policy* (1998) 88.
4 J. Dryzek, *The Politics of the Earth: Environmental Discourses* (2005, 2nd edn.) 93.
5 M.L. Martello and S. Jasanoff 'Globalization and Environmental Governance' in *Earthly Politics: Local and Global in Environmental Governance*, eds. S. Jasanoff and M.L. Martello (2004) 5.

76

them.'[5] In other words, in order to understand the complexities of globalized pressures and localized impacts there must be broader conceptions of the links between the two. Thus, cross-sectoral assessments can capture environmental changes across broad templates – spatial, temporal, and economic – whilst translating specified indicators into meaningful 'stories' for individuals within a local context. Applying such frameworks assists with the framing of complex environmental problems as part of a process of revealing information which helps us to untangle the exact nature of the inter-relationships between the global and local.[6]

The focus of this paper is the use of the Driver-Pressure-State-Impact-Response (DPSIR) framework for identifying and exploring the main aspects of these relationships within the context of challenges faced by Europe's regional seas. We examine the role and effectiveness of regulatory 'responses' in influencing the causal effects of some elements in those relationships. In doing so, we attempt to draw out some connections between local impacts and larger-scale socio-economic developments. Finally, we seek to evaluate the strengths and weaknesses of the DPSIR model. The perspective taken on the model and the issues arising is primarily that of law and policy, so that statistical aspects are only considered in broad outline.

EUROPE'S REGIONAL SEAS

Europe's regional seas (the Baltic, Black, and Mediterranean Seas and the North-East Atlantic Ocean) provide a useful case study for exploring local and 'global' factors in a number of respects. First, the seas are geographically 'local' in that their boundaries are fairly distinct, but at the same time, all are connected. Secondly, political governance is provided at a number of different levels: national (and sub-national); regional sea;[7] and broader region (EU). This network reflects in part the breadth of interested parties, with the coastline for 'Europe's' seas found on three continents. As awareness of the sources of environmental problems has developed, those interested parties have been brought into the political frameworks through expansion of the parties to the Conventions from littoral states alone to encompassing those upstream, with knowledge used and developed around those regional seas Conventions and their supporting structures.[8] The nature

6 D. Stanners et al., 'Frameworks for Environmental Assessment and Indicators at the EEA' in *Sustainability Indicators: A Scientific Assessment*, eds. T. Hàk, B. Moldan, and A. Dahl (2008).

7 Each of the regional seas has an international convention providing some level of policy and legal structure for environmental protection (the Bucharest (Black Sea), Helsinki (Baltic), Barcelona (Mediterranean), and OSPAR (North East Atlantic) Conventions).

8 D. Vandeer, 'Ordering Environments: Regions in European International Environmental Cooperation' in Jasanoff and Martello, op. cit., n. 5, p. 323.

of the environmental problems arising varies locally in the sense that whilst the main problems identifiable – chemical pollution, eutrophication, habitat loss, and unsustainable extraction (with emerging issues including those relating to climate change) – are common to all, their relative significance varies between and within each of the seas.[9] Similarly, the services provided vary, with functions such as recreation, waste disposal, fishing, and transport of variable importance across different localities. At the same time, functions such as climate regulation are of global significance. The effect of globalization processes and the localization of their impacts can be illustrated by a further pressure upon some marine ecosystems in the form of invasive species, which are a major cause of biodiversity loss. Increased levels of global trade have actuated increases in the transportation of goods through various means, including shipping.[10] The carriage of ballast water from one ecosystem locality to another provides the pathway for migration of species to new ecosystems, where the invasive presence is defined by the 'localness' of the ecosystem and its natural flora and fauna.

Regulation of the marine environment has traditionally been fragmented and reactive. The low visibility of marine ecosystem pressures has helped to make many marine issues a low priority for the EU, with a historic focus on the exploitation of the regional seas as a resource through instruments such as the Common Fisheries Policy. These perceptions are given an institutional basis through legal concepts such as the Exclusive Economic Zone. Awareness of the catastrophic collapse in many fish stocks has helped to shift some policy attention to sustainability issues, though intervention at the international level has been similarly sporadic, in forms such as the UN Drift Net Moratorium. Some of the regulatory responses which have acted to mitigate pressures on regional sea environments have been in the occasionally serendipitous form of 'co-' or 'by-'products of actions directed at other targets, such as air pollution. Regulatory responses at all levels are effected through localized implementation, further frustrating attempts to anticipate causal outcomes. The ecosystem approach to ecological management which has gathered momentum over recent years[11] has been applied recently to broad marine management in the EU Marine Strategy Directive,[12] which attempts to understand and manage marine issues through such an approach.[13] This identifies humans and human activity as integral parts of biological organization, processes, and interactions. It tries to address the

---

9 For example, the Baltic and Black Seas are relatively enclosed with narrow straits, which makes eutrophication a particular problem, in contrast with the North-East Atlantic.

10 As well as tourism (see EEA, *Europe's Environment: the fourth assessment* (2007) 199).

11 W. Howarth, 'The Interpretation of "Precaution" in the European Community Common Fisheries Policy' (2008) 20(2) *J. of Environmental Law* 213.

12 Directive 2008/56/EC.

13 Art. 1(3).

uncertainties inherent in anticipating and addressing environmental problems, through the use of 'adaptive management'.[14] Its aims include the promotion of more integrated policies, across[15] and within national boundaries, with implementation through localized marine strategies.[16] The Directive requires assessment of the predominant pressures and impacts, including human activity, on the environmental status of marine waters,[17] including economic and social analysis of use made of those waters and the cost of their degradation.[18] Where it stops short, at least in its explicit provisions, is in asking questions about the influences driving those human activities which result in pressures and impacts upon the marine environment.

In the remainder of this paper, we will use a conceptual model (DPSIR) to ask some of those questions and illustrate the importance of the context which they provide for the development of new policy responses and evaluation of historic interventions.

THE DPSIR MODEL

1. *The DPSIR model in outline*

The DPSIR model is a well-established framework[19] for use in trying to understand and respond to environmental challenges.[20] It is a useful mechanism used in the identification of causality chains which link underlying economic activities to environmental (eco)system stresses and thence on to state changes, impacts, and societal responses.[21] A simple type of causal matrix provided an early form of DPSIR model which the European Environment Agency adopted in an attempt to combine environmental data with some broader economic factors to produce various environmental

---

14 P. Gilliland and D. Laffoley, 'The Role of Marine Spatial Planning in Implementing Ecosystem-based, Sea Use Management' (2008) 32 *Marine Policy* 787–96.

15 Through the mechanisms and structures of the Regional Seas Conventions. in particular (Art. 6(2)).

16 As evidenced by the Marine Bill currently before Parliament.

17 Art. 8(1)(b) and Annex III.

18 Art. 8(1)(c).

19 Which builds upon the OECD Pressure, State, Response model: OECD, *Environmental indicators, a preliminary set* (1991). See, also, European Environment Agency, 'How We Reason', available at: <http://www.eea.europa.eu/documents/brochure/brochure_ reason.html>.

20 This paper refers to a modified DPSIR framework developed by Dr Philip Cooper, University of Bath, as part of the ELME Project. His paper on the development of this modified model is to be published separately.

21 D. Rapport and A. Friend, *Towards a comprehensive framework for environmental statistics: a stress-response approach*, Statistics Canada Catalogue 11–510 (1979).

indicators that communicate the state of the environment to the wider public.[22]

In broad terms, *drivers* can be conceived of as those human activities and the underlying factors influencing them which create or increase *pressures* on the natural environment. Those pressures comprise the direct manner in which human activities act upon environmental *states*, with state changes, such as the amount, or quality of a resource, resulting in *impacts* perceived by humans.[23] *Responses* comprise various forms of human action which seek to prevent, reduce, mitigate, remedy, or otherwise address such impacts. Drivers can include more *immediate* drivers, which influence pressures on environmental states directly, and *underlying* drivers which are those fundamental socio-economic activities responsible for the more immediate drivers.[24] In many cases, responses can be perceived as *reverse drivers*, though they can be directed at drivers, pressures, states or impacts. Where a pressure is in the form of land development, for example, the response might be to prevent or limit such development. Responses to impacts might be in the form of requirements for compensatory measures, or the closing of a public bathing water;[25] an example of how responses can be addressed directly to states can be found in the Water Framework Directive[26] which includes obligations on member states to meet certain water quality objectives, but leaves the means for achieving these up to the individual state.

The DPSIR framework does not seek to describe or evaluate the single elements which form its component parts. Instead, the strength of the DPSIR framework lies in its focus on 'the relationships between the elements that introduce the dynamics into the framework'. This focus thereby illuminates the complexity of the causal links that are instrumental in terms of environmental degradation.[27] In particular, the links between economic drivers and societal responses (including regulation) and environmental impacts provides a clearer picture of the effectiveness or otherwise of such responses. This monitoring of the effectiveness of responses is a critical factor when

---

22 European Environment Agency, *Europe's Environment: the Dobris Assessment* (1995) and see, generally, on the history of the development of the DPSIR framework, P. Gabrielsen and P. Bosch, *Environmental Indicators: Typology and Use in Reporting*, EEA Internal Working Paper (2003).

23 These impacts are not restricted to those which affect humans directly, and so do not reflect an anthropocentric approach. The need for human perception is simply a requirement for an effect to be incorporated within the model.

24 This distinction forms an important element of Cooper's modified DPSIR model, referred to in n. 20 above.

25 Whether a response directed towards an impact is a satisfactory facet of environmental management is questionable given that it suggests that the problem has not been identified in sufficient time.

26 Directive 2000/60/EC.

27 Gabrielsen and Bosch, op. cit., n. 22.

80

Figure 1. The DPSIR model

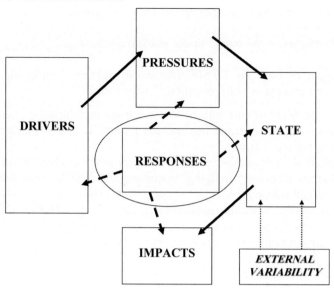

considering whether decoupling – the separation of the growth of so-called economic 'goods' from environmental 'bads' – is actually occurring.

A diagram of the DPSIR framework is provided at Figure 1, which also recognizes the influence of non-system exogenous variables. Although the links between different elements of the framework are represented here as linear, the actual nature of the relationships between the links in the chain is complex. In truth the relationships are dynamic in different ways. In many situations there are multi-casual links to the same impacts and the subtle interplay between these factors are difficult to discern. Critically, there are often no simplistic links between state changes and specific drivers. By their very nature, underlying drivers have an impact across regional and international settings. For example, widespread inward migration brought about by economic growth in one region (or through decline in another) can bring about a multiplicity of environmental pressures which cause impacts largely on a local level. In this sense, the pressures of economic globalization can be diffuse and undetectable in terms of direct causal links to the localized environmental degradation that results.

Once the elements of the model for a given system have been identified, time series data can be collected for appropriate indicators of those elements, in order to identify and analyse historic trends and relationships. Where it is not possible to elicit data directly on elements of the model, proxy indicators can be used.[28] Having constructed and populated a model with historic data,

---

28 The detailed empirical aspects of the DPSIR framework are beyond the scope of this paper, which considers the model in broad terms.

81

future projections can be undertaken, often combined with analysis of possible alternative futures, through scenario modelling.[29]

2. *An illustration of the model in the marine context*

An example of how the DPSIR framework operates within the marine environment context is eutrophication,[30] where the:

- *state* is the level of eutrophication (or nutrient enrichment);
- *pressures* which influence this include phosphorous and nitrogen loads entering marine waters;
- immediate *drivers* of those pressures are primarily levels of fertilizer use, wastewater disposal, dredging operations, and NO_x emissions from industry and transport;
- underlying *drivers* include population levels and Gross Domestic Product;
- *impacts* which result include loss of benthic flora and fauna, fisheries levels, health impacts (toxicity), invasive species (for example, jellyfish), and tourism depreciation; and
- *responses* have taken a variety of forms, including the Convention on Long-Range Transboundary Air Pollution[31] (at the global level), and the Urban Waste Water Treatment,[32] Nitrates,[33] Integrated Pollution Prevention and Control,[34] and Emissions Ceiling[35] Directives (at the EU regional level), with a variety of measures taken more locally.

The complexity of the relationships drawn together in this model is apparent. The immediate drivers are influenced by a broad spread of factors. For the waste water disposal aspects, the pressures are influenced by more localized phenomena than simple population levels. The concentration of populations is also an important influence, so that urbanization levels may act as a magnifying influence.[36] Levels of urbanization reflect the desire to live in an urban area, which may itself be influenced by a variety of factors. In some

---

29 See, for example, P. Cooper et al., 'Socio-Economic Scenarios of European Development and Integrated Management of the Marine Environment', University of Bath Working Paper (2008).
30 An increase in chemical nutrients (typically compounds containing nitrogen or phosphorus) in an ecosystem. This results in excessive plant growth and decay, with further effects including lack of oxygen and severe reductions in water quality, fish, and other animal populations.
31 1979.
32 Directive 91/271/EEC.
33 Directive 91/676/EEC.
34 Directive 96/61/EC.
35 Directive 2001/81/EC.
36 Which is reflected in the provisions of the waste water treatment directive where the nature of the local receiving medium may help to determine the treatment levels required of waste waters, but the concentration of populations in large agglomerations is particularly important.

82

contexts, it may be that economic inequalities are a major influence, whilst the attractiveness of perceived social benefits in various forms may be more or less persuasive. Other than in the most impoverished sectors of European society, it seems fair to say that the forces at play here are as much to do with individual preferences as with pure socio-economic needs, with the increases in economic wealth (identified in the model as GDP levels) freeing up decision making to these individual preferences. Similarly, when we consider another element of the model, fertilizer use, individual preferences combine with broader socio-economic factors in influencing driver levels. Levels of animal protein consumption tend to increase in line with levels of wealth. That correlation reflects personal choice in large part, but the effect on fertilizer levels is tremendously important, given the differential 'water footprints' in the form of relative acreage required for vegetable and animal protein production.[37]

3. *The decoupling of driver levels and their effects*[38]

The concept of *decoupling* lies at the heart of the link between the underlying drivers (in most cases related to the forces of economic globalization) and environmental pressures which lead to negative localized impacts. The phrase refers to the relative relationship between the growth in an economic variable in the form of relevant drivers and the increase in an environmentally relevant variable, normally, pressures.[39] One example is the link between growth economically as measured by GDP and the growth in the amount of biodegradable municipal waste being disposed of in landfill sites (which will, of course, have its own impacts). Decoupling occurs when there is a reduction in the growth of a pressure variable as compared to the growth in an underlying driver variable. The decoupling can be *relative*; where growth rates for the pressure and driver are both positive but the rate is lower for the pressure variable. Alternatively the decoupling can be *absolute* in circumstances where the growth rate of the environmentally relevant variable is zero or negative (that is, decreasing) whilst the economic variable is positive and increasing. Thus where the amount of waste going to landfill is falling whilst GDP is rising, there is said to be an absolute decoupling.

---

37 In the region of 5–10 times the acreage for animal protein, depending upon the type of vegetable protein comparator.

38 OECD, *Indicators to Measure Decoupling of Environmental Pressure from Economic Growth* SG/SD (2002)1/Final, see: <www.un.org/esa/sustdev/natlinfo/indicators/idsd/pdf/decoupling_environment_&_economy.pdf>.

39 It is possible to study the link between drivers and responses and even state changes although the main disadvantage of doing so is that the relevant time variable is often much longer in terms of assessing environmental state changes than in measuring changes in pressures. This can, of course, lead to certain difficulties where state changes are seen over very long periods (for example, in relation to groundwater quality).

83

The eutrophication example above also identifies how responses have often been designed to mitigate the effects of the human activities which cause pressures on the environment through breaking, or weakening, the relationships between them. The usual techniques for achieving this are regulatory requirements and technological developments, often working in combination. In the case of nutrient loads from waste waters, the response works by requiring treatment at waste-water plants before discharge to the sea. Thus technical standards are imposed by regulatory requirements which reduce nutrient loads from discharges, even though the volume of those discharges may continue to increase. This decoupling can be of more immediate drivers from underlying factors, such as the relationship between transport levels and economic growth, or of the pressures which result from those activities, such as the NO_x emissions from road transport activities. The latter is an example which demonstrates very clearly the effects of decoupling responses, and which relates to the most significant source of NO_x load for the marine environment. Data for passenger transport demand,[40] numbers of cars, trucks, buses, and coaches,[41] and other indicators show steady and significant increases between 1991 and 2001. These reflect a close relationship between GDP levels and transport activity. Over the period 1990 to 2004, however, the NO_x emissions from road transport in the member states declined by 38 per cent.[42] Whilst similar reductions were achieved from rail transport, NO_x emissions from shipping and aviation increased considerably, though the overall NO_x emissions from transport reduced significantly over the 1990 to 2004 period. Regulatory responses introduced include fuel[43] and vehicle standards, together with less direct influences in the form of air quality standards[44] in combination with technological developments and the roll out of these in order to achieve those standards. Thus, the most substantial factor was the requirement for new vehicles to have catalytic converters,[45] combined with the renewal of the vehicle fleet.

4. *Identifying the scale of challenges – tourism*

The DPSIR model identifies some of the relationships between drivers and their potential consequences quite clearly. The potential decoupling effect of responses in mitigating the effects of increased driver levels has also been

---

40 EEA, *Passenger transport demand (CSI 035)* (2005).
41 EEA, *Indicator Fact Sheet (TERM 2006 32)* (2005).
42 id.
43 Such as Directive 98/70/EC.
44 Such as the Air Quality Framework Directive (96/62/EC), and influence of the UNECE Convention on Long Range Transboundary Air Pollution.
45 Required from the early 1990s by Directive 70/220/EEC, and the amendments made by, among others, Directive 91/441/EEC.

illustrated. One of the strengths of the DPSIR approach is that it helps to identify the scale of the challenges faced through highlighting the level of decoupling which is required in a given area if that strategy for responses is to be pursued successfully. Taking the example of the tourism sector, pressures on marine ecosystems include urbanization and development of sensitive areas, water consumption and abstraction, beach and coastal waters disturbance, litter production, and concentration of waste water discharges. Tourist activity is fragmented and growth is often concentrated in specific environments, creating localized pressures.[46] Responses have been limited, with virtually no responses addressed to the activity of tourism itself.[47] The economic importance of tourism activities to many areas of Europe has helped to restrict the focus of policy to prevention or mitigation of the effects of activities in the most sensitive areas, whilst the primary tourism policy focus remains economic benefits.[48] We can identify indirectly relevant responses addressed to pressures and impacts in forms such as water quality standards and environmental assessment of large-scale projects, together with some broad policy measures such as intergrated coastal zone management strategies. The personal-choice aspect of tourism activity has been the subject of a limited response in the form of the eco-label award scheme.[49]

By contrast with the rather fuzzy picture of responses, the scale of predicted driver increases is very clear. The factors influencing the growth in tourism experienced to date and the anticipated future increases are a combination of socio-economic aspects and personal choice. As tourism represents one dimension of leisure activity, two fundamental factors which influence the activity are the amount of time which individuals have for leisure and the choices open to them. The economic factors include levels of wealth and relative costs of activities. In Europe, we have seen (at least until very recently) fairly steady increases in GDP, whilst at the same time relative costs of air travel have decreased. The opportunities for tourism activity have also increased through demographic changes, with an aging population, where the proportion of retired people has increased. These factors have contributed to the facilitation of personal choices through providing the opportunity by which individuals can express their preferences for more frequent, though shorter, holidays, development of second homes in coastal areas, and so on. These personal choices then aggregate to produce social expectations of increasing travel and tourism, which help to reinforce increases in demand for tourism.

---

46 EEA, op. cit, n. 11, p. 341.
47 Although there is a constitutional basis for taking action in 'the sphere of tourism' at European level under Article 3u of the Amsterdam Treaty.
48 Tourism policy being directed by DG-Enterprise.
49 Being the first product group to be included under Regulation 1980/2000.

On the global level, demand for international tourism increased by an average of 3.8 per cent per year in the 20 years to 2001.[50] Tourist arrivals are predicted to grow on average by 4.1 per cent per year globally, with those for Europe predicted for growth below that average, but still at 3.1 per cent.[51] The number of international tourist arrivals in Europe in 2006 was 458 million, with the predicted number for 2020 717 million.[52] The strongest growth within Europe is expected in the East Mediterranean region, where predictions are for levels double those of the European average,[53] and the Mediterranean coast is expected to see around 300 million tourists in 2025 (up from 135 million in 1990),[54] demonstrating that the localized pressures may be significantly magnified within regional averages. In the light of these predicted increases, and the powerful social factors underlying them, the lack of clarity in responses raises some questions about the likely prevention or even serious mitigation of marine degradation, amongst other concerns, such as the sustainability of the transport methods used.

THE NATURE OF 'RESPONSES' IN THE DPSIR MODEL

Direct responses can be conceived as those with a direct link to the identified drivers. In the example of eutrophication, the inadequate treatment of sewage was identified as a driver and a possible indicator for that driver is the number of households connected to secondary waste-water treatment facilities. Provision of such facilities in urban areas is a direct result of the implementation of the Urban Waste Water Treatment Directive, and so the link between the UWWT Directive and the increase in the number of households connected to secondary treatment facilities is direct and clear. Thus, the importance of direct responses is that there should be clear evidence of their effectiveness (or otherwise) in identifiable data. Where such a relationship is not observed, alternative explanations may be needed.

In other areas, such as tourism, there may be no responses aimed directly at issues such as the growth of international movements. Instead, drivers and pressures may be influenced indirectly by responses directed at states or impacts. An example of an indirect response is the Environmental Impact Assessment Directive[55] which may not shape the extent or location of

---

50 EEA, *Indicator Fact Sheet Signals 2001 – Chapter Tourism: YIR01TO07 Tourism expenditures of private households* (2001).
51 See UN WTO, *Tourism 2020*, the UN World Tourism Organization's predictions for growth to 2020, using 1995 as a base year.
52 EEA, op. cit., n. 10, p. 346.
53 World Tourism Organization, *Tourism 2020 Vision: Volume 4 (Europe)* (2001).
54 EEA, *Tourism Indicators*, at <www.eea.europa.eu/themes/tourism/indicators>.
55 Directive 85/337/EEC (as amended).

urbanization but does provide a mechanism which may, together with other responses,[56] cumulatively prevent further development in more sensitive locations. The increasing preference in recent years for integrated approaches to environmental problems has resulted in the development of integrated responses, particularly in relation to 'soft' law and guidance. Examples include the integrated coastal zone management strategy[57] and thematic strategies in areas such as the sustainable use of pesticides.[58] Such diffuse measures are often difficult to link to data trends (either historic or future) because of their general nature. Cross-sectoral responses, which are broad in application yet specific in obligation, generally take the form of legal measures in which the regulatory impact is felt across widely different sectors in different ways, such as the Integrated Pollution Prevention and Control Directive.[59] They include detailed procedural and/or substantive requirements which apply to certain prescribed activities or sectors but the manner in which such requirements are applied may be variable depending upon such things as detailed technical standards or sector-specific thresholds. Accordingly, although there may be a correlation between such indirect responses and drivers, there is no necessary direct connection between any individual driver and cross-sectoral responses so that establishing relationships is unlikely.

The nature of responses and their interaction within causal chains is one of the more opaque elements of the model. The cause and effect of NO_x emissions and policy responses outlined above is identifiable in the sense that it is possible to pinpoint specific responses and then outcomes which follow a predictable pattern. Whether there are external variables which distort perception of these relationships is, of course, one issue. A strength of the DPSIR model is that some of those variables are 'captured' for consideration, so that factors such as economic decline resulting in a reduction of industrial output are taken into account. A difficulty, however, is that different types of responses will, of course, differ in the directness of their impacts, and so be more or less identifiable in influencing outcomes.

Responses can include a broad range of actions undertaken at various levels of governance. Identifying the breadth of potentially relevant responses introduced at those varying levels and subjecting them to analysis for incorporation into the DPSIR framework can be a daunting task. The relative homogeneity provided through EC law in a number of areas can provide some assistance. This may contribute to a regionalization of perspectives, with local diversity in preferences and policies left out of the

---

56 Such as inter-coastal zone management policies (see COM(2000) 547 final) and Directive 92/43/EEC on the conservation of natural habitats.
57 id.
58 COM(2006) 373 final.
59 Directive 96/61/EC, op. cit., n. 34.

pictures presented. It does, however, reflect the increasing interdependence of the different layers of environmental regulation. There are clear links between international, European, national, and sub-national responses relating to marine ecosystems. Whilst certain drivers and pressures are thought to require action at an international or regional level (for example, marine matters or transboundary pollution) others are considered more appropriately dealt with at national or even local level (for example, planning policy), but within a broad coordinating framework. This globalization (or at least regionalization) of responses illustrates Martello and Jasanoff's link between responses as methods of solving environmental problems and the way in which those problems are perceived.

The link between responses and drivers varies within and between different sectors. In many sectors, there are less direct responses (at least at the level of European policy), whether for reasons of Community competence or otherwise, to drivers or pressures. In others, however, the link between responses and drivers is very close. Perhaps the clearest example here is the Common Fisheries Policy (CFP) where the driver of fishing effort is influenced by demand and the CFP, but the level of demand for many species of fish is such that by far the most important influence is the CFP, with some more limited factors such as fuel costs of more marginal relevance.

SOME DIFFICULTIES WITH DPSIR

The scale of increases predicted for many drivers calls into question the effectiveness of reliance on responses directed to other elements in the DPSIR model. But drivers in the form of population levels and economic growth are issues of huge political sensitivity, which may be too broad for interventions to be justified on the grounds of protecting the marine environment. By asking the question what it is that drives the forces of marine degradation, the DPSIR model illustrates the fundamental factors at play. Factors such as population levels, internal and external migration, economic growth, urbanization, and related increases in consumption involve some core questions of socio-economic policy. Some, such as migration, are political hot potatoes. Others, such as economic growth, are considered manageable goods whose value is rarely challenged, so that it is the undesirable effects of activities which are addressed, rather than activities themselves, reflecting some notions of sustainable development. Many also raise questions of individual freedom of choice. For such reasons, attempts at 'management' through responses is generally a no-go area. Before looking at how the effects of these factors might be influenced, some other difficulties with DPSIR will be identified.

1. *Limits on data*

The DPSIR model can require extensive statistical data, which is one of the most obvious challenges in using it for empirical analysis. The nature of the model, incorporating both socio-economic and physical factors, makes the data needs multi-dimensional. The breadth of data sources required is also increased where the boundaries of a given ecosystem are drawn more widely. It is perhaps inevitable that there will be gaps in data available in most models. The nature of the relationships explored is also problematic in that many of these may be non-linear and identifiable cause and effect may be elusive. In some cases, elements of the model may be observed as moving in the same way, with an implicit causal relationship. Establishing the nature of that relationship may be impossible in all but the most general terms, however. Again, this problem is exacerbated where the inter-connectedness of ecosystems is examined, with the corresponding increase in complexity of relationships. In some cases, the value of the DPSIR model may lie more in the collection of contextual data than in attempts at predictive modelling. As mentioned earlier, identification of variables can help to avoid distortions in perceptions of the success or otherwise of introducing responses. The effect of past responses may be identifiable through examination of data, such as connections to secondary waste-water treatment works, nutrient loads, and nutrient levels in specified areas. Apparent ineffectiveness might also be explained by analysing factors such as population levels, where some decoupling might be achieved but a 'net' increase in pressures and so on still result. Alternative explanations for perceived effectiveness may also be produced where reduced pressures, state changes, or lower impacts may not be (wholly) the result of responses.

2. *Complexity of ecosystems*

The DPSIR model necessarily simplifies and limits the scope of the ecosystems and the causal chains considered. In reality, the relationships which it attempts to illustrate are intricate. Indeed, the construction of a model may be helpful for evaluating the effectiveness of responses in one context, but once the issues and relationships are taken out of isolation, they quickly become unmanageable. As an example, the DPSIR model which might be constructed to explore responses to the issues of climate change would include familiar fundamental drivers such as GDP and population. State changes might include those pertinent to the marine environment; similarly, impacts may then include those relating to marine ecosystems. When we look at likely responses, the model quickly generates an additional level of complexity. Interventions in the form of the EU Emissions Trading Scheme and proposed Carbon Capture and Storage Directive,[60] and policies on renewable energy are designed to act as reverse drivers in relation to

---

60 Directive 2003/87/EC and proposals in COM(2008) 18 final.

climate change, decoupling carbon emissions to the atmosphere from energy and industrial production. Beyond the effects of climate change felt by marine ecosystems, however, those responses operate in a completely different manner in the marine environment. Offshore wind farms and carbon storage facilities represent new (or increased) pressures, resulting in impacts such as habitat loss. A further anticipated effect of responses is increased production of biofuels, potentially increasing nutrient loads entering marine waters. Thus, the same response can act as a reverse driver in one model representing certain dimensions of an ecosystem, and a positive driver in other models/dimensions. Further responses in the form of habitat protection cut across the causal chains, but that pervasiveness is a source of uncertainty in the models themselves; the increase in pressures can be identified but likely effect of such measures cannot. Attempting to take into account these factors produces an unworkable set of causal chains, but omitting them runs the risk of ignoring important influences.

3. *Regional limitations – the export effect*

Construction of a DPSIR model raises some spatial concerns. The most immediate is the geographical breadth of the model, where relevant factors may include the perceived range of ecosystems, hydrological factors, or geopolitical connections. Whatever the scale drawn, it is likely that the model will be incomplete through a failure to capture and take account of less easily connected events and outcomes. The strength of demand for fish, with pressures and impacts managed within European waters by the CFP, means that certain responses will have the effect of displacing, rather than properly reducing or mitigating pressure levels. Regulation of fishing and/or fish farming within the regional seas will not in itself address demand for those products. Unless effective trade restrictions are imposed, which may be problematic, it is likely that demand will be met from other sources. In our globalizing world, those sources may be geographically distant, with implications for transportation activity. Perhaps more of a concern is that production (or extraction) activities elsewhere may be undertaken using lower standards, and exerting pressures on more fragile and/or valuable ecosystems. The localization of impacts from demand from one region in another may, therefore, magnify the unsustainability of that demand, whilst distorting perceptions of those impacts through geographical dislocation. A similar displacement of impacts, again to potentially more vulnerable localities, can be found in the export of material for recycling. In the United Kingdom, the creation of a market in evidence of meeting recycling obligations through export to cheaper recycling facilities abroad effectively removes large amounts of waste arisings out of the United Kingdom data whilst still capturing the beneficial effect of recycling.[61] This has the effect

61 (2006) ENDS Report 376.

90

of increasing overall recycling rates whilst doing nothing to increase recycling capacity in the United Kingdom.[62]

WHAT ABOUT PERSONAL CHOICES?

The observation was made earlier that many of the fundamental driving forces influencing degradation of the marine environment comprise the aggregation of individual choices. The traditional difficulty of influencing these factors has been that of coordinating effect. The impact of a change in an individual decision, or set of preferences, is imperceptible on the global driver. It is only when a large number of switches take place that the influence becomes observable through aggregated effect. When one looks to identify such synchronizing influences, the most obvious forces of economic globalization have been those in the corporate sectors, where it is increased consumption, and corresponding production, which has been coordinated, with resultant increases in perceived wealth (to the benefit of some more than others). Thus the strongest forces have been towards economic growth, with related increases in activities, such as international trade, migrating and urbanizing populations, and so on. We have, however, also seen increasing coordination of efforts to address the disbenefits of economic globalization, connecting individual and localized preferences through NGOs, and broader civil society, together with some governmental action. Issues such as fair trade have been transformed from localized impacts and awareness to broader consumption changes through widening awareness influencing individual choices. Some of the artefacts of globalization in the form of communication technologies have played a part in bringing disparate knowledge of some impacts and their underlying causes together, presenting opportunities for synchronization. A variety of institutions can play roles in promoting coordination, as well as producing and disseminating the information which may influence decisions. Development of multinational institutions and agencies is a further feature of globalization which can be harnessed for coordinating effect, with recognition of the interdependence of economic issues resulting in close cooperation in governmental responses to global liquidity problems. A problem with some preferences is that the means of satisfying them are not apparent or do not exist; where certain infrastructure is required,[63] for example. Here the localized coordination of preferences can illustrate the demand for a level of provision which provides a platform for the wider expression of broader preferences. Coordination and

---

62 For example, between 1998–2001, 30 per cent of the increase in the recycling rate for packaging came from exports of waste. See European Union Committee, Thirty-third Report, *Packaging and Packaging Waste: Revised Recovery and Recycling Targets* HL (2001–2) 166.
63 As in the case of some sustainable transport modes.

91

development of 'infrastructure' can also nurture social expectations in a positive way, such as developing cultures of waste recycling, just as readily as driving expectations of more frequent and exotic travel.

The political obstacles to directing responses at fundamental driving forces were identified above. The relative 'elasticity' in driver levels, whereby perceptible effects of a response may be felt only from sustained and varied investment of efforts also contributes to the unattractiveness of taking action directly against those underlying forces. Their fundamental nature means, however, that their influence is manifested across a range of ecosystems and issues. Thus a shift in diet from animal to vegetable protein, coordinated as a means of addressing climate change,[64] would have wider positive effects, including eutrophication levels in Europe's regional seas. Those wider effects may combine positive and negative aspects in different contexts, but construction of models like the DPSIR model can help to assess the various consequences.

CONCLUSIONS

In many ways, the tension between economic globalization and ecological localization reflects the contested nature of sustainable development itself.[65] At the heart of this tension lie methodological challenges concerned with understanding complex relationships, collecting and synthesizing and interpreting large amounts of data. The development of sustainability indicators has been a response to this challenge and the use of the DPSIR methodology is just one way of producing meaningful indicators. This methodology has its glaring imperfections but represents an attempt at understanding the role that the forces of globalization play in creating localized ecosystem degradation. In the case of Europe's regional seas, such an assessment and action plan is woefully overdue. The danger is that in the absence of developing and communicating such frameworks, the disconnection between the global and local is not properly appreciated at the individual level. There is no inevitability that economic growth will only lead to the expression of narrow consumerist preferences. More money and time off work does not necessarily mean more weekend breaks with consequent short-haul flights within Europe or an increase in coastal urbanization as a result of more second homes. Individual preferences can be selected upon the basis of the common good – where notions of environmental citizenship and individual responsibility inform decisions rather than a blanket reliance upon market forces and narrow consumer interests. Part of the development of the DPSIR

---

64 Recently called for by Dr Rajendra Pachauri, Chair of the UN Intergovernmental Panel on Climate Change.

65 W. Beckerman, 'Sustainable Development: Is it a Useful Concept?' (1994) 3 *Environmental Values* 191–209.

framework is to increase understanding of the link between global and local, as a way of developing the individual's preference-formation framework. The benefits of the DPSIR framework are that it sends relatively clear messages to policy-makers and individuals.

The complexity of the systems studied in DPSIR models and the causal chains within them, together with issues such as lack of adequate data for some elements of the models constructed makes their value as predictive tools limited in many cases. Even in such cases, however, those models do help to provide a deeper, contextualized understanding of systems and the relationship between their different elements, both socio-economic factors and physical states. Whilst they may raise more questions than the answers they provide, those questions can help to analyse the effects and effectiveness of regulatory responses, whilst highlighting the powerful underlying forces which drive the problems being addressed. The scale of predicted developments in some of those forces and their anticipated effects felt down socio-economic causal chains is such that a pervasive question raised in relation to the drivers of marine degradation is whether the preferences of individuals, influenced by social relations at various levels, can be co-ordinated so as to influence those drivers. Further questions which then arise are whether, or the extent to which, such coordination or more direct responses regarding drivers should be the role of government. If those kinds of responses are felt inappropriate, then it is the activities of non-state organizations and individuals that will need to perform this vital function. For, given the scale of many challenges in terms of predicted driver increases, the prospect of continued reliance upon the mitigation of undesirable effects through the decoupling of pressures from drivers, and impacts from pressures is an unhappy one.

93

JOURNAL OF LAW AND SOCIETY
VOLUME 36, NUMBER 1, MARCH 2009
ISSN: 0263-323X, pp. 94–109

Framing the Local and the Global in the Anti-nuclear Movement: Law and the Politics of Place

CHRIS HILSON*

This article examines the politics of place in relation to legal mobilization by the anti-nuclear movement. It examines two case examples – citizens' weapons inspections and civil disobedience strategies – which have involved the movement drawing upon the law in particular spatial contexts. The article begins by examining a number of factors which have been employed in recent social movement literature to explain strategy choice, including ideology, resources, political and legal opportunity, and framing. It then proceeds to argue that the issues of scale, space, and place play an important role in relation to framing by the movement in the two case examples. Both can be seen to involve scalar reframing, with the movement attempting to resist localizing tendencies and to replace them with a global frame. Both also involve an attempt to reframe the issue of nuclear weapons away from the contested frame of the past (unilateral disarmament) towards the more universal and widely accepted frame of international law.

INTRODUCTION

The literature on social movements or contentious politics has, for some time now, sought to explain why it is that certain movements adopt particular strategies, ranging from political lobbying, through litigation, to demonstrations and civil disobedience. In this line of analysis, the strategy or 'repertoire of contention' is thus the dependent variable and the independent variables which might account for strategy choice include, among others, political opportunity, legal opportunity, resources, ideology, identity, and framing. Thus, for example, a social movement organization (SMO) might decide to rely on lobbying as a strategy because political opportunities are

* School of Law, University of Reading, Foxhill House, Whiteknights Road, Earley, Reading RG6 7BA, England
c.j.hilson@reading.ac.uk

viewed as particularly favourable; similarly, litigation might be chosen where legal opportunities through the courts seem promising.

The aim of this paper is to examine two related instances of legal mobilization by the anti-nuclear movement. First, it looks at 'citizens' weapons inspections' at various nuclear sites in the United Kingdom including, for example, the Atomic Weapons Establishment (AWE) at Aldermaston in Berkshire, which seek to adopt a similar type of international-law based inspection regime for weapons of mass destruction that the UN had enforced on Saddam Hussein's Iraq. Second, it explores civil disobedience cases involving acts of criminal damage and often also trespass onto nuclear sites, in which activists have essentially invited arrest with a view to raising defence arguments about the international law legality of nuclear weapons in the local criminal courts.[1]

The paper begins by examining a range of variables which might explain why the anti-nuclear movement adopted the above, law-related strategies. However, it then proceeds to focus on just one of these variables – framing, which involves the purposeful construction of meaning or the 'politics of signification'[2] – examining in particular how both strategies involve an attempt to resist, re-code and to benefit from a 'politics of place'.

THE CASE EXAMPLES

1. Citizens' weapons inspections

The idea of citizens' weapons inspections arose from around the time preceding the Iraq war when UNSCOM[3] weapons inspectors were mandated to search for weapons of mass destruction held by Saddam Hussein. Peace campaigners were struck by the apparent hypocrisy of the fact that these inspections were authorized by the UN, with the five permanent members of the Security Council themselves deploying nuclear weapons.[4] As a result, an international network of groups employing citizen weapons inspections

---

1 Note that many protestors would contest the framing of the damage as 'criminal' and also the characterization of their action as 'civil disobedience' – instead arguing that they are acting to prevent crime and that they are obeying a higher law (or even, for certain religious protestors, that it is a matter of 'divine obedience' – see S. Nepstad, *Religion and War Resistance in the Plowshares Movement* (2008) 61). Similar civil disobedience action (followed by successful jury acquittal) has also been taken recently in relation to climate change: see, for example, <http://www.greenpeace.org.uk/blog/climate/coal-kingsnorth-six-on-trial-20080828>.

2 R. Benford and D. Snow, 'Framing Processes and Social Movements: An Overview and Assessment' (2000) 26 *Annual Rev. of Sociology* 611, at 613.

3 The United Nations Special Commission established under resolution 687 of 3 April 1991 of the UN Security Council to carry out inspections of Iraq's weapons of mass destruction.

4 <http://www.motherearth.org/inspection/index_en.php>.

95

developed, ranging from international groups such as Greenpeace International,[5] through national groups like Friends of the Earth UK, the Los Alamos Study Group (United States),[6] Bombspotting (Belgium),[7] Friends of the Earth Flanders and Brussels,[8] and Trident Ploughshares (United Kingdom),[9] through to local groups such as the Aldermaston Women's Peace Camp[10] and the Gloucestershire Weapons Inspectors.[11] Many of these groups fall under the umbrella of Abolition 2000, a global network aimed at abolishing nuclear weapons which has a Citizens' Weapons Inspection Working Group designed to 'support citizen groups who inspect sites and report their findings to the public, United Nations, national governments and other interested parties'.[12]

Citizen inspections are designed to bring openness and transparency to the typically secretive siting of nuclear weapons in predominantly Northern countries which are not subject to UN inspections. Justification for the inspections is often legally-based: inspectors are typically portrayed as upholding international law, with reference often made to the 1996 International Court of Justice (ICJ) Advisory Opinion on the Legality of the Threat or Use of Nuclear Weapons.[13] The inspections themselves are typically carried out by ordinary citizens but have occasionally included Members of Parliament[14] and celebrities.[15] Inspectors often dress up for the occasion in white boiler suits reminiscent of the news coverage of 'official' expert, scientific inspection teams in Iraq. They are invariably denied access to the relevant facility, but in most instances, an inspection report[16] is nevertheless completed, posted on the web, and sent to the relevant authorities.

5 <http://www.greenpeace.org/international/news/citizen-inspections>.
6 <http://www.lasg.org/inspections.htm>.
7 <http://www.bomspotting.be/>.
8 <http://www.motherearth.org/>.
9 <http://www.tridentploughshares.org/>.
10 <http://www.aldermaston.net/>.
11 <http://cynatech.co.uk/gwi/14-dec-Fairford.htm>.
12 <http://www.abolition2000.org/site/c.cdJIKKNpFqG/b.1316401/>.
13 (1996) 35 ILM 809 and 1343.
14 For example, in the United Kingdom, at Aldermaston in 2006, Norman Baker MP. See also the United States, where (Canadian) Vancouver East Member of Parliament Libby Davies led an inspection team at Bangor nuclear submarine base in Washington state.
15 Such as Anita Roddick, the (now deceased) Bodyshop founder, at Aldermaston in 2006.
16 Model report forms are available at <http://www.motherearth.org/inspection/inspection5.php>.

96

2. Civil disobedience

It would be misleading to seek to draw too great a contrast between citizen weapons inspections and civil disobedience, since some citizen inspections also involve civil disobedience.[17] However, for the most part, weapons inspections involve lawful and symbolic non-violent direct action, whereas the aim of civil disobedience actions is actively and openly to break the law and to invite arrest, which is accepted without resistance.[18] The relevant actions generally involve acts of alleged criminal damage to try to gain entry to nuclear establishments, which, if successful, will be followed by alleged offences of aggravated trespass and, typically, further acts of criminal damage to 'war' equipment.[19] In the United Kingdom, many of the actions are undertaken by individuals associated with the Trident Ploughshares movement. Although not a Christian organization, the name of this stems from the biblical reference of turning swords into ploughshares, which often underpins the nature of the damage activity undertaken: in many instances, individuals have been arrested for hammering and thereby seeking to disable aeroplanes, submarines, and other 'war machines'. When brought before the criminal courts, the individuals then typically seek to raise a defence to the relevant criminal charges that they are acting to prevent a breach of international law by the United Kingdom. Again, reference is often made here to the illegality of nuclear weapons under international law based on, among other things, the ICJ Advisory Opinion.

IDEOLOGY

It is no surprise to find groups such as Greenpeace and Trident Ploughshares behind both types of action above. Ideologically, Greenpeace has its roots in the Quaker movement and elements of Quakerism, such as bearing witness to an unlawful and/or immoral act and speaking the truth to power, can be seen in both the weapons inspections and the acts of open and accountable civil disobedience (which characterized Greenpeace's very first whaling actions). Although expressly non-religious in the United Kingdom,[20] the

---

17 M. Finn, 'Citizens Inspect Aldermaston' in A. Zelter (ed.), *Trident on Trial: The Case for People's Disarmament* (2001) 71.
18 For the distinction between symbolic non-violent action and civil disobedience, see A. Carter, *Direct Action* (1962) (cited in P. Routledge, *Terrains of Resistance* (1993) 33).
19 The term 'war' equipment is a conscious reframing made by many in the movement of the more standard use of 'defence' in such contexts.
20 See, further, Nepstad, op. cit., n. 1, pp. 190–1, who explains that, in contrast with the United States, where the Plowshares movement has a strong Catholic underpinning, there was a conscious choice made in the United Kingdom Ploughshares movement to adopt a more inclusive, secular tone in order to maximize participation.

97

history of the Ploughshares movement can also be traced back to Christian and Quaker influences,[21] and a number of British Ploughshares activists are committed to these faiths. Both Greenpeace and the Ploughshares movement are also influenced by Gandhian ideology of non-violence (*ahimsa*) and his *satyagraha* (the truth force) actions against British colonial authority such as the famous salt march protest against the 1882 Raj Salt Act.

It is thus quite clear that ideology – in other words, ideas, values, and beliefs about the world – plays a part in the choice of movement strategy.[22] This type of open, accountable action lies in stark contrast with the type of covert 'ecotage' employed by more radical wings of the environmental movement such as Earth First! or the Earth Liberation Front.[23] Such groups often fail to see the point of transparent and accountable Ploughshares-type action, seeing their role instead as one of avoiding arrest by an oppressive state and destroying as much of the environmentally harmful (for example, GM) material as possible without invited interference. Similar tensions can be found within the anti-nuclear movement itself. At Faslane, for example – the key Scottish Trident submarine base – in addition to a significant Ploughshares presence, there is also a Peace Camp,[24] which is concerned with creating an alternative lifestyle as well as engaging in anti-nuclear activity.[25] The ideology of the camp also has strong anarchist elements, leading many within it to question the Ploughshare reliance on state-based, court strategies.[26]

POLITICAL AND LEGAL OPPORTUNITY

The idea of political opportunity structure (POS) or political opportunity (PO) has been used for some time to help explain the rise of new social movements at particular times and also their use of protest as a particular strategy.[27] However, such 'political process' theories tended to underplay or ignore the role of law and litigation-based strategies in their analyses. In recent years, the idea of legal opportunity structure (LOS)[28] or legal

---

21 id.
22 S. Buechler, *Women's Movements in the United States: Woman Suffrage, Equal Rights, and Beyond* (1990) 85.
23 A. Nocella and S. Best, 'A Fire in the Belly of the Beast: The Emergence of Revolutionary Environmentalism' in *Igniting a Revolution: Voices in Defense of the Earth*, eds. A. Nocella and S. Best (2006).
24 Faslane Peace Camp, at<http://faslane.co.nr/>.
25 D. Heller, 'Resolving Culture Conflicts' in Zelter, op. cit., n. 17, p. 165.
26 id., pp. 166–7.
27 For example, see H. Kitschelt, 'Political Opportunity Structures and Political Protest: Anti-Nuclear Movements in Four Democracies' (1986) 16 *Brit. J. of Political Science* 57; S. Tarrow, *Power in Movement: Social Movements, Collective Action and Politics* (1994).
28 E. Andersen, *Out of the Closets and Into the Courts: Legal Opportunity Structure and Gay Rights Litigation* (2005).

opportunity (LO)[29] has thus been developed alongside POS/PO in order to bridge this gap and to provide law with the focus it deserves when looking at mobilization.

Of course, one could argue that, in a general sense, political opportunity for the anti-nuclear movements in the new century should have been quite favourable. After all, in a post-Cold War environment, the greatest security threats now arguably come not from states but from terrorism, which nuclear weapons are particularly ill-suited to combating. And specifically in the United Kingdom, one might have thought that a Labour government with a number of former Campaign for Nuclear Disarmament (CND) members in the Cabinet, would be receptive to arguments about not proceeding with the renewal of the United Kingdom's Trident-based nuclear weapons programme.[30] However, this would be to ignore the role of global power politics and state interests: for the key nuclear powers, maintaining their nuclear presence is perceived as a prerequisite to continuing to play at the top table internationally. For New Labour, an anti-nuclear stance may also have appeared too much like Old Labour with associated concerns about electability.[31] For those reasons, it is perhaps not surprising that the decision to replace Trident was approved by the Westminster Parliament in March 2007, albeit with Conservative support. However, not all political opportunity within the United Kingdom is negative. Post-devolution, although the retention of Trident remains a reserved matter for the Westminster Parliament, the Scottish Nationalist Party (SNP) is very much anti-Trident and for a nuclear-free Scotland. There is little doubt that anti-nuclear protestors have seized on this difference and maintained both lobbying and protest activity to keep Trident in the public eye.[32] In emphasizing Scottish hostility to Trident, the aim is to maintain pressure on the Labour government, which has already lost considerable ground to the SNP in recent years.

What then of legal opportunity? Certainly at first sight, existing LO/LOS approaches will struggle to make sense of the actions taken here. Legal opportunities were arguably opened up in what Andersen has described as the 'legal stock'[33] sense by the ICJ's Advisory Opinion on nuclear weapons, which spelled out that the threat and use of such weapons would typically be in breach of international law. And, of course, both the citizens' weapons

---

29 C. Hilson, 'New Social Movements: The Role of Legal Opportunity' (2002) 9 *J. of European Public Policy* 238.

30 However, history may suggest otherwise – namely, the pro-nuclear stance of the Wilson government in the 1960s, despite considerable anti-nuclear sympathy within the Labour Party at the time.

31 L. Wittner, *Toward Nuclear Abolition: A History of the World Nuclear Disarmament Movement, 1971 – Present* (2003) 478.

32 'Faslane: Paying the Price of Protest' *Herald*, 2 October 2007, which details (in addition to the Ploughshares and Peace Camp activity at Faslane mentioned above) the 'Faslane 365' blockade campaign which took place during 2006–2007.

33 Andersen, op. cit., n. 28, p. 20.

99

inspections and the Ploughshares-type examples of civil disobedience have made reference to this Opinion and thus relied on this legal opportunity.[34] However, in other respects, the terrain of legal opportunity in play here looks very different to that examined in previous studies. These studies have, as Vanhala states, tended to examine proactive litigation where SMOs are the claimants commencing the relevant litigation proceedings.[35] While there is a recent example of this type of proactive litigation by the anti-nuclear movement in the shape of the *Marchiori* case, legal opportunity in the sense of judicial receptivity was weak there in so far as the relevant claim did not succeed in immediate, purely instrumental terms.[36] In contrast, the citizens' weapons inspections, though underpinned by a reference to international law, do not involve litigation and the courts at all. And while the civil disobedience cases do involve the courts, they are an example of what Harlow and Rawlings have termed 'reactive litigation',[37] where the social movement actors are not the claimants but rather the defendants, with the state being the party to have commenced proceedings, which are criminal rather than civil in nature.

In relation to these reactive civil disobedience cases, there is a marked difference in legal opportunity terms, between magistrates' courts and Crown courts (or their relevant Scottish equivalents). With the former, magistrates have tended to be extremely unreceptive to international law arguments and legal opportunity has thus been poor.[38] In Crown courts, however, judicial receptivity has been mixed. In some cases, judges were unwilling to allow international law evidence,[39] while in others, such as the Greenock case involving the 'Trident Three' described further below, they were more receptive to international law. However, even in cases where judges were unreceptive, juries remained free to take note of international law arguments and indeed, because of the unpredictability of juries, the

---

34 Indeed, Nepstad, op. cit., n. 1, pp. 188–90, traces the growth of the United Kingdom Ploughshares movement (and the origins of Trident Ploughshares) to the Advisory Opinion.

35 L. Vanhala, 'Anti-discrimination Policy Actors and their use of Litigation Strategies: The Influence of Identity Politics' (2009) 16 *J. of European Public Policy* (forthcoming).

36 *R (Marchiori)* v. *Environmental Agency* [2002] EWCA Civ 3, [2002] *Eur. Law Reports* 225.

37 C. Harlow and R. Rawlings, *Pressure Through Law* (1992) 162; Vanhala, op. cit., n. 35.

38 See, for example, D. Fairhall, *Common Ground: The Story of Greenham* (2006) 96; Heller, op. cit., n. 25, p. 167; A. Zelter, 'Our Story' in Zelter, op. cit., n. 17, pp. 260, 269, 275.

39 See, for example, the 1998 Burghfield case against Sarah Hipperson and three others before Reading Crown Court, arising from fence cutting at AWE Burghfield, where the judge (Mowat) apparently instructed the jury to ignore international law arguments that had been presented to them (S. Hipperson, *Greenham: Non-Violent Women v The Crown Prerogative* (2005) 80–6).

100

authorities have often been keen to keep cases away from the Crown courts wherever possible.[40] And for good reason it would seem: writing in 2001, Angie Zelter noted that, of the four major Trident Ploughshares jury trials in England and Scotland, three resulted in acquittals and one in a hung jury.[41] Juries and Crown courts, in other words, offer a potentially favourable legal opportunity, regardless of the disposition of the particular judge hearing the case.

As regards receptivity of judges in Crown court proceedings, the higher courts in both Scotland and England and Wales have since sought to close down the glimmer of legal opportunity offered by the more receptive members of the Crown court judiciary by ruling that international law arguments do not provide a justification defence in relation to criminal protest activity.[42] As Lord Hoffmann stated in the House of Lords in *R* v. *Jones*:

> the apprehension, however honest or reasonable, of acts which are thought to be unlawful or contrary to the public interest, cannot justify the commission of criminal acts and the issue of justification should be withdrawn from the jury. Evidence to support the opinions of the protesters as to the legality of the acts in question is irrelevant and inadmissible, disclosure going to this issue should not be ordered and the services of international lawyers are not required.[43]

What impact these higher court rulings have had on more recent case outcomes will require further empirical investigation. However, as intimated above, defendants – though perhaps only those representing themselves – will still be tempted to put arguments about international law before juries, which may well continue to take them into account, even if formally directed not to. Legal opportunity has thus been dented by the relevant rulings, but perhaps not dealt a fatal blow.

RESOURCE MOBILIZATION

Unlike political and legal process approaches, which stress the role of external opportunities to movement mobilization, resource mobilization theory[44] examines the internal resources available to groups.[45] The argument

---

40 See, in relation to Greenham, S. Roseneil, *Disarming Patriarchy: Feminist and Political Action at Greenham* (1995) 108, who notes that there appeared to be an attempt to keep cases within the summary justice system in order to avoid the possibility of acquittals by sympathetic juries.

41 A. Zelter, 'People's Disarmament' in Zelter, op. cit., n. 17, p. 53.

42 In Scotland, see *Lord Advocate's Reference No 1 of 2000* [2001] JC 143. For England and Wales, see *R* v. *Jones* [2006] UKHL 16, [2007] 1 A.C. 136.

43 *Jones*, id., at [94].

44 J. McCarthy and M. Zald, 'Resource Mobilization and Social Movements: A Partial Theory' (1977) 82 *Am. J. of Sociology* 1212; J.C. Jenkins, 'Resource Mobilization Theory and the Study of Social Movements' (1983) 9 *Annual Rev. of Sociology* 527.

45 Kitschelt, op. cit., n. 27, pp. 59–60.

is that SMOs must be able successfully to mobilize resources from the public in order effectively to engage in collective action. As applied to strategy choice, it has been argued that protest is typically cheaper as a strategy, calling on fewer financial resources than litigation or political lobbying.[46] Vanhala has argued that while this is perhaps true of proactive litigation, it is not true of reactive litigation of the civil disobedience type,[47] which typically requires little or no actual financial expenditure by the individual apart from a time commitment and potentially the payment of a criminal fine.

In fact, the picture is more complex here. It is true that both the citizens' weapons inspections and the civil disobedience case examples lie at the cheaper end of the financial resource spectrum, despite the latter being litigation-based. However, while proactive litigation is generally resource intensive for the larger interest groups within a movement, at a lower level, members of the movement may be able to benefit from legal aid or *pro bono* legal support. Thus, resources do not fully explain recourse to civil disobedience-type, reactive litigation, because proactive litigation may in practice be equally 'cheap' to some within the movement. This was indeed the case in the proactive *Marchiori* judicial review case mentioned earlier, where the claimants were supported either by legal aid in the case of the individual (Emanuela Marchiori), or by *pro bono* public interest lawyers in the case of the interest group (Nuclear Awareness Group).

FRAMING

Vanhala has pointed to a need, in assessing strategy choice, to develop a holistic account, based on a range of explanatory variables rather than just one or two such as political and legal opportunity and resources.[48] In drawing up such an account, she suggests that those who have studied legal mobilization have tended to ignore framing as an important variable.[49] Framing is, as Benford and Snow put it, 'meaning work'.[50] It is a process in which social movements are 'actively engaged as agents in a struggle over the production of mobilizing and counter-mobilizing ideas and meanings'.[51] It is thus a contentious process in so far as 'it involves the generation of interpretive frames that not only differ from existing ones but that may also challenge them'.[52] In looking at the use of litigation as a strategy by the

---

46 For example, Hilson, op. cit., n. 29.
47 Vanhala, op. cit., n. 35.
48 id.
49 id. Though compare, for example, M. Smith, 'Framing Same-sex Marriage in Canada and the United States: Goodridge, Halpern and The National Boundaries of Political Discourse' (2007) 16 *Social & Legal Studies* 5.
50 Benford and Snow, op. cit., n. 2, p. 613.
51 id.
52 id., p. 614.

disability movement, Vanhala's argument is that the way the movement had reframed the issue of disability from being a medical condition to a rights-based one led naturally to its using litigation in the courts as a strategy.[53]

My claim here is that framing is similarly crucial to the two different forms of legal mobilization here: international law-based citizens' weapons inspections and civil disobedience resulting in reactive litigation. It has been suggested that, where contradictory ideologies are at play, a social movement may need to engage in a process of reframing or 'keying' so as to meet at an accepted ideological point.[54] Just as Vanhala suggests that the disability movement engaged in such a process, so too, one can argue, did the anti-nuclear movement. During the 1970s–1980s, the British anti-nuclear movement, spearheaded by CND, largely campaigned for unilateral nuclear *disarmament* – an ideology at loggerheads with the government appeal to the ideology of nuclear *deterrence*. In contrast, actions like the citizens' weapons inspection and civil disobedience followed by court-based defences have sought to reframe matters, stressing more the illegality of the government's position on nuclear weapons as a matter of international law. While there were elements of such an approach in earlier decades such as at Greenham, this legal reframing became a more powerful possibility after the legal opportunity presented by the ICJ Opinion in 1996. In place of the clearly divergent and irreconcilable ideological positions of unilateral disarmament versus deterrence, one now had a form of immanent critique, where the movement were able to confront the government for failing to play by the accepted and ideologically apparently neutral rules of international law as confirmed by the ICJ.

THE POLITICS OF PLACE

However, just as Vanhala argues that framing has been missing from the litigation literature, my contention is that insufficient attention has been paid by it to geographical notions of spatiality. The interface between geography and social movements has received increased attention in recent years, with numerous studies examining how scale, space, and place affect and are affected by collective action.[55] Needless to say, there have been numerous

---

53 Vanhala, op. cit., n. 35.
54 D. Snow and R. Benford, 'Mobilization Forum: Comment on Oliver and Johnston' (2000) 5 *Mobilization* 55.
55 See, for example, B. Miller, *Geography and Social Movements: Comparing Antinuclear Activism in the Boston Area* (2000); W. Sewell, 'Space in Contentious Politics' in *Silence and Voice in the Study of Contentious Politics*, eds. S. Aminzade et al. (2001); Routledge, op. cit., n. 18; D. Martin and B. Miller, 'Space and Contentious Politics' (2003) 8 *Mobilization* 143; G. Franquemagne 'From Larzac to the Altermondialist Mobilisation: Space in Environmental Movements' (2007) 16 *Environmental Politics* 826.

disputes about the precise meaning and relationship between these various spatial terms. For example, there is a tendency to see place as territorially bounded, local, and particular, and in that sense in direct contrast to space, which is associated with the unbounded, global, and universal.[56] Authors such as Massey contest this view, arguing that place is really just a coming together of socially constructed relational networks – in other words space – at particular nodes.[57] On this account, place is just a snapshot view of space: far from being opposites, the relational dynamics of the two are the same.

Nevertheless, like Leitner et al.,[58] the position adopted here is that all of these spatialities potentially matter to social movement strategy and it is therefore important to examine them all. One can agree with Massey that, in theory, the distinction between place and space is overdrawn, while at the same time appreciating that social movements often thrive on emphasizing distinctions and conflicts.

1. Citizens' weapons inspections

Beginning with the citizens' weapons inspections, these can be seen as a continuation of the problematizing of place first instigated by the anti-nuclear women's camps at Greenham Common in the 1980s. In Cresswell's terms,[59] Greenham involved women who were 'out of place' and it was this apparent jarring which made their protest all the more powerful. Thus, on the one hand, they were women out in the public sphere protesting rather than behaving themselves as wives and mothers within the typical nuclear family home. But in addition, they were also women forming local communities of place in the camps outside the base, in contrast to the predominantly male, patriarchal, abstract, and global[60] space inside the nuclear base itself. Unlike Greenham, the citizens' weapons inspections do not involve an attempt to create a community of place. However, like Greenham, they rely on the politics of spatiality by seeking to prick the normalization of such nuclear establishments within their local landscapes. As Couldry has noted of Greenham, '[f]or existing residents of the area, the camp publicized a

---

56 A tendency described (though not shared) by, for example, D. Massey, *Space, Place and Gender* (1994) 5, 152–6; and A. Escobar, 'Culture Sits in Places: Reflections on Globalism and Subaltern Strategies of Localization' (2001) 20 *Political Geography* 139.

57 Massey, id., p. 154.

58 H. Leitner et al., 'The Spatialities of Contentious Politics' (2008) 33 *Transactions of the Institute of British Geographers* 157.

59 T. Cresswell, *In Place/Out of Place: Geography, Ideology, and Transgressions* (1996) 99.

60 Nuclear weapons being, as Couldry observes, the ultimate example of weapons of global significance and concern (N. Couldry, 'Disrupting the Media Frame at Greenham Common: A New Chapter in the History of Mediations' (1999) 21 *Media, Culture and Society* 337, at 348).

104

disturbing aspect of their immediate environment that had been naturalized.'[61] And as the Los Alamos Study Group has similarly stated in relation to citizens' weapons inspections, 'the verification process serves as a popular check against illicit government activities, and the perpetuation and normalization of potentially dangerous policies.'[62] In spatial terms, nuclear establishments often become an invisible part of their local communities: they become swallowed by surrounding place. What the citizens' weapons inspections seek to achieve is to reframe this localizing scalar effect by using the theatre of an international weapons inspection more normally associated with 'truly' international places like Iraq. The sense of performance (with people often dressed up in expert white radiation protection suits and hard hats) is important to such events[63] and, as performance, may strike many as the theatre of the absurd.[64] However, therein, at the same time, lies its power and its weakness: the appearance of incongruity – of the event seeming 'out of place' in Cresswell's terms – is counter-hegemonic but perhaps at the same time underlines the sheer weight of the hegemonic force of the existing politics of place.

2. Civil disobedience

As for the civil disobedience case example, this too involves the politics of spatiality. There is a number of senses in which this is so. First, lawyers and those studying litigation have tended to ignore the 'material geography' of the court buildings themselves.[65] Court buildings exist in particular locales and this setting and place matters to the deployment of litigation as a strategy. The spatiality of the court matters – not just in terms of court architecture, which has been studied,[66] but also in terms of its place and scale. For many protestors, the court is simply another site for enacting the theatre of direct action.[67] For that reason alone, the location of the court buildings matter. This can be seen in the context of the actions of the so-called 'Trident Three', who in 1999 committed sabotage on a floating

61 id., p. 341.
62 <http://www.lasg.org/inspections.htm>.
63 For the importance of performance in environmental protest, see B. Szerszynski, 'Performing Politics: The Dramatics of Environmental Protest' in *Culture and Economy After the Cultural Turn*, eds. L. Ray and A. Sayer (1999).
64 Witness reaction on YouTube to videos of the Aldermaston citizens' inspection, with some comments referring to the protestors as 'numpties' and such like: <http://www.youtube.com/watch?v=9-SILV3JB44&feature=related>.
65 Couldry, op. cit., n. 60, p. 338 makes a similar observation about the locale of media production space such as studios, which I have applied here to courts.
66 See, for example, L. Mulcahy, 'Architects of Justice: The Politics of Courtroom Design' (2007) 16 *Social and Legal Studies* 383.
67 See, for example, R. Johnson, 'Alice Through the Fence: Greenham Women and the Law' in *Nuclear Weapons, the Peace Movement and the Law*, eds. J. Dewar et al. (1986) 163; Fairhall, op. cit., n. 38, p. 94.

scientific laboratory (*Maytime*) on Loch Goil in Scotland, which was involved with maintaining the crucial acoustic silence of the Trident nuclear submarine fleet. John Mayer, one of the defence lawyers in their subsequent prosecution, highlights how it was probably no accident that they ended up being placed for trial initially in Dunoon, where their alleged crime had taken place – a 'sleepy' island town in the West Highlands, 'remote from the big cities of Glasgow and Edinburgh [which] would ensure that the trial passed off with as little fuss as possible'.[68] In the end, according to Mayer, because the complexity of the trial looked likely to swamp the Dunoon court for weeks, it was eventually sent to the nearest mainland town, Greenock – itself rather remote and described by Mayer in terms of it being 'a town of faded glory'.[69] Thus, where the court is geographically within the country matters in terms of the publicity the case is likely to attract. In the event, as Mayer observes, this decision to try the case 'well out of the way' seriously backfired because the local Sheriff (Margaret Gimblett) instructed the jury to find the accused not guilty.[70] Where the court is within the particular town or city itself may also make a difference: in the case of Greenock, for example, Mayer describes how the location of the Sheriff Court is 'in an out-of-the-way street, almost an aside to what is happening in the town'.[71] This too will impact on publicity.

Second, where a court is located will influence the social profile of its relevant actors – whether those actors are local magistrates or members of the jury. Certain Crown courts are preferred by defence lawyers because juries there are more likely to be drawn from social classes which are likely to treat police evidence with some caution. Within the context of the civil disobedience cases under examination here, Sarah Hipperson – a Greenham protestor – felt that the hostile reception shown to the Greenham women's arguments by West Berkshire Magistrates' Court in Newbury could in part be traced to the fact that the lay magistrates were drawn from the conservative, local area.[72] This area was indifferent to Cruise missiles, but very much against the intrusive 'mess' of the camps and the presence of visibly 'different' women around the town.[73]

Next, as Creswell has forcefully argued, places are important in defining socially acceptable norms of behaviour.[74] What is normal is, in other words, constructed geographically: what is normal behaviour for one place may thus be regarded as out of place in another. We have seen this above in the context of the Greenham women at the airbase, where their gendered camps

68 J. Mayer, *Nuclear Peace: The Story of the Trident Three* (2002) 100–1.
69 id., p. 135.
70 id., pp. 258–60.
71 id., p. 135.
72 Hipperson, op. cit., n. 39, p. 61.
73 Roseneil, op. cit., n. 40, pp. 128–35.
74 Cresswell, op. cit., n. 59, p. 105

appeared out of place alongside the equally, but oppositely, gendered airbase. However, this out-of- placeness can also be seen in relation to the presence of anti-nuclear protestors within the criminal justice system. Many of the actors and commentators on magistrates' court cases involving both Greenham women in the 1980s and, more recently, anti-Trident activists in the 1990s-2000s, have remarked on the often unruly behaviour of the defendants, in marked contrast to the usual hierarchy and order expected within courts as reverential places. As Fairhall notes, at Greenham, when magistrates tried to cut short women trying to put forward lengthy justifications for their actions, the latter:

> responded either by talking on regardless, or perhaps breaking into song. The solemn rituals of the law were being mocked, or at least ignored. There was pandemonium in court, not silence.[75]

And, at both Greenham and in recent Trident cases, defendants and sympathetic movement supporters attending court would often fail to obey the usher's call to rise, instead remaining seated, particularly if the court had itself failed to show respect to the defendants by failing to listen appropriately to arguments about justification for their actions.[76]

This sense of the protestors being out of place within the criminal justice system can be found not only within the courts, but also in prison, where many anti-nuclear protestors have ended up over the years – occasionally for the gravity of their initial offences – but more often than not for refusing, as a matter of principle, to pay the typical fines imposed for criminal damage convictions. In prison, the protestors are often regarded by other prisoners and prison officers as out of place – not this time because of their behaviour while in prison (though occasionally for this),[77] but because of the very different nature of the 'criminal' actions which brought them there.[78] In this sense, they are out of place because prison is constructed as an appropriate place for 'proper' criminals and not for 'political prisoners' like the protestors.[79]

There is a further important sense in which the actions of many of the anti-nuclear protestors in court appear out of place, and one which returns us once again to the central issue of framing. As mentioned briefly above, many protestors – particularly since the ICJ Advisory Opinion – have sought to raise collateral, international law defences to charges brought against them in local criminal courts.[80] Here again there is a scalar incongruity along the

75 Fairhall, op. cit., n. 38, p. 95.
76 Hipperson, op. cit., n. 39, pp. 61–2; Zelter, op. cit., n. 17, pp. 262, 282–3.
77 See, for example, Fairhall, op. cit., n. 38, p. 97.
78 id., pp. 96–7; M. Armstrong, 'Prison Thoughts 1' in Zelter, op. cit., n. 17, p. 127.
79 Though interestingly, one of the protestors, Rebecca, did not see herself as out of place – seeing her fellow prisoners as also in a sense 'political' – see Fairhall, op. cit., n. 38, p. 97.
80 Though of course not all defences raise international law points – see, for example, Hipperson, op. cit., n. 39, p. 81 (self-defence).

lines of that seen above in relation to citizen weapon inspections. Just as it may seem odd to have an international law inspection more often associated with places such as Iraq in a local setting such as the Atomic Weapons Establishment at Aldermaston in Berkshire, so too it seems odd to hear arguments about international law in local criminal courts. Here then, it is not so much the defendants themselves but rather the nature of the arguments raised by them (or, if represented, by their lawyers) which appear out of place: local courts are more used to hearing run-of-the-mill cases involving local criminals than the exotica of cases with 'foreign' defendants raising complex, international law-based defence arguments. The place for international law, many might think, is in 'truly' international court settings such as The Hague. At most, and perhaps increasingly often these days, one might expect to see international law arguments being made before higher national courts. However, it still seems an unexpected affront to the system for such arguments to be heard before a local criminal court. This perhaps goes some way to explaining why, as we saw earlier, most magistrates' courts – both during Greenham time and more recently – have tended to ignore international law arguments. They are out of place in such courts. It may also help to explain, again as we saw earlier, why the higher courts in both Scotland and England and Wales have since placed a firm brake on the ability to raise such arguments as justificatory defences for criminal protest activity.

In terms of framing, a number of observations can be made. First, by deliberately framing their defences in terms of international law in parochial, local court settings, there is again a sense of the theatre of the absurd at play here: the striking scalar juxtaposition undoubtedly adds a degree of power to their case in a rhetorical sense while, at the same time, reducing its power in strictly legal terms because of its bravura, 'out-of-place' absurdity. Second, one might point to a tension in the context of the account given earlier of how reframing can be seen as a way of bridging ideological gulfs. On the one hand, there is a certain consistency here with such an account in so far as the prosecution's attempts to frame the actions of protestors as, say, criminal damage – a very spatially localized form of crime – are resisted and reframed in globalized terms by the protestors as efforts to prevent criminal breaches of international law in accordance with the Nuremberg principles.[81] However, on the other hand, Angie Zelter – one of the key founder members of the United Kingdom Ploughshares movement – has also sought to reframe 'criminal damage' in terms of 'people's disarmament'.[82] This not only lacks a globalized, international frame, but also involves a step back towards the contested ideological waters of the intractable disarmament

---

81 See, for example, Zelter, op. cit., n. 17, pp. 48–52.
82 id. See, for example, the title of the book itself and also pp. 47, 52. On p. 52, she simultaneously also refers to the other frame of 'nuclear crime prevention'.

versus deterrence debate. In this respect, there is a potential for inconsistencies to creep in to different forms of framing.

CONCLUSION

The argument that has been made in this article is that, in studying the use of law by social movements, issues of space, place, and scale matter. Geography is, in other words, crucial to legal mobilization. We have seen this in a number of respects. However, for the purposes of the current issue, the most noteworthy example lies in relation to the use of international law in both citizens' weapons inspections and civil disobedience court cases. In both of these contexts, international law is relied upon as a frame for two reasons: first, because it presents an apparently more neutral framing to movement claims than previous, contested calls for unilateral disarmament; and second, in relation to the politics of place, because it enables the anti-nuclear movement to attempt to resist localizing tendencies and to reassert issues as properly global ones. However, as we have seen, this international or globalized reframing, in the particular local contexts in which it is employed (military bases, criminal courts), is at the same time potentially a source of strength and weakness. The power of the frame derives from the scalar contrast it involves and seeks to close up. However, for some people – perhaps many – the scalar contrast may lead them to feel that the frame is simply too much 'out of place' and therefore in the realms of the absurd.

JOURNAL OF LAW AND SOCIETY
VOLUME 36, NUMBER 1, MARCH 2009
ISSN: 0263-323X, pp. 110–28

Globalizing Regulation: Reaching Beyond the Borders of Chemical Safety

Veerle Heyvaert*

This article argues that although globalization can benefit both exporters and importers of regulation in absolute terms, it may turn the globalization of regulation into a game with relative winners and losers. Using the EU REACH Regulation of chemicals as a case study, it explores the normative, social, economic, and strategic reasons that push the EU to promote the global adoption of REACH. Notwithstanding its attractions, rules globalization may result in a mismatch between global norms and local priorities, particularly for developing countries. It reduces regulatory diversity, and amplifies the strengths but equally the weaknesses of the dominant regulatory framework. While it can foster international trade through mutual recognition of regulatory decisions and the development of trans-national regulatory frameworks, it increases the likelihood of conflict and trade flow desequilibria. The article calls for further careful consideration of rules globalization, so that harmonization does not come at the expense of local interests and values.

INTRODUCTION

What propels the globalization of health and environmental regulation, and what are the likely consequences of regulatory globalization processes? These two questions, which form the backbone of this article, inquire into the fundamental nature of 'rules globalization'. Whereas market globalization is characterized by a free flows of goods, services, labour, and capital across national borders, rules globalization refers to the regional or global diffusion

* Law Department, London School of Economics and Political Science, Houghton Street, London WC2A 2AE, England
V.Heyvaert@lse.ac.uk

I am grateful to Rob Baldwin, Damian Chalmers, Elizabeth Fisher, Maria Lee, and Eckhard Rehbinder for comments on an earlier version of this article. Any mistakes are mine.

of normative frameworks. Rules globalization assumes many shapes and forms, from entirely privately orchestrated initiatives by, typically, firms agreeing to adhere to voluntary codes of practice, such as the Responsible Care programme in the chemicals sector,[1] to states being persuaded to import mandatory regulatory frameworks developed and adopted by other states. This article concerns itself with the latter variety. I will argue that, just as the influx of imported goods has profound and sometimes disruptive effects on local production and domestic markets, so does the importation of foreign regulatory norms and procedures put pressure on local regulatory priorities, cultures, and practices. The article identifies five challenges that rules-importing countries, and in some cases both importers and exporters of regulation, are likely to face. First, there is the risk of a mismatch between global norms and local regulatory priorities. The second and third challenges address the risks generated by increasing regulatory uniformity, namely, the development of 'regulatory monocultures' and the amplification of both strengths and weaknesses of a dominant regulatory approach. The fourth and fifth challenges consider the process of rules importation as a first step in the development of transnational regulatory governance, and contemplate some of the trade-offs between regulatory sovereignty and transnational recognition of domestic rule making. In identifying these challenges, the aim of the article is not to condemn rules globalization as necessarily pernicious, but to take a preliminary step towards a discussion of responsible and responsive models of rules globalization, that reconcile global agendas with local needs and capacities.

GLOBALIZING REGULATION: REACH AS A CASE STUDY IN GLOBAL NORM DEVELOPMENT

The 2006 EU Regulation on the Registration, Evaluation, Authorisation and Restriction of Chemicals (REACH Regulation)[2] is a rewarding field to study questions of rules globalization, as it is a quintessential example of contemporary health and environmental regulation that addresses global risks. Moreover, REACH is a regulatory framework for which globalization is positively advocated by the EU, and actively contemplated by non-EU countries. This paper does not offer a full overview of the regulation's provisions or the institutional framework in which they operate; instead, it will concentrate on those features relevant to the discussion of rules globalization as they come up.[3]

---

1 See <http://www.responsiblecare.org>.
2 [2006] OJ L396/1.
3 For a fuller treatment of the regulation's provisions, see J. Scott, 'REACH: Combining Harmonization and Dynamism in the Regulation of Chemicals' in *Environmental Protection: European Law and Governance,* ed. J. Scott (2009); C.

111

Briefly, REACH aims to improve chemical safety while strengthening innovation and competitiveness in the European chemicals market. This goal is targeted through the adoption of a 'no data, no market' approach: chemicals, whether old or new, may only be produced or marketed within the EU if they have been registered with the European Chemicals Agency (ECHA). Registration is conditioned upon the supply of technical and testing data, provided by the private sector. Private data production and supply is intended both to foster the self-regulatory prowess of the chemicals industry, and to flag up chemicals that may require regulatory follow-up. Further assessment of chemicals of concern is organized through a substance evaluation process, where the European Commission, in consultation with the member states, draws up priority lists of chemicals for assessment, delegates the task of risk assessment to the member states, and uses the resulting risk assessments and recommendations to determine whether and which chemical risk reduction measures are indicated. Under the regulation, risk reduction measures assume two main forms: first, an authorization requirement for chemicals 'of very high concern', which requires private applicants to prove that the chemical risks in question are adequately controlled or minimized; and, second, the adoption of marketing and use restrictions, which, for instance, cap the concentration in which a chemical may be marketed. The REACH Regulation is more demanding, with greater scope for regulatory restrictions, than non-EU chemical safety frameworks such as the United States' Toxic Substances Control Act (TSCA). Moreover, as both the 'no data, no market' and authorization provisions condition market access upon production of data (registration) or proof of safety, REACH is said to embody a precautionary approach to chemical risks.[4]

WHY EXPORT RULES?

European hopes for REACH to become a world standard for chemicals management are well documented. As early as 2003 – more than three years before the regulation's enactment – then Environment Commissioner Wallström spoke of her aspirations for REACH to go global.[5] The passing of time has done nothing to cool these ambitions. If anything, confirmations of REACH's potential to be exported beyond EU boundaries to regions as diverse as Norway, Switzerland, Japan, Korea, Canada, New Zealand, and

Garcia Molyneux, 'Current Survey: Chemicals' (2008) 8 *Yearbook of European Environmental Law;* V. Heyvaert, 'No Data, No Market. The Future of EU Chemicals Control Under the REACH Regulation' (2007) 9 *Environmental Law Rev.* 201.

4 See V. Heyvaert, 'Guidance Without Constraint: Assessing the Impact of the Precautionary Principle on the European Community's Chemicals Policy' (2006) 6 *Yearbook of European Environmental Law* 31.

5 Communication by Mr Liikanen and Ms Wallstrom – Chemicals Orientation Paper, 1 April 2003. See Garcia Molyneux, op. cit., n. 3, p. 441.

China[6] have become so commonplace that the rationality of the enterprise is often assumed unquestioningly.[7] This paper does not to take the export of REACH for granted but inquires, first, why the European Union wants to push this expansion programme and, second, why non-EU countries would adopt an EU model for their own chemicals management. Thus, we can obtain a fuller understanding of the forces driving the globalization of regulatory regimes generally, which will help to uncover potential problem areas emerging in the wake of globalization, and to identify additional policy fields where globalization is likely to occur in the coming decades.

A first reason why the EU, and most visibly the Commission, wants to promote REACH as a global standard may be their belief in its inherent superiority as a regime to foster innovation and competitiveness on the chemicals market, while guaranteeing an acceptably high level of health and environmental protection. Cynics might balk at the naivety of this assumption; however, if ever a policy were to inspire true belief in its policy makers, to the extent of championing it beyond internal borders, it just might be REACH. The European Commission, led in this respect by DG Environment and supported by a small but influential cohort of member states, was a staunch defender of the regime since its inception.[8] The European Parliament identified REACH as the single most important dossier ever to be discussed within its walls.[9] Arguably, the vehement opposition to the REACH Proposal, stemming both from the chemicals industry which, during the early stages of negotiation, tended to portray REACH as a death warrant for private enterprise,[10] and from foreign governments which denounced REACH as an exercise in unabashed protectionism,[11] consolidated the EU's allegiance to the project and strengthened the institutions' belief in their new approach to chemicals' management. In the course of its gestation, REACH became symbolic of the new, European, precautionary style of risk regula-

---

6 See L. Koch and N. Ashford, 'Rethinking the Role of Information in Chemicals Policy: Implications for TSCA and REACH' (2006) 14 *J. of Cleaner Production* (2006) 31, at 40.

7 'Q&A on the New Chemicals Policy, REACH', MEMO/06/488, 13 December 2006, published on the Internet at <http://europa.eu/rapid/pressReleasesAction.do?reference =MEMO/06/488>, asserting that 'the EU has taken a constructive international leadership role on chemicals safety and REACH has the potential to inspire new standards worldwide.' See, also, H. Selin, 'Coalition Politics and Chemicals Management in a Regulatory Ambitious Europe' (2007) 7 *Global Environmental Politics* 63, at 88; and J. Zielonka, 'Europe as a Global Actor: Empire by Example?' (2008) 84 *International Affairs* 471, at 474.

8 Commission White Paper, *Strategy for a Future Chemicals Policy* COM(2001)88, 27 February 2001.

9 See C. Garcia Molyneux, 'Current Survey: Chemicals' (2007) 7 *Yearbook of European Environmental Law* 331.

10 See D. Pesendorfer, 'EU Environmental Policy Under Pressure: Chemicals Policy Change Between Antagonistic Goals?' (2006) 15 *Environmental Politics* 95, at 105.

11 V. Crawley, 'U.S., Other Nations Concerned by European Chemicals Rules' *Washington File,* 1 August 2006, at <http://www.america.gov/>.

tion. Thus, the promotion of REACH began to transcend the debate on the soundness of this new chemicals management policy in itself, and presented itself as a unique opportunity to defend the legitimacy and authority of the EU as a risk regulator.

Belief in the soundness of REACH, and the corresponding desire to promote it as a global standard, attain further relevance when we consider that a number of the chemical risks that REACH addresses are commonly known as 'global risks'.[12] Environmental damage caused by unregulated, or poorly regulated, use of chemicals may threaten biodiversity, which affects not only the region where it occurs but the global community. Some substances, such as persistent organic pollutants, migrate easily, causing health risks in areas far removed from the places where they were manufactured, used, or discarded. To the extent that global risks pose local threats, the EU's promotion of REACH falls within its internal mandate of pursuing a high level of health and environmental protection for the EU region.[13]

So far, the EU's desire to export REACH has been related to factors that are characteristic of Europe's environmental policy, and chemical risk management more specifically. Additional motivations, however, transcend the area of environmental risk regulation. First, there are considerations pertaining to the EU's competitiveness on the global market. For regulated industries, new product regulations represent a cost. This is certainly the case for REACH, with its stringent standards of producer and user responsibility in chemicals management. Throughout the legislative process, the chemicals industry strenuously argued that the financial burden created by the new and extended data reporting, the testing and assessment provisions, and the authorization requirement would blight the chemical industry's competitiveness on the world market; an ominous prediction for a production sector that accounts for 7 per cent of all EU manufacture and employs two million people, not counting those employed in downstream sectors.[14] Industrial lobbying did achieve the alleviation of some of the initially planned regulatory requirements, although it evidently did not succeed in staving off new, more stringent regulation altogether.[15] If regulatory cost cannot be avoided entirely, then at least the affected industry can try to ensure that none of its competitors escape it, leading it to put pressure on government, first, to strive for uniformity in product regulations and, second, champion the adoption of equally costly regulations abroad, so that local rules do not adversely affect the global competitive position of the domestic industry.[16]

---

12 D. King and A. Narlikar, 'The New Risk Regulators? International Organisations and Globalisation' (2003) *Political Q.* 337.

13 Article 174(1)(4) EC.

14 See <http://www.cefic.org/factsandfigures>.

15 Opinions on the extent to which the industrial lobby managed to dilute the REACH requirements are divided. Contrast Pesendorfer, op. cit., n. 10 with Selin, op. cit., n. 7.

16 D. Esty and D. Geradin, 'Environmental Protection and International Competitiveness – A Conceptual Framework' (1998) 32 *J. of World Trade* 5.

114

The quest for a level playing field for competition is a venerable justification for the adoption of harmonized product (and in some instances process) standards within the internal market,[17] and a similar reasoning now eddies beyond EU borders.

Successful globalization of REACH might help the EU to bolster not only its economic interest in having a competitive chemicals industry, but also the legitimacy and integrity of its approach to risk governance, of which REACH is a landmark example. As indicated earlier, REACH epitomizes the contemporary EU style of risk regulation; a style characterized by the privatization of risk identification and assessment functions; centralized decision making supported by national input via a committee structure; highly formalized procedures for the introduction and treatment of decision-making inputs, such as scientific expertise and interest-group contributions; and, most importantly, by its low thresholds for regulatory intervention, which are both justified and facilitated by an outspoken endorsement of the precautionary principle. In a world premised on the principle of free trade, which has found a powerful expression in the notion of market globalization and its defence as a force of global welfare maximization,[18] regulatory interventions are suspect; they are potentially disruptive obstacles to free flows of goods and services across the globe and, by inference, to all the hoped for economic and social blessings that should follow in the wake of trade liberalization. Being a highly regulated region, the EU is an experienced defendant in the world court of free trade, having had several of its health and environmental regulations (most famously the EU rules governing the commercialization of GMOs) challenged by non-EU countries and scrutinized by the World Trade Organization Dispute Settlement Body (WTO DSB).[19] Several WTO member countries have raised doubts about the compatibility of the REACH Regulation with WTO law,[20] and even though the EU has thus far dismissed these allegations as unfounded,[21] it may at some point be called to defend this position in the framework of an international trade conflict. In the event, the question will undoubtedly be raised whether REACH, and particularly its most intrusive, precautionary aspects such as the authorization and substitution requirement, constitutes a necessary and proportionate response to the risks caused by trade in

---

17 D. Geradin, 'The European Community: Environmental Issues in an Integrated Market' in *The Greening of Trade Law*, ed. R. Steinberg (2002) at 135.

18 See M. Wolf, *Why Globalization Works* (2005); J. Bhagwati, *In Defense of Globalization* (2004).

19 See Case (WT/DS26/AB/R and WT/DS48/AB/R) *EC – Measures Affecting Meat/Livestock and Meat Products (Beef Hormones);* and case (WT/DS291, WT/DS292 and WT/DS293) *EC – Measures Affecting the Approval and Marketing of Biotech Products (Biotech).*

20 'EU Chemicals Bill Under Fire From US-Led Coalition' *EUObserver.com*, 6 June 2006, at: <http://www.euobserver.com >.

21 See Selin, op. cit, n. 7, p. 82.

chemicals, or whether on the contrary it is excessive and illegitimate.[22] The answer to this question will have profound ramifications for the future of REACH and for the credibility of the EU as a risk regulator generally. In light of these phenomenally high stakes, the EU's promotion of REACH as a global standard is more than a missionary project inspired by belief in its soundness, a way of responding to the transboundary nature of global risks, and a strategy to preserve the competitive position of the EU chemicals industry; it is an attempt to find safety in numbers, a rounding up of allies with an eye to the battle ahead. After all, it will be a lot harder argue that a risk management regime is unnecessary, disproportionate, or unfair if it is endorsed by a significant proportion of the world population.

The above-described strategy, where the globalization of a regulatory regime is sought to increase its chances of survival against the pressures of deregulation, is an aspect of what Meunier and Jacoby call the 'defensive management' of globalization.[23] Others however have argued that the EU's aspirations in exporting regulation go beyond an interest in sheer survival, and constitute an exercise in empire-building.[24] The globalization of regulation (which has arguably become one of the Europe's most distinctive and abundant 'products') represents an attempt to reel other regions into the European sphere of influence. This vying for global influence happens at a crucial juncture in time when a constellation of phenomena – ranging from the internet revolution, the meteoric rise of India and China on the global market, the ascendance of complex and transboundary risks such as climate change on the global political agenda, to the waning intellectual and moral leadership of the United States – are said to presage a changing of the guard in global power relations. The export of regulation is therefore deployed as an instrument of European foreign policy;[25] a strategy to increase stability in the regions surrounding the EU through the regularization of public administration along a familiar format, and a way of creating kinship and

---

22 The WTO DSB has already brushed up against the precautionary principle, and the legitimacy of its implementation in EU regulatory decision-making, most notably in *Beef Hormones* and *Biotech* (see n. 19 above). So far, its responses to precaution have been qualified, claiming most famously in the *Beef Hormones* case that the principle did not, or more precisely not *yet*, amount to customary international law, but it has been equally unwilling to condemn it as a legitimate basis for regulatory decision making, leaving open the door for further consideration in future cases. See I. Cheyne, 'Gateways to the Precautionary Principle in WTO Law' (2007) 19 *J. of Environmental Law* 155.

23 S. Meunier and W. Jacoby, 'Europe and the Management of Globalization: Defensive and Offensive Responses to Globalization Pressures' (paper presented at the *Conference on Europe and the Management of Globalization*, 23 February 2007, Princeton University, at: <http://www.princeton.edu/~smeunier/conference_europeanization.htm>).

24 Zielonka, op. cit., n. 7.

25 See H. Mayer, 'Is It Still Called "Chinese Whispers"? The EU's Rhetoric and Action as a Responsible Global Institution' (2008) 84 *International Affairs* 61, at 63.

interdependence by opening scope for cooperation and exchange, in which process the EU, as the original architect of the regulatory format, is poised to take a central role. Following this line of reasoning, the promotion of REACH as a global norm for chemical risk management is but one aspect in an encompassing strategy of offensive globalization management.

WHY IMPORT RULES?

The EU may want to export, but why are other countries willing to assume new and, in the case of REACH, singularly demanding sets of rules and regulations? Perhaps they are swayed by the EU's frequently proclaimed belief in the superiority of REACH as a chemical risk management approach over previous and alternative regimes. The fact that the EU is actively lobbying foreign governments to contemplate the adoption of REACH might even be used as an excuse by the latter to 'sell' a beneficial but controversial measure to its domestic constituencies.[26] Finally, Lazer points out that the export of regulatory regimes can have a self-perpetuating effect. As proliferation is equated with success, adoption by some countries triggers further expansion.[27]

An additional factor to consider is that, even in times of shifting global power relations, the EU is still a good friend to have. For poor and developing countries, regulatory approximation may improve its standing vis-à-vis the EU generally, and more particularly improve trade relations and technical and intellectual exchanges with the EU. This is most emphatically the case in EFTA countries, where the adoption of European regulation virtually constitutes a 'payment' for the benefits of being included in the EU's free movement zone.[28] But even beyond the EEA, EU regulation can prove an attractive investment. For example, it is conceivable that the adoption of REACH, or at least a REACH-type approach to chemicals regulation, might improve developing countries' chances of securing funding for capacity building and technological development under the Stockholm Convention on Persistent Organic Pollutants,[29] since it signals a clear intention on the part of the developing countries to establish and operationalize a

---

26 Compare A. Moravscik, 'Why the European Community Strengthens the State: Domestic Politics and International Institutions' Centre for European Studies Working Paper Series 52 (1994).

27 D. Lazer, 'Global and Domestic Goverance: Models of Interdependence in Regulatory Policymaking' (2006) 12 *European Law J.* 455, at 466.

28 D. Chalmers, *European Union Law* (2006), at 35; A. Tovias, 'Exploring the "Pros" and "Cons" of Swiss and Norwegian Models of Relations with the European Union: What Can Israel Learn from the Experience of these two Countries?' (2006) 41 *Cooperation and Conflict* 202, at 211–12.

29 Stockholm (Sweden) 22 May 2001 (entered into effect 17 May 2004), see <http://www.pops.int>.

stable regulatory and administrative structure that will facilitate the country's compliance with POPs-related provisions. REACH-compliant countries might find their credibility as risk regulators strengthened, not only in the eyes of the EU as a potential donor in health and environmental development projects, but also in those of international funding organizations such as the Global Environment Facility (GEF).

Finally, the pressure that the EU chemicals industry puts on EU institutions to promote REACH as a world standard, so that the global competitive disadvantage of bearing a high regulatory cost is gradually diluted as competing industries in more and more regions are subjected to equivalent burdens, is matched by the pressure exerted by industries located in non-EU countries to ratchet up local standards to the EU level. The 'race to the top' or 'California effect' has become a familiar term in political studies, and refers precisely to the phenomenon of countries tightening up health and environmental standards to match stricter foreign standards.[30] For a race to the top to occur, certain conditions must be met. First, the country upholding the more stringent standards must be able to close its borders to products that do not meet its regulatory prescriptions.[31] Second, the country with the toughest regulation must constitute a desirable export market. In the case of REACH, both conditions are fulfilled: the EU is a highly desirable export market for third-country chemicals producers, and the REACH provisions apply both to domestically manufactured and imported chemicals. As industries located in third countries that plan to export, or continue exporting, to the EU cannot escape REACH's grasp, it is in their interest to lobby for the adoption of identical, or at least compatible, standards domestically. One reason is to avoid the dual or multiple burdens of dealing with different regulatory regimes internally and externally, which causes great inefficiencies in industrial production and management. A second reason is remove the indirect advantage that non-EU exporting companies might gain over their competitors on the domestic market, or other export markets located outside the EU, as a consequence of their lighter regulatory burden.

In conclusion, the pressures for approximation may be less pronounced for the potential importers of regulation than for its originators, but they are nonetheless significant. This is certainly the case for REACH, where the regulation in question governs an economically very important sector, and where the health and environmental consequences of inadequate regulation are potentially disastrous. It is therefore not surprising that, two years after REACH's entry into force, the idea of it developing into a world standard is gaining clout across the globe.

---

30 D. Vogel, 'Trading Up and Governing Across: Transnational Governance and Environmental Protection' (1997) 4 *J. of European Public Policy* 556.
31 J. Golub, 'Globalization, Sovereignty and Policy-Making' in *Global Democracy: Key Debates*, ed. B. Holden (2000) 179, at 185.

Market globalization stirs spectacularly divergent reactions in its commentators. Some credit it with the capacity to eradicate world poverty, misery, and injustice; others denounce (or, in some cases, welcome) it as a cataclysmic step towards the decline and fall of Western civilization. It stands to reason that rules globalization, too, provokes heated debate, and controversy is bound to flare even higher as rules globalization gradually migrates from the realm of the conceptual to that of the applied. The final sections of this paper contribute to the debate on the desirability of globalizing regulation by identifying five challenges that exporting and particularly importing governments will need to confront in the wake of globalization projects. The analysis indicates that, particularly for poorer, less technically advanced countries, the REACH regime is likely to produce a lower pay-off in terms of both global market access and improved health and environmental protection. While in absolute terms it may still make sense for less developed countries to accede to the global norm, the globalization of regulation benefits stronger states and industries much more than the weaker ones, making this a game with relative winners and losers.

Before reviewing the five challenges, it needs to be made clear that this article starts from the assumption that, leaving aside the case of the EFTA countries, where the importation of the EU REACH framework will amount to a full normative and institutional assimilation, global convergence around REACH will happen initially through a process of rules approximation. Rules importing countries are expected to take over the REACH standards and procedures, but embed them within the domestic institutional structure. The identified challenges therefore need to be understood with reference to this assumption of regulatory convergence. The final section of the discussion, however, does venture beyond this model, and preliminarily maps out some challenges of institutional convergence.[32]

1. *Global norms to address local priorities*

However adamantly the EU professes the virtues of REACH as a global norm, the REACH Regulation was incontrovertibly developed with European public and private interests firmly in mind. Whether it necessarily responds to the public policy priorities of countries outside the European region is debatable. Desmond King and Amrita Narlikar recently observed that:

---

32 For a fuller discussion of globalization models under REACH, see V. Heyvaert, 'Regulating Chemical Risk: REACH in a Global Governance Perspective' in *Regulating Chemical Risk: Multidisciplinary Perspectives on European and Global Challenges*, eds. J. Eriksson, M. Gilek, and C. Rudén (2009, forthcoming).

both the existence of international regulation and its direction are determined crucially by the balance of interests expressed in power relations. Risks that threaten the weak and have only marginal effects on the powerful often fail to reach the agenda of international regulation.[33]

Putting to the side for a moment the economic and global political pressures towards rules importation, it is indeed questionable whether the potential health and environmental impacts of the production, marketing, and use of industrial chemicals reach a sufficiently high level of concern in some of the world's poorer regions to warrant the introduction of an expansive and highly sophisticated risk management regime, particularly when we factor in the many acute threats to basic health and welfare with which developing countries contend.

Even if chemical risks of the type controlled by REACH attain a sufficiently high level of salience to warrant new or stronger regulatory intervention, the REACH approach to chemicals management may not be most effective response for countries with limited public resources. On the plus side, the privatization of data production and risk assessment responsibilities alleviates the regulatory burden, making REACH more easily transportable than risk regimes that rely predominantly on public data gathering and assessment. To the extent that the information production and distribution under REACH results in pre-emptive management decisions, for instance, safer handling and use of chemicals as a result of more and better information being passed down the production chain, privatized data production and assessment has a positive knock-on effect on management. On the other hand, the EU implementation of REACH shows that public administration must play an important facilitating and supporting part in the registration scheme, which implies a change rather than reduction of public responsibility.[34] Early data from the EU indicates that ECHA is already buckling under the weight of the administrative design that REACH has called into life,[35] hardly an encouraging omen for other, less affluent administrations. Moreover, the substance evaluation and authorization tasks are structured around a typical EU, highly formalized and strongly expertise-dependent, mode of decision making.[36] The introduction of decision-making protocols that outstrip the technical capacity of the rules-importing country fundamentally jeopardizes the legitimacy of the risk governance regime, which exposes itself to alternate indictments of sub-standard or irresponsibly slow decision-making.

---

33 Desmond King and Amrita Narlikar, 'The New Risk Regulators? International Organisations and Globalization' *Political Q.* (2003) 345.
34 See, for example, the mandate of the UK REACH Competent Authority, set out at <http://www.hse.gov.uk/reach/compauth.htm>.
35 'EU Chemicals Agency "Could Go Bust by 2011"' *ENDS Europe Daily*, 14 July 2008.
36 M. Lee, *EU Environmental Law. Challenges, Change, and Decision-Making* (2005) 79–97.

2. Superweeds in the regulatory landscape

Following on from the previous observations, we might question the inherent desirability of globally dominant regulatory frameworks that successfully outcompete alternative models.[37] We know from the physical world that the survival of the fittest comes at a price; not only through the reduction of diversity and the corresponding impoverishment of our environment and culture, but also by increasing our dependence upon the continued success of a single variety of a species. Similarly, global reliance on a singular model of regulation reduces diversity in the regulatory landscape.[38] If we accept regulation as a cultural phenomenon,[39] then the globalization of regulation raises similar concerns of cultural imperialism to the worldwide diffusion of major brands that push local production to extinction. Also, the globalization of regulation may limit opportunities for comparative learning and exchange, which narrows the basis for review and reform.[40] In areas such as risk regulation, where review and reform processes are an integral part of the regulatory design, this could lead to sub-optimal regulatory outcomes.

We might note with some relief that the comparison between organic and regulatory superweeds falls down on the point of irreversibility. Plant or animal varieties, once pushed to the point of extinction by hardier competitors, cannot be brought back to life. By contrast, regulatory frameworks continue to be open to diversification and change, even if they have gone through a period of 'monoculture'. This, however, seriously underestimates the compelling power of regulatory path dependency.[41] A detailed assessment of the resilience of regulatory frameworks exceeds the scope of this article, however, it is readily observed that, once a state has made the substantial commitment to adopt and implement REACH, creating a range of new institutions, functions, and corresponding interests in the process, it would be supremely difficult and disruptive to undo the exercise. Reform is rarely revolutionary. The very reform process that led to REACH within the

---

37 Compare G. Peters, 'Policy Reform: Is Uniformity the Answer?' (2003) *Political Q.* 421.

38 For a dissenting opinion, see E. Fisher, 'The Perfect Storm of REACH: Charting Regulatory Controversy in the Age of Information, Sustainable Development, and Globalization' (2008) 11 *J. of Risk Research* 541, at 555, placing a stronger emphasis on the receiving environment's capacity to process and modify imported rules through the prism of local legal and political culture. Note, however, that local differentiation could result in stronger tensions in the area of equivalence claims and mutual recognition (see below).

39 Compare J. Abraham, 'Regulatory Science as Culture' (2002) 11 *Science as Culture* 309, at 310.

40 V. Heyvaert, 'Codification and Centralisation of Environmental Law: a UK Perspective' (2005) *Rivista Italiana di Diritto Pubblico Comunitario* 1329.

41 See K. Heine and W. Kerber, 'European Corporate Laws, Regulatory Competition and Path Dependence' (2002) 13 *European J. of Law and Economics* 47; C. Hood, H. Rothstein, and R. Baldwin, *The Government of Risk* (2001) at 68.

121

EU exemplifies this. While we should not downplay the relevance of the changes that REACH brings, it is interesting to note that the core dynamics of risk decision making (such as prioritization through substance-by-substance evaluation, carried out by member states on behalf of the Commission; reliance on single-substance risk assessment; emphasis on short-term toxicity testing over epidemiology and ecological monitoring) are essentially conserved, even though they constituted some of the most contested features of the previous framework.[42] The resilience of this procedural format of the EU chemicals management regime is particularly concerning when we recall that it is closely linked to those aspects of REACH which might be far less suitable for application in non-EU regions.

3. *Globalization of strengths and shortcomings*

We have identified the potential mismatch between global norms and local priorities and the erosion of regulatory diversity as challenges to the desirability, even the legitimacy, of rules globalization. Naturally, the extent to which we are willing to put up with these challenges will depend heavily on the effectiveness of the proposed regulatory regime. In other words, if the adoption of REACH as a global norm indeed succeeds in, first, lowering the health and environmental risks caused in the process of chemical production, processing, trade, and use and, second, eliminating barriers to transnational trade in chemicals, then this might outweigh the risks of regulatory impoverishment and of substantive and procedural unsuitability of the global norm to local needs. REACH's potential contribution to the market liberalization objective is analysed in the next section. First, we consider the link between the globalization of REACH and improved health and environmental protection.

It is early days yet, but we can already make a few observations concerning the likely contributions of REACH to health and environmental protection within the EU. Prima facie, the enforcement of REACH would have to fail spectacularly for it not to result in a higher level of chemical data production than its notoriously ailing predecessor, or any other existing chemicals control framework.[43] In a sector where the ability to regulate effectively is vitally dependent on data availability, this is a crucial benefit.

However, when we look beyond the bare minimum expectation of increased information production, the skies cloud over. A number of leading scientists in Europe take a discouragingly dim view of the quality of the information that will be generated in compliance with the REACH prescriptions as a basis for better health and environmental decision making.

---

42 Heyvaert, op. cit., n. 4, pp. 51–7.
43 A. Warhurst, 'Assessing and Managing the Hazards and Risks of Chemicals in the Real World – the Role of the EU's REACH Proposal in Future Regulation of Chemicals' (2006) 32 *Environment International* 1033.

122

For instance, the decision to exclude substances produced below one tonne pm/py causes unease, since production volume is a plausible but still highly imperfect heuristic for expected exposure.[44] A considerable range of chemicals that pose unacceptable risks may continue to escape our notice as they are produced in below-threshold volumes. Even more damningly, the chemical tests prescribed for toxicity and ecotoxicity assessment are no longer state-of-the-art, and can only give the most rudimentary insight into a chemical's toxicity.[45] The situation is particularly dire for environmental impact prediction, since the REACH format creates few incentives for the integration of ecological information, which can significantly affect risk assessment predictions, and does not address synergic chemical effects, even though ecosystem exposure to a single substance virtually never occurs in practice.[46] The upshot is that while generally agreeing that REACH will bring improvements over the previous risk control framework, many see REACH as a partially missed opportunity to reassess and improve the scientific and technical strands of the hazard identification/risk assessment/ evaluation/risk management tapestry.[47] If such concerns invite us to, at the very least, reflect critically on the quality and the legitimacy of REACH in the EU, they should be taken all the more seriously when considering the EU's attempts at managing globalization by promoting REACH internationally.

4. Transnational recognition of regulatory decisions

If the diffusion of REACH as the standard for global market regulation greatly contributes to chemical trade liberalization, then this might balance out the potential negative consequences of rules globalization discussed in sections 1 and 2 above. Considering the prominence of the chemical industry in the debate on rules globalization, the extent to which a transnational adoption of the REACH approach will facilitate the free flow of chemicals across borders could arguably constitute an even stronger justification for the globalization of REACH than the prospect of improved health and environmental protection in rules-importing states (which, as revealed in the preceding section, may be less easily attainable than assumed).

As was the case for health and environmental protection, there is a bare minimal level of contribution that the globalization of REACH could hardly fail to bring about. As the registration, authorization, and marketing

44 id.
45 M. Breitholz, 'REACH – Can Ecology and Economy be Combined in this Process?', paper presented at the Research Conference on Regulating Chemical Risk: Science, Politics and the Media, Stockholm, 16–17 August 2007.
46 V. Forbes, 'How Can Ecology Inform Chemical Regulation and Risk Assessment', paper presented at the Research Conference on Regulating Chemical Risk: Science, Politics and the Media, Stockholm, 16–17 August 2007.
47 Koch and Ashford, op. cit, n. 6.

conditions for chemicals in different markets become more and more alike, manufacturers and importers will be able to 'cut and paste' a significant proportion of the dossiers prepared for, say, EU registration when drawing up applications to be submitted in New Zealand or Korea. Similarly, if different countries impose identical concentration limits for certain dangerous substances in chemical preparations, manufacturers producing according to the dictates of one state can more easily export to others. However, it is reasonable to predict that, with increasingly similar registration and authorization requirements, pressures will mount for regulatory authorities to avoid duplication altogether, and instead recognize the validity of each other's regulatory decisions.[48] This prospect, attractive as it may be for particularly the large chemical enterprises that market their products internationally, unleashes an onslaught of challenges and complications.

A first question revolves around the extent of regulatory similarity required to make a finding of equivalence, which happens in case-by-case judicial determinations, or to grant mutual recognition, which refers to a general agreement between states to recognize the validity of and give extraterritorial application to regulatory determinations made by either party in a particular policy area.[49] Internally, the EU has extensive experience with both, as questions of equivalence of regulatory requirements have arisen before the European Court of Justice,[50] and mutual recognition remains pivotal for the functioning of the internal market.[51] The EU experience illustrates the many controversies that disputes over equivalence, and even more so mutual recognition, throw up. Assessments of equivalence inevitably entail questions on the lengths to which host states should go to accommodate applicants who have already passed regulatory hurdles in their home state, for instance, by recognizing translations of original documents as authentic, or by recognizing foreign certification of testing laboratories.[52] Within the EU, a duty for member states to facilitate assessments of equivalence can be derived from Article 10 EC's requirement of loyal co-operation, but expectations beyond EU borders are more vaguely defined.[53] As to mutual recognition, the EU's regulatory history delivers a forceful message that this approach can only thrive in an environment of mutual trust, which is a rare commodity indeed. Giandomenico Majone's study of EU

---

48 Compare with developments in pharmaceutical sector, discussed in J. Abraham and T. Reed, 'Trading Risks for Markets: the International Harmonization of Pharmaceuticals Regulation' (2001) 3 *Health, Risk & Society* 113.
49 J. Trachtman, 'Embedding Mutual Recognition at the WTO' (2007) 14 *J. of European Public Policy* 782.
50 Case 272/80, *Frans-Nederlandse Maatschappij voor Biologische Producten* [1981] ECR 3277.
51 See S. Schmidt (ed.), 'Special Issue: Mutual Recognition as a New Mode of Governance' (2007) 14 *J. of European Public Policy* 667 and following.
52 Case 272/80, op. cit., n. 50.
53 Trachtman, op. cit., n. 49, p. 782.

regulation of pharmaceuticals shows how insufficient trust between national regulators led to the disruption and eventual demise of the regime of mutual recognition of pharmaceutical approvals as initially conceived.[54] With every main amendment to the regulatory framework for pharmaceuticals – initiated chiefly in order to overcome tensions and disputes stirred up between member states by the expectation of mutual recognition – decision-making powers were increasingly concentrated at a centralized, transnational level. This example offers a number of important lessons for the globalization of REACH and its consequences. First, we should probably not assume that a higher level of trust reigns between EU and non-EU regulators, than in the EU internally. If anything, there is likely to be an even greater trust deficit internationally than regionally. A high probability exists therefore that expectations of mutual recognition will frequently be dashed by a host state's refusal to honour them, thus multiplying the opportunities for international trade conflicts to erupt. Moreover, the conflicts would touch politically raw nerves, since what would be called into question would not be the appropriateness of the (globalized) risk regulatory regime, but the way in which the home state interprets, implements, enforces, and manages it. Rather than querying the effectiveness of one particular set of rules to govern a public policy area, mutual recognition disputes call into question the competence and aptitude of the regulator and supporting administration in itself.[55] Mutual recognition disputes can paralyse trade flows, or distort them into a crisscross of one-way streets, if more powerful states and regions are able to obtain mutual recognition for their regulatory decisions while successfully challenging requests for the application of mutual recognition from abroad. Such development could, again, consolidate the already advantageous position of chemical industries located in the wealthier regions. Finally, returning to the observation that mutual recognition deficits can trigger a push towards greater centralization, as it did in the case of EU pharmaceuticals approval, we might wonder whether a similar fate awaits chemical regulation, only now on a global instead of European scale. The prospect of an emergent transnational regime for chemical risk regulation is discussed further in the final section below.

There is also the thorny question of the compatibility of mutual recognition agreements with international law, and WTO law in particular. In a recent article, Joel Trachtman opines that mutual recognition arrangements could be construed as contravening the most favoured nation principle in WTO law.[56] This article will not focus on this new and burgeoning debate in

---

54 G. Majone, 'Mutual Trust, Credible Commitments and the Evolution of the Rules of the Single Market' (1995) EUI Working Paper RSC 95/1, 16–17.
55 See G. Betlem, 'Cross-Border Private Enforcement of Community Law' in *Compliance and Enforcement of European Community Law*, ed. J. Vervaele (1999) at 7–12.
56 Trachtman, op. cit., n. 49, pp. 790–4.

international law; however, since rules globalization is likely to fuel calls for mutual recognition, we should be aware of the possibility that the WTO will be confronted with challenges to the legitimacy of mutual recognition arrangements in the foreseeable future.

The last and, in my view, most important factor to consider, bears on the potentially destructive impact of assessments of equivalence and/or mutual recognition on the participatory elements of the REACH framework. Expertise-dominated as they are, the decision-making processes under REACH do carve out some space for public input. For instance, interested parties get a chance to comment on authorization applications.[57] Even though the practical impact of public participation might be constrained in areas such as chemicals control, characterized by both strong economic interests and high levels of scientific complexity, at least the opportunity exists under REACH to bring to the fore risk considerations that defy quantification or monetization, and that express those localized and culturally distinct concerns about risk that otherwise easily slip through the mazes of EU-wide assessment and evaluation exercises. Equivalence assessments or mutual recognition could erode the already modest role of civil society in risk decision-making, since they could compel states to recognize and give effect to decisions that have been made, possibly with, possibly without the home state's civil society input, but in any event without consideration by its own people. Thus, global regulatory approximation and its 'one-stop-shop' consequences threaten the democratic, participatory legitimacy of the risk regulatory framework, cutting off the avenues through which local health, environmental, and other socio-economic concerns are channelled, however imperfectly, into globalized decision-making processes.

5. *Truly transnational regulation*

A fifth and final challenge of rules globalization invites us to contemplate whether the global diffusion of the REACH approach is the end goal, or a half-way point in the development of transnational risk governance. Will the adoption of REACH as a global norm lead to transnational institutional convergence and centralization of decision-making power? It is early days, but several factors certainly hint that transnationalization may be in the offing. First, the EU's own risk regulatory history is one of growing institutional centralization, with chemicals management reform as a prime example.[58] A second factor to consider is the attractive economies of scale governments can achieve by pooling resources for expertise and administration. In dauntingly costly areas such as chemicals management, the relief

---

57 V. Heyvaert, 'The EU Chemicals Policy: Towards Inclusive Governance?' in *European Risk Governance – Its Science, Its Inclusiveness and Its Effectiveness,* ed. E. Vos (2008).
58 See Heyvaert, op. cit., n. 32.

brought by centralization may well be worth the sacrifice of a degree of decision-making autonomy, particularly for countries with modest admini- strative capacity.[59] A centralized decision-making structure may also appeal to enterprises affected by chemicals risk regulation. Beyond the expanded opportunities for data sharing and one-stop shopping that centralization creates, the larger players in the chemicals market in particular might gain a competitive advantage by virtue of their greater experience and more firmly established connections at the international policy level. For civil society organizations that struggle to gain footing at the local level, too, the move towards centralized decision making opens up new channels for influence, allowing them to concentrate their efforts and develop more cohesive engagement strategies.

If the future of risk governance is, indeed, transnational, then questions of how to reconcile local inputs, interests, preferences, and anxieties surround- ing chemical risks with global risk management acquire even greater urgency than in a climate of international harmonization. The EU experience in this area, epitomized in the field of GMO management but equally drawn from other risk-control areas such as chemical safety and pesticide control, suggests that the path towards such reconciliation is as treacherous as it is tortuous.[60] When we consider some of the factors commonly thought to play a major part in the complex relation between the local and the European in risk governance, such as the differences in risk preference between different EU states, the relative obscurity of the new, ever-growing institutional framework for risk control for those not professionally familiar with it, and the regulatory distance between the locus of decision-making and the public affected, they are of the kind that will be even more pronounced at trans- national than EU level. Correspondingly, the challenge of giving a credible voice to local risk preferences within a transnational risk governance structure will be that much greater still.

CONCLUSION

Europeanists easily get an impression of déjà vu when discussing the prospect of rules globalization. The process of harmonizing risk regulation in the internal market raises many similar challenges of, for instance, accommodating divergent member state interests and priorities within the development and implementation of Community-wide risk management

---

59 id. Compare P. Kjaer, 'Rationality within REACH? On Functional Differentiation as the Structural Foundation of Legitimacy in European Chemicals Regulation', EUI Working Papers, Law 2007/17, fn. 94, published on the Internet at: <http:// cadmus.iue.it/dspace/handle/1814/6948>.
60 See D. Chalmers, ' "Food For Thought": Reconciling European Risks and Traditional Ways of Life' (2003) 66 *Modern Law Rev.* 532.

strategies, or of maintaining a precarious balance between the trade-related advantages of approximation on the one hand and local autonomy over risk decision making on the other, to those that are presently unfolding in the global arena. The European experience will therefore be invaluable when we consider the challenges cursorily sketched above in greater depth, and pursue the debate on strategies to bridge the distance between the local and the global and, hopefully, avoid rules globalization from becoming a game with all too predictable winners and relative losers. Yet it would be a regrettable mistake to assume that the EU experience has taught us all we need to know about rules globalization and stop there. The differences in power, wealth, capacity, interests, and priorities between rules-exporting and -importing states globally are much starker than those dividing different EU member states. Moreover, the mature and highly developed legal and institutional framework of the EU offers a range of tools, practices, and procedural channels through which the relative iniquities produced by rules European-ization can be identified and mediated. In contrast, the scattered and embryonic nature of the law and institutions of global risk governance gives far less protection to the relative losers of rules globalization. It remains, therefore, vitally important to continue our inquiries into the local impact of emergent global norms, and to look for productive responses to identified challenges.

JOURNAL OF LAW AND SOCIETY
VOLUME 36, NUMBER 1, MARCH 2009
ISSN: 0263-323X, pp. 129–44

The Globalization and Re-localization of Material Flows: Four Phases of Food Regulation

ROBERT LEE* AND TERRY MARSDEN*

Over three phases of regulation, the paper traces a narrow range of regulatory interest in food, focusing largely on food safety and the handling of periodic food crises. We suggest that these crises were early indications of the problems in sustaining increasingly unsustainable modes of food production through global supply chains and that United Kingdom/EU regulation acted in part as a palliative, cloaking the wider systemic disorders. We go on to suggest that, as resource pressures become increasingly apparent in world food systems, a further fourth phase of food regulation will need to pay much greater attention to the resilience, sustainability, and security of food supply.

INTRODUCTION

Modern food supply systems are marked by their high degree of liberalization. For over twenty years, from the mid-1980s onwards, food prices in the United Kingdom fell at the same time as the food retail sector rejoiced in the ability of the globalized food supply systems to deliver a plentiful supply of increasingly technologically novel foods.[1] Yet this apparently successful pattern has been undermined by two growing doubts. The first is that the capacity of these systems carried a price of not infrequent disruption in the form of food crises, almost as though, in Beck's terms, nature rebelled

* *ESRC Centre for Business Relationships, Accountability, Sustainability and Society (BRASS), Cardiff University, 55 Park Place, Cardiff CF10 3AT, Wales.*
LeeRG@Cardiff.ac.uk
MarsdenTK@Cardiff.ac.uk

1 M.C. Appleby, N. Cutler, J. Gazzard, P. Goddard, J. A. Milne, C. Morgan, and A. Redfern, 'What Price Cheap Food' (2003) 16 *J. of Agricultural and Environmental Ethics* 395.

129

against the strains of the technocratic pressures.[2] The second is that, partly as a result, the systems were subject to increasing contestation as doubts about their sustainability persisted. Indeed, through much of these twenty years, the corporately organized system of food production and consumption has been locked in a battle to maintain its legitimacy in the face of both crises and misgivings.

Unsurprisingly, across this period, regulation has proved equally dynamic, shifting from public to private sector as earlier state regulation is displaced by a highly complex model of food governance significantly dependent on the management and policing of private supply chains.[3] In addition, the focus of regulation moved from its initial, primary concern with food hygiene and local public health to an emphasis on the containment of food risk, largely corporate-led and delivered within the private contracting of the supply chain. In the next iteration of development, the public sphere re-engages with this private activity, though not at nation-state level, as food regulatory systems become more international and centralized, mapping onto the global activity of food supply. Moreover, these systems are not truly public, because they remain highly dependent on private interest regulation of the sourcing and provenance of food. These three identifiable stages of development are outlined below, but to these we would now add a fourth, emergent and prospective stage of regulatory change involving a shift from concerns about food safety and quality to concerns about food security.

The second and third stages developed in response to food crises such as the onset of BSE in British cattle combined with its transfer into CJD in the human population, a possibility grudgingly accepted at a somewhat late stage for purposes of risk management. Ironically, just as regulation beds in, and, through the third stage, is institutionalized, the second area of doubt concerning the food system supply model, as to its sustainability rather than its safety, begins to rear its head. This happens as the system finds itself unable to continue on the path of ever-falling food prices and finally hits real resource constraints. This paper wishes to review the first three defined phases of food regulation, exploring, with some hindsight, their limited scope and purpose before asking how those models may need to adapt to respond to the immediate new concerns. This is less than easy to predict, not least because the dominant model of food supply has proved remarkably resilient to shocks and disorder, but it is just possible that the latest round of pressures are different in nature to the food crises of the earlier era.[4]

---

2 See U. Beck, *Risk Society: Towards a New Modernity* (1992) in which Beck argues that while seeking to increase power over nature, paradoxically humankind is exposed to much greater risk, and see J. Gray, 'Nature Bites Back' in *The Politics of Risk Society*, ed. J. Franklin (1997).

3 See T. Marsden, A. Flynn, and M. Harrison, *Consuming Interests: The Social Provision of Foods* (2000).

4 A. Flynn et al., *The New Regulation of Food: Beyond the Food Crisis*, to which the authors have contributed and which is to be published by Routledge in 2009.

The Food Safety Act 1990[5] best represents the first phase of regulation even though ironically we are quickly into the second phase soon after its passage. The Act is wide ranging not least because it applies to the entire food supply chain including production, processing, storage, distribution, and sale within all food premises. It is very much concerned with food hygiene, and may be described as a system of food assurance, with the main offences under the Act covering food which is: substandard; injurious to health; unfit; contaminated; or mis-described. It is archetypal 'command and control' regulation with significant powers open to enforcement agencies to serve improvement or prohibition notices, seize foods or close premises. It contains a 'due diligence' defence of taking reasonable precautions and exercising due diligence to avoid the commission of an offence.

As an inspection process, it is dependent upon a science-based approach rooted in hygiene and health, though it carries an assumption that food and agricultural production systems are safe and that the subject of regulation is the aberrant behaviour of mis-selling a bad product. By testing for and isolating such conduct, government seeks to deliver public health and food quality assurance policies. This established regulatory approach, with its on-site monitoring reinforced by a graduated scheme of penalties for breaches, positions state agencies (such as local authority environmental health officers) as the key agents in ensuring the integrity of the food supply sector. It is the type of provision easily recognized by public lawyers in a variety of fields, which, on the face of it, is state-led control of a regulated food industry, though which in reality is open to capture by that regulated community.

In earlier work, *Consuming Interests*,[6] this process of capture is documented. Agencies find it difficult in practice to exercise comprehensive control over large parts of the retail food sector given the dominance of a few large supermarket chains, their global and increasingly complex supply lines, and political pressures for lighter-touch regulation. Command and control turns to compromise as the process of inspection and enforcement transforms into a model described as 'supportive audit' of the activities of the larger retailers. These corporate retailers are privileged in this respect as different sectors and sizes of the food trade are subjected to different regulatory forms. Their omnipresence in the United Kingdom exposes flaws in the consistency of this mode of regulation as the supermarkets voice concern at the disparate forms of treatment across localities within the United Kingdom. What begins

---

5 Significantly, for our purposes, the Act followed the salmonella crisis of the late 1980s – see T. Lang, 'The Complexities of Globalization: The UK as a Case Study of Tensions within the Food System and the Challenge to Food Policy' (1999) 16 *Agriculture and Human Values* 169, at 177.

6 Marsden et al., op. cit., n. 3.

as a local model is nationalized;[7] what is written in law as inspection becomes a 'systems' audit, as models of supervision of the food retailers becomes a matter of negotiation. Evidence-based processes driven by local inspection give way to external central checks of the supermarkets' own quality control systems in a manner which depends on both a high degree of trust and an expectation that the retailers' own checks and standards easily out-perform anything demanded at the minimum legal level.

Retail sales of groceries in stores of the major retailers in the United Kingdom amounted to 16 per cent of total consumer expenditure in 2006, an increase of 17 per cent from 2000. The number of product lines supplied by the 'big four' increased by 40 per cent, whilst real prices of food declined by 7.3 per cent. By 2006, 72 per cent of all grocery sales took place in supermarkets, an increase from 67 per cent in 2000, with sales increasing by 26 per cent over the same period.[8] As we move towards this level of significant market dominance of the major food retailers, the second phase of regulation develops. This is driven by reliance on the private interest in using quality assurance to maintain market position, and a complex framework of cooperation and competition emerges as the retailers seek to present a united front in establishing regulatory reliance on their own systems while developing supply chains which compete fiercely against each other in different combinations of both price and quality. There is no obvious point at which the first phase of state-led corporate monitoring and control evolves into a second phase dominated by supply chain management, and food standards strategies, designed and applied by the large multiple food retailers. However, as suggested above it seems likely that by the time of the passage of the Food Safety Act in 1990, it was already past its sell-by date as a regulatory model, because this shift was readily observable. It produces, however, a dual system of regulation with more traditional command-and-control approaches applying to non-corporate producers and smaller outlets whilst private-led regulatory oversight of supply chain management becomes ever more entrenched for those within the large retail supply chains.

For a time this corporatist model seemed to deliver rewards for both government and retailers. Tight supply chain management drove down prices influencing government in the direction of a largely laissez faire approach. The looser form of regulation offered enough to legitimate the state's role as overseer of cheap food supply, while offering the food industry a licence to globalize in order to meet that supply. There are shortcomings, however, of the two-tier approach in this second phase. Global sourcing of food limits the regulatory reach of national government agencies and increases their

---

7 In a somewhat belated recognition of this, Part 2 of the Regulatory Enforcement and Sanctions Act 2008 allows regulated enterprises to opt for a 'primary authority' as the lead regulator – reflecting the de facto position for larger retailers for some years now.
8 Figures taken from Flynn et al., op. cit., n. 4.

dependence on private-interest models. The space for gaps between the tiers is problematic, especially when in the 1990s a series of multifarious food crises generated a series of shocks to the consumer. These crises, and particularly those arising out of the long-standing nature of BSE, were seen as indicative of government (rather than governance) failure.[9] They re-opened questions about the room for public interest in private interest models. They made clear the difficulties of the nation-state in protecting its consumer population under conditions of global supply. They tended to suggest a shortfall in institutional structure and, in particular, perhaps structures in which 'good science' could overcome previous technologically driven failures apparently inherent in some of the food crises.[10]

In the increasingly globalized food market, the crises also generated difficult questions concerning the extent to which bio-security concerns might find legitimate restrictions on the free flow of food goods. This was particularly true in relation to the European Single Market given the trade in (for example) livestock. The need to draw clear lines on when action was legitimate and proportionate[11] drove a new era of food regulation in Europe. This demonstrates marked features of centralization, Europeanization, consumer focus and reliance on rational scientific assessment. While at national level, the United Kingdom Food Standards Agency is set up as an independent, science-based institution, almost simultaneously there is the significant passage of decision making to the European Food Safety Agency, which seeks to assert its authority on the basis of its risk-management structures. Both agencies reflect in their establishment the need for governments to restate a new (consumer-based) public interest in food, to rid pre-existing institutions (like MAFF in the United Kingdom) of the public stigma of being the handmaidens of the corporate food sector, and to give greater emphasis to scientifically-based risk management and risk communication.[12] A key conundrum for governments remained: how to re-institutionalize food (thereby quelling consumer concerns over food safety) at the same time as continuing to promote it as a vibrant and rapidly integrating sector in the European economic market.

To some degree the development of this third phase of regulation contains problematic features. On one hand it serves trade liberalization and further retailer-led internationalization of supply chains. Regulation facilitates the free movement of food products by eliminating barriers within the single market constructed in the name of risk management. At the same time one

---

9 S. Dealler, *Lethal Legacy: BSE – the Search for Truth* (1996).

10 P. Van Zwanenberg and E. Millstone, *BSE: Risk, Science, and Governance* (2005).

11 Arising out of WTO disputes such as *Beef Hormones* and *Biotech Products* – see the summary in D. Orden, and D. Roberts, 'Food Regulation and Trade under the WTO: Ten Years in Perspective' (2007) 37 *Agricultural Economics* 103.

12 See Commission of the European Communities, *White Paper on Food Safety*, COM (2000) 719 final.

significant effect has been to stimulate the private regulation of food quality by the growth of retailer-led food quality protocols[13] which lie above and beyond baseline EU and national regulatory systems. Other jurisdictions, and particularly the United States of America, would claim that many of these institutional structures have the effect of further defending barriers erected around the European market. Yet, to the extent that they resolve arguments concerning national veto on food imports, these institutions and institutional arrangements serve the liberalization agenda, while forming a reassertion of public interest regulation, thereby, to some degree, reining in the neo-liberal licence. Indeed, a key area of tension in this model concerns the revised public and private responsibilities for consumer welfare with regard to food goods, and how this rebalances both productionist and consumerist interests. Therefore, this most recent phase of food regulation blurs further public and private regulatory boundaries making it more difficult to establish the territories of each sector. In this sense, it is a more hybrid governance model, in which both the public and private sectors strive to codify, rationalize, and regulate the safety and quality of foods. They do so at the same time as attempting to maintain the growth and vitality of a technologically driven intensive food production and processing system; one which is becoming all the more dominated by highly concentrated private sector actors. In this sense, the hybrid model, however sophisticated it becomes, also remains vulnerable to continuing food crises. As we shall see, it is, despite its dominance, increasingly exposed as a palliative solution to the inherent vulnerabilities that are generated by the intensive food system.

STRESS AND SUSTAINABILITY

It is the intention of the latter part of this paper to highlight a likely fourth phase of regulation in which concerns with food safety reorientate themselves towards questions of food security. Before doing so, we will attempt to make the case that the same stresses in the food system underlie both sets of concerns about safety *and* security. For in both cases, the concerns are generated because elements of the modern food system are increasingly unsustainable. The first part of this thesis is that food and bio-security crises are a feature, and arise out, of the nature of modern food production and supply systems. No matter how much the liberalized food system makes claims of technological sophistication, paradoxically, it has not proved capable of overcoming periodic shocks to its structure. Even in our third phase of regulation, for instance, food scares and safety issues are only

---

13 Such as GlobalGap, formerly EurepGap. and see M. Hatanaka, and L. Busch. 'Third-Party Certification in the Global Agrifood System: An Objective or Socially Mediated Governance Mechanism?' (2008) 48 *Sociologia Ruralis* 73.

134

contained under the surface. The more integrated, mobile, and technologically sophisticated the food production framework becomes, the more it
seems to invite periodic crisis. Indeed the main pressures on the evolving
regulatory models have been the need to support the advanced capitalist,
corporate-governed, food production and consumption system, in its delivery
of the economic benefit of cheap food, while coping with an unremitting
series of traumas that undermined public and consumer confidence, thereby
threatening the legitimacy of the regulatory effort. In dealing with these
contingencies, as in the case of foot and mouth disease, efforts have been
expended to deal with the immediate crisis which have deflected wider
questions of how food is produced, processed, distributed, sold, and eaten. In
short, the intensive system of production and supply was taken as given, with
regulatory agencies aiming to uphold consumer confidence in this system
through increasingly elaborate sets of private and public standards.[14]

Over a long sweep of history, agriculture, as a production process, has
shown itself to be incredibly robust. Entirely dependent on nature,
agricultural production works through natural processes of propagation,
reproduction, and growth. Moreover, agriculture is a part of nature, shaping
as it does our landscape, topography, and biodiversity. It has, then, both a
transformative capacity in the production and manipulation of foods, and a
requirement, if only to produce future harvests or continued agricultural
production, to conserve soils, stock, and the balance of rural resources.
Working with the land and with other natural capital, there is an in-built and
intuitive need to ensure a replication of natural cycles in a sustainable
manner such that these are ecologically, economically, and socially conserved. Agriculture and the environment need to be mutually supportive and
harmonized across seasons, geographies, terrains, and habitations. Moreover,
this is vital if, as required, production is capable of infinite reproduction, at
least by the shifting and marshalling of resources over time as a process of
good agricultural management.

This is such a well-established model that it allows practices to be
measured against it. Among a growing number of observers and commentators, across not only developed but increasingly too in developing
countries, under pressures of feeding global markets, there are progressive,
nagging doubts about the sustainability of modern, intensive agricultural
practices when measured in this way. In the inexorable drive for ever more
intensive production, essential principles may have been left behind. Rather
than natural harmony, it has been suggested that there has been a 'metabolic
rift' indicating practices that simply are not sustainable in the longer term.[15]

---

14 For a comprehensive analysis of standard setting in the contemporary food system,
   see J. Bingen and L. Busch, *Agricultural Standards: the Shape of the Global Food
   and Fiber Systems* (2006).
15 J.B. Foster, 'Marx's Theory of Metabolic Rift: Classical Foundations for
   Environmental Sociology' (1999) 105 *J. of Sociology* 366.

As illustrated by earlier work on the foot and mouth outbreak of 2001, the intensification of the system creates complex risks along its supply chains. Then, the vast movements of live animals across thousands of miles not only 'manufactured the risk' of animal disease but rendered impossible the effective control of the disease once the outbreak was established. Even though animal movements were halted, by then diseased animals had dispersed to all quarters of the United Kingdom and also to the Netherlands and the Republic of Ireland. Interestingly, once foot and mouth disease became so entrenched that responsibility for its combat passed to the Cabinet Office, the consumer interest in policy development to cope with the outbreak was represented only by the retailers.[16] We would argue that this is typical of the hybrid model, in that, during the passage from the first to the second and third phases of development, public and private interests combine in sophisticated, complex networks that tended to marginalize consumer interest in the name of serving up cheap food. The true nature of this governance enterprise is that it is driven not by consumer interest but by an economic model which suggests that driving down cost is a good in its own right. Though pursued in the name of liberalization, this is mere dogma, as the sector as a whole does not operate in true markets because of the persistence of subsidy and the quasi-monopolistic position of the dominant major retailers.

Again, this may be demonstrated by reference to GM crops. There has been little consumer support for GM food in the European market. In the United Kingdom, the issue was subject to the largest ever exercise in public consultation[17] which showed, among other things, 85 per cent of respondents thought that GM crops would benefit producers not ordinary people and 93 per cent felt that GM technology was driven more by the pursuit of profit than the public interest. Stunned initially by these findings and widespread press support for the public understanding of the issues, the government announced it would listen.[18] Yet commercial growth of GM crops will begin in this year and government has derided the idea of a ban as an 'easy way out' which will harm the United Kingdom science base. The issue, for present purposes, is not whether goods or bads will flow from genetic modification of crops; the simpler point is that the government line follows and supports the technocratic hyper-intensive model of production when seen to be in contest with consumer interest. As for the United Kingdom science base, it is interesting to observe that the technologies are specifically applied to bolster the present system and to provide a palliative to minister to

16 D. Campbell and R. Lee, 'Carnage by Computer: The Blackboard Economics of the 2001 Foot and Mouth Epidemic' (2003) 12 *Social and Legal Studies* 425.
17 Public Debate Steering Board, *GM Nation: The Findings of the Public Debate* (2003).
18 The background to this is explained in R. Lee, 'GM Resistant: Europe and the WTO Panel Dispute on Biotech Products' in *Ethics, Law and Society*, eds. J. Gunning and S. Holm (2005) 131.

the vulnerabilities of the system, to sustain the unsustainable. Indeed, Marsden has argued that the dominant role of private and public research in applied animal sciences is to address the technical problems generated by intensively housed livestock production.[19]

It is a central part of our thesis that food crises that focused the regulatory effort on safety arose out of the concentration and intensification of agri-food production, particularly from repeated attempts to compress the temporal production periods of animals and plants while at the same time significantly extending the spatial movements of foods which then transgress under-pinning local ecologies. The results, as with BSE arising out of a change in the natural diet of the livestock, are reverberations as the natural order is distorted and bent to a breaking point. So too, as with foot and mouth disease, as the logistics of food supply move from the local rearing and processing model to one in which production activities are concentrated but spatially dispersed, the risk of the development, mutation, and spread of diseases is heightened both geographically and biologically. Efforts at food governance have done little, perhaps nothing, to counter these trends.[20] Rather, as the food industry has become the largest, most integrated manu-facturing sector in the EU, local and even national interests in regulation have diluted as a pan-European corporate-driven supply of food has shifted the geographies of regulatory effort.

Notwithstanding regular food crises, the food production system has manifested considerable resilience in working with public agencies to pro-duce a system of food governance which, while addressing safety concerns through scientific scrutiny, allows the continuing (re)generation of profit through continued unsustainable practice. This is the key dynamic which lies at the heart of the hybrid model in the third phase of food regulation. It is a dynamic which reproduces capital accumulation through the constant processing, marketing, and 'value-adding' of food goods, at the same time as maintaining a public regulatory system to ameliorate public concerns, and continues to allow a widening array of foods goods to satisfy consumer choice. This dynamic creates, for what seems to be a sustained period of time, relatively declining food household costs (in advanced countries at least) which contribute significantly to inflation targets and macro-economic goals. Hence, the hybrid model provides more than a rational basis for delivering food safety and quality; it provides a regulatory basis to legitimate a particular set of market and corporate opportunities for shifting and relocating both power and profits to those private actors which lie closer to the consumer-end of the food supply system. Consumerization is thus both a public and private concern, and in its continued attempts to create value and

19 T.K Marsden, *The Condition of Rural Sustainability: European Perspectives on Rural Development* (2003).
20 D. Campbell and R. Lee, 'The Power to Panic: the Animal Health Act 2002' (2002) *Public Law* 382.

profits by providing never-ending and relatively cheap food choices to mass consumers in advanced countries, it simultaneously devalorizes many of the production systems upon which such food 'choices' ultimately lie.[21] The trick has also been to obscure and to distance the alleged benefits of consumer choice from their real social and ecological consequences. Nevertheless the continued 'manufactured risks' continue to unfold.

One way of viewing these regulatory processes, then, is to consider how the wider external deficits of ecological harms are indeed converted into surplus in the hands of the modern food production system. To some degree, this was possible because the costs manifested themselves as risks which materialized in a manner that was both temporally and spatially unpredictable, and not always with obvious links to the conditions of agri-food production. Meanwhile, retailers have proved very nimble in accommodating alternative visions of food production (organic, local, and so on) and representing these to the consumer as a widening of food choices while remaining rooted in a dominant paradigm of intensive, integrated agri-food production. This is a process which some scholars have termed 'conventionalization' as new forms of branding and 'quality' protocols are developed in ways which attempt to 'nichify' alternatives to the conventional system. Hence there has developed considerable debate about real or partial alternatives to the prevailing system, at the same time as re-enforcing a consumerist ideology based upon consumer sovereignty and liberal markets.[22]

THE FOOD SYSTEM AND RESOURCE SHORTFALLS

Notwithstanding the considerable resilience of the prevailing regulatory system to accommodate growing tensions, since 2007 it is possible to observe the ending of a twenty-year, uninterrupted trend of falling food prices, and the emergence of volatility in global food markets. This may not be a short-term hiccup prior to the restoration of 'business as usual', given

---

21 Work now on rural development signifies the devalorization of local and regional food production systems as a major feature (see J.D. Van der Ploeg and T.K. Marsden (eds.), *Enlarging the Theoretical Understanding of Rural Development: Exploring the Rural Web* (forthcoming)). Debates about the long-running farm 'cost-price squeeze' and the widening gaps between farm gate and retailer checkout prices provide illustrations, while on the international development agenda are growing concerns about the marginalization of many rural regions and peoples as a result of the growth of export agricultures.

22 The degree to which the 'alternative' sector is appropriated and conventionalized by the prevailing system has become a key question in recent agri-food studies debates: see J. Guthman, *Agrarian Dreams? The Paradox of Organic Farming in California* (2004) and W. Friedland, *"Chasms" in Agrifood Systems: Rethinking How We Can Contribute'* (2008) 25(2) *Agriculture and Human Values* 197.

available evidence to suggest that food production systems may be hitting up against resource limits. It does not seem to be coincidence that rising prices for food coincided with significant increases in the price of oil. The hydro-carbon inputs to the food system are multifarious but fertilizers may account for two-thirds of those inputs alone before energy used for processing or transportation.[23] Highly intensive growing faces this type of input cost just as the cost benefits of concentration begins to be off-set by the escalating price tag of transferring food across significant distance. Fuel for transport is relevant in another sense; oil shortage has encouraged the diversion of food crops, especially maize, rapeseed, and sugar cane, for bio-ethanol and bio-diesel transport fuels. With the availability of this new and more lucrative market, land is switched to biomass production and away from food crops. The recent focus on bio-fuel production has clearly affected food prices, perhaps contributing as much as 75 per cent of recent price rises.[24]

Mol suggests that it is extremely difficult to mitigate new social vulnerabilities arising out of bio-fuel production because it involves a change in power relations under globalization in which new trade alliances are formed between oil traders and developing countries and their small-scale farmers.[25] This does not mean that the capital will flow back to these communities; it is perfectly possible that the resource base for bio-fuel production will be exploited while control will remain in an agro-industry well versed in consolidation through horizontal and vertical integration in the global markets. Indeed, one envisages a model of intensive monoculture in the supply chain in a manner already prevalent in food supply chains that has yet to prove advantageous to the growers. It is difficult for a national government like the United Kingdom to change this pattern of global trade flows or influence the trading countries even if it wished to do so in the name of food security or sustainability, though the United Kingdom subscribes to EU targets that aim for a contribution of 6 per cent of bio-fuels by 2010 and 10 per cent by 2020.[26]

If deficiencies in oil production generate disruptions in the food supply system, of no less concern should be growing water shortages. The reliance on water for agricultural production is rarely appreciated fully, although it accounts for some 70 per cent of drinkable water usage.[27] This means that

---

23 World Bank, *World Development Report 2008: Agriculture for Development* (2008): <http://siteresources.worldbank.org/INTWDR2008/Resources/WDR_00_book.pdf> 66.

24 A. Chakrabortty, 'Secret Report: Biofuels Caused Food Crisis' *Guardian*, 4 July 2008 – referring to an internal World Bank report.

25 A. Mol, 'Boundless Biofuels? Between Environmental Sustainability and Vulnerability' (2007) 47 *Sociologia Ruralis* 297.

26 Department for Transport, *UK Measures to Promote Renewable Transport Fuels* (2006).

27 UNESCO, *The Second UN World Water Development Report: Water, a Shared Responsibility* (2006).

food traded across borders involves also the transfer of embedded water – often from areas of relative water shortage to areas where it is more plentiful. The dependence on irrigation in many producing countries is vital and inextricably linked with agricultural productivity. But under climatic pressures and with growing desertification, not all irrigation practice is sustainable, involving as it does depletable aquifer stocks. Patterns of water stress created by climate change and population growth are noticeably increasing. Climate change itself and associated unpredictable and unreliable weather patterns form a risk factor in ensuring the growth and harvesting of produce. At the same time agricultural and particularly livestock production add to global warming through greenhouse gas emissions.

Levels of livestock production are increasing as, in countries with developing economies, diets change as people become wealthier. This 'nutrition transition' involves a protein exchange as people shift from traditional diets of vegetable, staple foods to become meat eaters. This vastly increases the take-up of food stocks since, to take a simple example, four kilos of grain could go into producing 1kg of pork.[28] The rates of increase in countries such as China in meat consumption is already placing significant demands on available animal feed, water, and grazing land to the point that, as China well realizes, these countries may be forced to import a portion of their feed and livestock products to meet future demand, adding to the global prices for food. These trends are reinforced by growing urbanization, patterns of food consumption in urban environments, and a fracturing of people's relationship with the land.

As pressures grow on food production, attention must turn also to issues of sustainable consumption. As people become more affluent, they modify their diets, eating more sugars, soft drinks, meat, and dairy – a diet which is likely to increase risks of modern disease such as heart disorders, obesity, and diabetes. In addition, levels of food waste rise. The British government calculates that consumers throw away more than a quarter of all food produced. According to a WRAP study of food waste, consumers in England and Wales waste 6.7 million tonnes of food each year.[29] Any relative efficiency in the supply chain is negated by food waste in the home. It has been estimated that British consumers consume (or waste) food that represent six times more than the available land and sea.

Responses to growing demand for food raise questions about the elasticity of food supply. On one hand, in real terms, food production worldwide continues to rise even though historically there was a greater amount of land given over to agricultural use. On the other hand, the rate of growth in output

---

28 In addition to other inputs, see L. Horrigan, R. Lawrence, and P. Walker, 'How Sustainable Agriculture Can Address the Environmental and Human Health Harms of Industrial Agriculture' (2002) 110 *Environmental Health Perspectives* 445–56.

29 More than two-thirds of this thrown away whole, untouched, and unopened: WRAP, *The Food We Waste* (2008).

is decelerating, implying the need to bring more land into production. It seems that there is land available for agricultural production but this may be restricted in its geography and its contribution may be modest when placed against rates of population growth. Add to this the uncertainties of climate change and water availability, and the prediction might be that although there can and will be some supply-side response to rising food prices, there are doubts about temporal framework both in terms of the time taken to respond and the durability of that response. For the moment, measured in terms of days of consumption, world grain stocks stand now at half the levels of the mid-1980s and are lower than at any time since the 1970s.

Recently stakeholders have suggested that these trends are more than 'just a blip' in which high prices prove to be a temporary phenomenon but that persistent food inflation and even food crisis are more plausible, future scenarios.[30] All of this is having an effect already on global markets with some countries imposing export bans on foodstuffs. Countries are beginning to position themselves within world trade structures in order to ensure food supply. The best example is that of China, which has pursued a number of bilateral agreements to secure essential supplies such as oil, minerals, and now agricultural products to support its economic growth. The ending of the Doha Round in disarray signals the depth of the divisions over the direction of agricultural trade in particular; any solution based on reduction of subsidy may be further away than ever as agricultural production is strongly encouraged.

TOWARDS A FOURTH PHASE OF REGULATION IN THE UNITED KINGDOM?

Under the new resource pressures, it can be argued that the interests and focus of government(s) will have to shift for reasons more profound than those in the three phases of food regulation. If earlier phases have proved effective and somewhat evolutionary palliatives whereby private and public interests, however contested, have reached some form of compromise in managing inherent food risks, whether of production or consumption, now the real social, economic, and ecological 'externalities' are being exposed. In short, these externalities are both far more global in reach and local in impression. They also manifest clear resource interdependencies between food production, fuel, energy, water, carbon, and waste. The fourth regulatory challenge is far more diverse and less susceptible to control than the earlier phases, representing new challenges for private, public, and civil

---

30 S. Ambler-Edwards et al., *Food Futures: Rethinking UK Strategy* (2009). The authors were part of the research team for this Chatham House study; the latter part of this paper draws upon that research.

141

interests. These relate far more widely to: global and local rights to resource use; the allocation of those rights; the powers of extracting value from those rights. The irony is that these 'uncontrollables' have been unleashed by the sophisticated 'hybrid' model, at the same time that this compromising model attempts to manage them.

Under these new conditions, whilst the regulatory role of the British government has ceded territory to private-interest regulation in the second phase, and Europe in third phase, it may be necessary to reclaim some lost ground as the concern becomes not one of food safety but of food security. Food security is an awkward label for a country in relative food 'surplus', concerned with problems of child obesity and food waste. Nonetheless, there is a comparison with energy security; just as we do not believe the country will be plunged into darkness, so too there is no reason to envisage wide-scale starvation. As with energy, however, we may become concerned with those suffering food poverty alongside fuel poverty. The type of appre-hension about where energy is sourced and the stability and reliability of supply might too become equally applicable to food. These forces are likely to become too strong for government to ignore. In addition, the concept of food security can be broadened in an advanced country context to incor-porate questions of the sustainable access to the right sorts of food at the right time and in the right place. Rising food costs have become a political issue, as with energy. This has forced the government to consider a wider more strategic approach to food policy across its whole set of departments.[31]

In the public interest there may need to be a greater level of planning of the food supply system. This is a new term missing in earlier phases of regulation based upon neo-liberal assumptions as rising resource costs and externalities expose the chimera of free-market rhetoric and policy with regard to the operation of food markets. Indeed, the earlier phases with their narrow focus on food safety and quality, and expectations of private sector responsibility for food provision, may be drawing to a close. This paper has suggested that the configuration of production and consumption over recent years has provided a partially legitimate basis for the grinding down of both natural and social capital in a manner that is not capable of being sustained. In this sense, the successive phases of food regulation, as we witness them, are part of an ecological and social zero-sum game. They may, in short, be irreversible within near generational time frames.

The initial tensions inherent in the system as indicated by occasional calamity or catastrophe are now manifested in more enduring conundrums of food supply. Government may become interested once more in the type of system that produces and delivers food beyond a notion that competition will deliver, when that concept was too narrowly drawn to internalize the hidden

---

31 See Cabinet Office, *Food Matters: Towards a Food Strategy for the 21st Century* (2008).

ecological and social costs. This is not to say that government alone will assume this responsibility. In global supply chains led by multinational players, this hardly seems plausible, but government influence and even leadership of a hybrid model may be possible. An agenda of change must relate both to the deployment of resources and modes of consumption. The latter is problematic in the context of consumer expectations of cheap food, driven over a generation by a system in which external costs went unallocated. Difficult decisions must be made about the values underpinning change. To what extent can agro-technologies deliver ecological modernist gains? To the extent that this is possible, there is a clear soft-law role for government in funding and influencing appropriate research and development, though this may entail public spending in an era of recession. But what of values that might see themselves in opposition to technology, whether labelled GM free and/or organic? And to what degree will fair trade goods have room to penetrate a market bedevilled by higher prices?

These questions begin to shape a programme in which the capability, ecological resilience, and function of the food supply system becomes a central point of United Kingdom and EU policy and scholarly debate. The results of that debate must deliver a revised policy framework for food and a new institutional capacity to deliver. It also suggests that the private sector too will have to re-examine business models and relationships in ways which moderate the excessive resource use inherent in former systems. Questions of food waste, transport, and logistics, excessive energy consumption, and carbon and water footprints will become key concerns for international retailers and food processors, as they consider the management of material flows and redistribution of costs and benefits along their supply chains. In doing so, they will also need a supportive and facilitative regulatory framework extending beyond earlier phases of regulation. As pressures for food safety, quality, and welfare increase rather than diminish, new sets of relationships will need to be forged between the private and public actors. These will need to incorporate and manage the resilience and sustainability of the food supply system and shape both competitiveness and consumer expectations. National government will have to take a more proactive lead in promoting sustainable and healthy consumption, whilst also setting a framework within which the private sector can deliver more healthy and sustainable choices.

A major question of our ongoing research with Chatham House[32] concerns whether the private and public sectors and the extant regulatory systems which surround them have the capability or capacity to meet these new challenges. With hindsight, the earlier phases of regulation of food supply supported a process of devaluation of the food supply base and its increasing dependence upon imported material flows. Add to this the

32 Ambler-Edwards, op. cit., n. 30.

143

diminution of the public research and development base in agri-food, from Thatcher onwards, and it is difficult not to conclude that those regulatory systems significantly depleted the overall resilience and capability of the United Kingdom's national food supply system. National self-sufficiency in foodstuffs continues to decline. Since 1995 self-sufficiency in all has decreased by 21.2 per cent and the trade gap in food, feed, and drink has widened by 66.6 per cent.[33]

In times of plentiful and relatively cheap supply from around the world it is easy to accept the neo-liberal view that any declines in national self-sufficiency of supply can be efficiently met by increasing imports without necessarily increasing overall dependence or resilience. Moreover, the positive advantages rather than the disadvantages for the consumer can be heralded as part of expanding consumer choice delivered by the neo-liberal agenda. Both the corporate retailers and successive governments have promoted these sets of conditions. Now, with wider questions concerning the very availability and scarcity of basic resources – land, water, energy, skills – and the volatilities and indirect effects this is having on global markets, levels of national resilience may be doubted.

A key challenge is for a new vocabulary which puts sustainability and resilience of national and regional food supply systems in the context of existing patterns and processes of globalization and, more specifically European integration, to recalibrate both the globalization and the re-localization of food supply. This is not necessarily a contradiction: in order to keep effective markets and supply chains functioning in the future it will be necessary to consider the health of their material flows. As such, the regulation of food supply has a key role to play in creating a new set of partnerships between national, regional, and international trading relationships. This analysis of the fourth phase of regulation suggests that piecemeal strategies are no longer sufficient. Rather, the new ecological and resource conditions, which are generating a wider and deeper concern for global (and local) food security, demand systemic and convergent government and private sector responses. New paradigms and new forms of partnership between the private and public sectors both need to play a proactive role in rebuilding the resilience of food supply. In this sense, if the overall response to the turmoil and turbulence recently experienced is to continue 'business as usual', it will only forestall a far deeper food and resource crisis in the future and serve to ignite political and national conflicts surrounding food rights and insecurity.

---

33 Defra, *Food Statistics Pocketbook* (2007).

JOURNAL OF LAW AND SOCIETY
VOLUME 36, NUMBER 1, MARCH 2009
ISSN: 0263-323X, pp. 145–66

The New Collaborative Environmental Governance: The Localization of Regulation

NEIL GUNNINGHAM*

This article examines the new collaborative environmental govern-ance, an enterprise that involves collaboration between a diversity of private, public, and non-government stakeholders who, acting together towards commonly agreed goals, hope to achieve far more collectively, than individually. Such an approach appears to blur the familiar sharp boundaries that separate 'the state' from civil society, yet we still know very little about exactly what this blurring of public and private adds up to, and what its implications are. This new form of governance is examined through the lens of three Australian case studies. Each of these studies involves participatory dialogue, flexibility, inclusiveness, transparency, institutionalized consensus-building practices, and, at least to some extent, a shift from hierarchy to heterarchy. The paper examines the relationships between new and old governance, the architecture of these new initiatives, the role of the state, and the importance of negotiating in 'the shadow of hierarchy'.

I. INTRODUCTION

The 'new governance' has many dimensions and spans many spheres of social policy. One of the most important of these spheres, and one where there has been more policy experimentation than most, is that of environmental protection and natural resource management.

* Regulatory Institutions Network and Fenner School of Environment and Society, Australian National University, Canberra, ACT 0200 Australia, and Cardiff Law School, Cardiff University, Law Building, Museum Avenue, Cardiff CF10 3AX, Wales
Neil.Gunningham@anu.edu.au   GunninghamN@cardiff.ac.uk

I am grateful for the comments of Darren Sinclair and Geoff Lawrence and of my collaborators on the broader project of which this is a part, Cameron Holley and Clifford Shearing. I am also indebted to an Australian Research Council Discovery Grant, without which the empirical work for this project would not have been possible.

145

Precisely what is meant by 'the new governance' as it relates to environment, or indeed to other social issues, is a moot point. As de Búrca and Scott point out,[1] the term is defined more by what it is not, than by what it is. And where it is defined, this is often done in such broad terms that it does little to narrow the scope of inquiry or to identify what is distinctive about this form of governance.

For present purposes, 'new governance' in the context of environmental protection will be treated as involving a cluster of characteristics: participatory dialogue and deliberation, devolved decision-making, flexibility rather than uniformity, inclusiveness, transparency, institutionalized consensus-building practices, and a shift from hierarchy to heterarchy. Not all these characteristics need to be present for a particular experiment to be regarded as involving new environmental governance, but the more characteristics that are present, and the stronger the form in which they are present, the greater is the claim to be regarded as falling within this category.

Such a definition is consistent with the broad spirit of the new governance literature which recognizes that a shift is taking place in the role of the nation state, which has moved substantially away from top-down command-and-control regulation to a much more decentralized and consensual approach which seeks to coordinate at multiple levels, and which is distinctively polycentric.[2] This approach, in turn, provides greater scope for non-state actors to assume administrative, regulatory, managerial, and mediating functions previously undertaken by the state.

Normatively, new governance is claimed to be more responsive, legitimate, and effective than top-down approaches because deliberation, cooperation, and learning at local level may lead to responses which better take account of local circumstances, build on local knowledge and capacities, and result in greater stakeholder ownership and 'buy in'. It is also, arguably, better able to transcend jurisdictional boundaries than traditional approaches.

Little is known about the preconditions for the success of new collaborative environmental governance initiatives. Many scholars are concerned that collaborative initiatives in the United States of America are producing disappointing results but have only limited data as to why this might be so.[3]

---

1 G. de Búrca and J. Scott (eds.), *Law and New Governance in the EU and the US* (2006).
2 D. Trubek and L. Trubek, 'The coexistence of New Governance and Legal Regulation: Complementarity or Rivalry?' (2005) 542 (paper presented at Annual Meeting of Research Committee on Sociology of Law).
3 T. Abel and M. Stephan, 'The Limits of Civic Environmentalism' (2000) 44 *Am. Behavioral Scientist* 614–28; C.W. Thomas, 'Habitat Conservation Planning' in *Deepening Democracy: Institutional Innovations in Empowered Participatory Governance*, eds. A. Fung and E. Wright (2003); A. Camacho, 'Can Regulation Evolve? Lessons from a Study in Maladaptive Management' (2007) 55 *UCLA Law Rev.* 293–358; M. Lubell, 'Collaborative Environmental Institutions: All Talk and No Action?' (2004) 23 *J. of Policy Analysis and Management* 549–73.

146

Much remains to be done in mapping progress, identifying what works and what doesn't and why, and in providing a better understanding of how to match types of institutional and governance arrangements with particular environmental problems.

This article examines three Australian experiments in the environmental sphere that have more claim than most to involve new governance mechanisms: Environment Improvement Plans, Neighbourhood Environmental Improvement Plans, and with Regional Natural Resource Management bodies. In Part II, the three case studies are described. Mindful that new governance initiatives are often influenced by, reactive to, and contain remnants of, governance modes that preceded them, each case study begins with a short summary of relevant prior developments. It continues by describing the central features of the new initiative and by seeking to identify what is distinctive about its architecture. Part III evaluates the effectiveness of each of the three case studies and examines the particular characteristics which have impacted upon their success or failure. It considers the role of the state and the importance of negotiating in 'the shadow of hierarchy'. Part IV concludes.

The empirical work on which this article is based involved 27 semi-structured interviews conducted by the author and/or other members of the research team with community, industry, and Victorian Environment Protection Authority (EPA) representatives in relation to eight ongoing Environmental Improvement Plans, and with 15 respondents (local government, community volunteers, local environment groups, state government agencies, Victorian EPA officers, and industry) involved in Neighbourhood Environment Improvement Plans. With regard to Regional Natural Resource Management, interviews were conducted with 11 stakeholders directly connected with regional/sub-regional bodies (for example, advisor, member, staff, regional farmers), with 12 representatives of government bodies involved in the programme (for example, federal, state, local, science), and with seven representatives of non-government bodies (for example, peak industry and conservation bodies). For each of the three case studies, sub-cases were selected to ensure they provided rich information on how each of the programmes operates, dimensions of interest to new environmental governance theory and, where possible and pertinent, variations in the different contexts and conditions involved.

II. TOWARDS THE NEW ENVIRONMENTAL GOVERNANCE: CASE STUDIES

1. Environment improvement plans

At the risk of over-simplification, pollution control from the 1970s involved regulatory agencies imposing command-and-control regulation primarily

147

targeted at large point-source polluters. However, this approach softened with the ascent of neo-liberalism, and of neo-liberal mentalities which assumed that many problems that were previously thought to require direct state intervention could instead be dealt with by some combination of deregulation, privatization, voluntarism, outsourcing, and/or use of market mechanisms.[4]

By the 1990s the regulatory state was in retreat, regulatory agencies were by and large contracting, and environmental policy became increasingly characterized by a preference for voluntary and negotiated agreements and environmental partnerships (particularly in Western Europe), or for 'regulatory flexibility' initiatives (particularly in the United States) which sought less intrusiveness in the affairs of industry, greater efficiency, and greater industry self-regulation.[5]

At around the same time as this shift was beginning to take place in North America and Western Europe, the Australian state of Victoria introduced a new policy instrument, the Environment Improvement Plan (EIP). This instrument was designed to reduce polluting emissions from major industrial sites. As described by the Victorian Environmental Protection Authority (hereafter 'the EPA') an EIP:

> ... is a public commitment by a company to enhance its environmental performance. The plan outlines areas of a company's operations to be improved and is usually negotiated in conjunction with the local community, local government, EPA and other relevant government authorities. Where possible, an EIP contains clear timelines for completion of improvements and details about on-going monitoring of the plan. Improvements may include new works or equipment, or changes in operating practices. Monitoring, assessments and audits are undertaken to plan and support these improvements.[6]

This initiative represented a significant departure from conventional command and control regulation in two key respects. First, it emphasized a systematic approach to pollution prevention, a form of process-based regulation intended to influence management practices, to 'make industry think', and to encourage greater self-management. Second (and more important for present purposes), it involved a significant shift from the traditional bipartite relationship between regulators and regulatees to a tripartite approach involving disclosure of information to, and consultation with, local communities.

Put differently, the EIP process is designed to involve a more *collaborative* approach to regulation. Such an approach characteristically devolves authority to an organization comprising government, business, non-government, and community stakeholders who work together cooperatively

---

4 N. Gunningham and P. Grabosky, *Smart Regulation* (1998) ch. 2.
5 N. Gunningham and D. Sinclair, *Leaders and Laggards: Next Generation Environmental Regulation* (2002) ch. 6.
6 Victorian Environmental Protection Agency (VEPA), 'A Question of Trust: Accredited Licensee Concept' (1993) 1.

as decision makers, implementers, and monitors of the governance of an environmental problem.[7] This emerging approach to environmental regulation assumes that there are more gains to be made through cooperation, dialogue, and utilizing multiple sources of knowledge and abilities than by adversarial and government-dominated modes of regulation. For example, the active participation of local stakeholders in regulatory decision-making and monitoring processes is more likely to be sensitive to the complexities of an environmental problem and its local context than centralized regulatory decision-making.[8]

The collaborative approach under an EIP involves the participation of the polluting enterprise, the environmental regulator, local government, local non-government stakeholders, and interested local citizens through the vehicle of a Community Liaison Committee (CLC). As members of a CLC, the stakeholders collectively participate in and are given responsibility for defining and assessing the aspects of the enterprise's environmental performance that are to be regulated in the local area. They also develop, monitor, periodically review, and adjust a plan which governs improvements to the enterprise's environmental performance. The resulting plan stands as a form of agreement between stakeholders for a settled period of time. At the end of that period there is a complete review and reauthorization of a new plan.

Victoria is not alone in progressing down this alternative regulatory path, and has since been followed by several other Australian jurisdictions. But it was the pioneer, and remains the leading exponent, of this approach in Australia. Significantly, this initiative was introduced a considerable number of years before the rash of regulatory flexibility initiatives that emerged in the United States under the Clinton-Gore administration and which have since decayed under the Bush administration. As such, the EIP is a much more mature regulatory experiment than, for example, the defunct Project XL, the now revived Performance Track or, at state level, the 'Green Tier' initiative in Wisconsin. As such, it provides both an interesting example of an emerging regulatory architecture and is suggestive of both its strengths and limitations.

The architecture of the EIP is based on three interconnected and mutually reinforcing central pillars: (i) process-based requirements (which prompted reflexivity on the part of companies and encouraged them to develop more effective internal management and planning); (ii) community participation and oversight (including access to information which was crucial in achieving change); and (iii) agreed environmental targets and the threat of

---

7 B. Karkkainen, 'Collaborative Ecosystem Governance: Scale, Complexity, and Dynamism' (2001/2002) 21 *Virginia Environmental Law J.* 189–244.

8 J. Cohen and C. Sabel, 'Directly-Deliberative Polyarchy' (1997) 3 *European Law J.* 313–42; and B. Karkkainen, 'Information-forcing regulation and Environmental Governance' in de Búrca and Scott, op. cit., n. 1.

149

direct EPA intervention if these are not met. As we will see below, these components contributed to achieving substantially improved environmental outcomes, and the absence of any one of them would have seriously weakened the overall strategy.

Although the EIP has a credible claim to be treated as an example of the new environmental governance, it is in many ways a transitional instrument, rather than one that encapsulates new governance in its fullest form. Specifically, although the EIP involves much greater flexibility, the active involvement of the community in decision making, monitoring, and enforcement, and a genuine dialogue between the main stakeholders, all this is underpinned by a very traditional form of command-and-control regulation and a hard- rather than a soft-law approach.

Certainly the EPA views the EIP as an opportunity to 'regulate from a distance', leaving the community and the regulated company to engage in the dialogue that will lead to agreed performance targets, and the community to act as the first line of monitoring and enforcement. Nevertheless, it is absolutely clear that the regulator retains a fundamentally important role should dialogue between the other stakeholders not result in positive outcomes, or should commitments by the regulated entity not be honoured. Indeed, it is precisely because all sides are very much aware of the EPA's capacity to return to its traditional command-and-control role, that negotiation is likely to succeed – a classic example of bargaining in the shadow of hierarchy.

2. Neighbourhood environmental improvement plans

By the late 1990s, the nature of the environmental challenges confronting environmental protection agencies was also changing. First-generation problems such as the emissions of large enterprises were substantially under control, only to be replaced by much more complex second-generation problems. These included sediment and nutrient run-off from broad-scale agriculture, storm-water discharges containing animal faeces and street litter, petrochemicals washed off roads, and the polluting discharges of numerous small and medium-sized enterprises. These were very difficult to detect, involved multiple small polluters, and did not lend themselves to traditional regulatory solutions.[9] Environmental policy makers began to search for policy instruments that were better suited to address such multi-faceted environmental challenges. However, they had to do so in a political and ideological environment in which direct regulation was out of favour and in which there were serious budget constraints.

It was in this political and regulatory environment that the Victorian EPA decided to introduce Neighbourhood Environmental Improvement Plans

9 Gunningham and Grabosky, op. cit., n. 4, pp. 5–7, 41–7.

150

(NEIP). Notwithstanding the similar nomenclature, the NEIP is a far more ambitious and innovative policy instrument than its EIP predecessor. It not only abandons command and control in favour of collaboration and community-based decision making, but specifically engages with diffuse and complex environmental problems involving multiple actors at a neighbourhood geographic scale.

The NEIP instrument was developed in response to one of the central second-generation environmental challenges confronting environmental agencies and policymakers: the cumulative impact of multiple sources of pollution at a local level. For example, an urban neighbourhood might have an air pollution problem caused by the collective discharges of one or two medium-sized industrial sites, a variety of small commercial enterprises, motor vehicles, and emissions from lawn mowers and wood heaters. Often, these diverse and diffuse sources of pollution have an overall environmental impact far exceeding that of the traditional villain, namely, large industrial enterprises.[10] Furthermore, these types of environmental challenges tend to be multi-faceted and located on a particular geographic scale, with both the problems and their likely solutions being primarily at a local level. While the traditional policy toolkit does include some options for addressing such problems, it does so typically only on an ad hoc basis. In any event, regulators are so vastly outnumbered by the multitude of wood heater owners, plastic bag litterers, small and medium-sized enterprises, and so on, that the range of credible policy responses is substantially constrained.

For such reasons, the Victorian Minister for Environment and Conservation made the case in 2001 for a more holistic, locally-based approach to complex environmental problems known as NEIP. In particular she argued that: 'local communities and state and local government agencies need a new tool to help them address local environmental issues in a more useful and cost-effective way'.[11] Soon after, the NEIP was introduced into the Victorian Environment Protection Act 1970. Although no working definition of what NEIP might involve was provided in the Act, the relevant second-reading speech notes that NEIP is:

> a statutory mechanism to enable those contributing to and those affected by local environmental problems to come together in a constructive forum. In this forum, the members of the local community, including residents, industry and local government, can agree on the environmental priority issues for the neighbourhood. They can then devise a plan to address their agreed environmental issues in a practical manner.[12]

---

10 Groundwork, *Small Firms and the Environment: A Groundwork Report* (1998).
11 The Hon S. Garbutt, 'Environmental Protection (Liveable Neighbourhoods) Bill 2000 (Vic) 2nd Reading' (Hansard Extract, Legislative Assembly, 2 November 2000, p. 2), available at <http://www.epa.vic.gov.au/projects/NEIP/docs/protec.pdf>.
12 id.

Gunningham, Holley and Shearing's research[13] suggests that the architecture of the NEIP involves five interrelated features:

(a) *Addressing complex environmental problems at neighbourhood level:* echoing 'place based' or ecosystem based approaches to environmental regulation,[14] NEIP is intended to address environmental problems such as 'the cumulative impacts of many small sources of pollution, or working towards a sustainable neighbourhood'[15] and/or problems 'where there is no other program or plan tackling that issue, or existing efforts are ineffective, not linked, under-resourced or are at crossed purposes'.[16] In particular NEIP is intended to overcome the long recognized scale mismatches between environmental problems and governmental jurisdictions by providing the flexibility to develop institutional structures and frame solutions at the scale at which environmental problems manifest themselves.[17]

(b) *Facilitating community based processes of decision making and action:* NEIP is intended to provide opportunities for the community (broadly defined) to play a greater role in environmental decision-making. According to the late Brian Robinson (former chairman of the EPA and source of many of its greatest innovations), NEIP was 'conceived as a means of grass roots empowerment in the development of sustainable communities'.[18] Familiar examples in the regulatory literature and in practice of how such 'community' discourses have or should be adopted by governments include the Third Way political philosophy in the United Kingdom,[19] and Osborne and Gaebler's principle of 'community owned government'.[20]

---

13 N. Gunningham, C. Holley, and C. Shearing, 'Neighbourhood Environment Improvement Plans: Community Empowerment, Voluntary Collaboration and Legislative Design' (2007) 24 *Environmental and Planning Law J.* 125–51.
14 See, for example, D. Tarlock, 'Putting Rivers Back in the Landscape: The Revival of Watershed Management in the United States' (2000) 6 *Hastings West-Northwest J. of Environmental Law & Policy* 167–98; and E. Weber, 'A new vanguard for the environment: Grass-roots ecosystem management as a new environmental movement' (2000) 13 *Society and Natural Resources* 237–59.
15 VEPA, 'Corporate Plan 2003–2005' (2003) 4.
16 id.
17 B. Karkkainen, 'Post Sovereign Environmental Governance' (2004) 4 *Global Environmental Politics* 72–96; and B. Karkkainen, 'Transboundary Ecosystem Governance: Beyond Sovereignty?' in *Public Participation in the Governance of International Freshwater Resources*, eds. C. Bruch, L. Jansky, M. Nakayama, and K. Salewicz (2005).
18 B. Robinson, 'A New Policy Paradigm for Environment Protection' (2004) 38 *Clean Air & Environmental Quality* 33–5, at 35.
19 A. Giddens, *The Third Way and its Critics* (2000).
20 D. Osborne and T. Gaebler, *Reinventing Government: How the Entrepreneurial Spirit is Transforming the Public Sector* (1992).

152

(c) *A reliance on voluntary collaboration:* Interconnected with NEIP's first two features is a third that emphasizes voluntary collaboration. Indeed, 'whole of community' approaches to complex environmental problems at a neighbourhood level implicitly stress collaborative solutions being developed between the multiple actors in the community who contribute to the problem and those who might contribute to its solution. Akin to a range of more collaborative approaches to regulation emerging around the world,[21] NEIP is designed to address issues 'which require concerted shared action'.[22]

(d) *An underpinning of contract:* The fourth characteristic of NEIP is emblematic of what Adam Crawford contends is the burgeoning trend of regulating social problems through 'contractual governance'.[23] As we discuss below, the NEIP is structured so that once the plan is approved by the EPA, the actions signed on by the partners are binding at law and are thus required to be met. While such signing on is voluntary, and no stakeholders will be required to participate against their wishes, those who do choose to participate nevertheless bind themselves to a form of agreement which is essentially contractual in nature. Such formal legal backing (be it contractual, court order, legislative or otherwise) is increasingly recognized to be an important factor underpinning the success of a number of similar collaborative and community-based processes internationally.[24] Nevertheless, the penalties for contractual breach are minor compared to those that could potentially be applied for non-compliance with command-and-control regulation.

(e) *Mobilizing new forms of resources:* The resources of state environment protection agencies are already substantially stretched, and in devising NEIP, it was not the intention of the EPA to take on substantial additional responsibilities. On the contrary, collaboration, voluntarism, community-based regulation, and contractual governance under the NEIP are all seemingly intended to facilitate and bind *others* to both (in Osborne and Gaebler's 'neo-liberal' terms) steering (setting goals and strategies and making decisions concerning NEIP development), and rowing (actual implementation and service delivery carried out under NEIP).[25] Put differently, NEIP's final characteristic is its capacity to mobilize *new* resources to achieve effective environmental outcomes, especially those of local stakeholders, who are to take a portion of the responsibility for making NEIP effective.

21 Karkkainen, op. cit., n. 7; and de Búrca and Scott, op. cit., n. 1.
22 VEPA, op. cit., n. 15, p. 7.
23 A. Crawford, ' "Contractual Governance" of Deviant Behaviour' (2003) 30 *J. of Law and Society* 479–505.
24 D. John, 'Civic Environmentalism' in *Environmental Governance Reconsidered*, eds. R. Durant, D. Fiorino, and R. O'Leary (2004).
25 Osborne and Gaebler, op. cit., n. 20.

153

From the above it will be apparent that NEIP arises out of an imaginative vision that goes well beyond traditional approaches to regulating complex environmental problems by seeking to build upon the five central characteristics. Arguably, it provides a 'new governance' innovative addition to a regulatory toolkit that until now contained only fragmented, ad hoc, and largely ineffective means of addressing complex second-generation environmental problems. However, it is important to note that NEIP is not in any way integrated with other policy tools that are available in that toolkit. It coexists rather than conflicts with them, but it does not seek to invoke them, should it prove inadequate in itself to achieve behavioural change on the part of at least some actors. There is no regulatory safety net and no attempt to obtain an optimal regulatory mix by developing complementary combinations of instruments (compensating for the weaknesses of some by building on the strengths of others) and this arguably is the greatest weakness in the NEIP structure. And unlike voluntary agreements that if carefully designed and crafted, can:

> play a useful role in 'lubricating' [the] policy mix; increasing flexibility, paving the way for new regulations without a stringent and brutal implementation, inducing industry to develop innovative approaches, [and] filling enforcement deficits,[26]

this is far from the case with NEIP.

3. Regional natural resource management

At the time of writing, an ambitious new governance experiment is taking place in the sphere of natural resource management (hereafter NRM) involving multiple stakeholders, multiple levels of government, and industry and civil society engagement, on a broad geographical scale. It is commonly referred to as the new regional-based approach to NRM (hereafter, regional NRM).

The context for this new development is the twin recognition (i) that NRM in Australia is in crisis – there are massive problems relating to rising water tables, increasing salinity, water scarcity, land clearing, loss of topsoil, diffuse pollution from broad-scale rural land use and biodiversity loss and (ii) that traditional approaches (and arguably some non-traditional approaches such as Landcare)[27] which purported to address this environmental challenge have failed to halt the extent of environmental degradation occurring in Australian farming systems.[28]

---

26 OECD, *Voluntary Approaches for Environmental Policy: An Assessment* (1999).
27 S. Paton, A. Curtis, G. McDonald, and M. Woods, 'Regional Natural Resource management: Is it Sustainable?' (2004) 11 *Aus. J. of Environmental Management* 259–67.
28 I. Grey and G. Lawrence, *A Future for Regional Australia* (2001).

154

Those traditional approaches have for the most part been based upon the provision of information and persuasion by government authorities whose fundamental role has been not to police agricultural producers, but to assist them to do the right thing. For example, regulation of agriculture focused on the promotion and development of the industry, and even when environmental concerns were raised, this did little to change the basic model of agricultural support rather than regulatory control. To the extent that regulation was imposed, the low public visibility of non-compliance further reduced what small risk of detection and sanctioning might have existed. Only relatively recently has the sanctity of private property, and the widely held view that a landowner is free to do whatever he or she wishes with their land, begun to yield to concerns for greater intervention in the wider public interest. The protection of native vegetation and the banning of land clearing are recent and controversial examples of this partial shift, but still represent the exception rather than the rule.

In the early years of the new millennium the Australian Federal government embarked upon a far-reaching new approach to NRM. Through $4.4 billion of government funding provided through the National Heritage Trust (NHT) and the National Action Plan on Salinity and Water Quality (NAP), NRM decision-making power is being devolved to the regional level. Fifty-six regional NRM bodies have been created across Australia at the initiative of the federal government. These bodies generally comprise a mix of community, rural, and other stakeholders, have formal office holders, and are responsible for undertaking NRM consultation, planning, and priority-setting. They must each develop a regional plan and regional investment strategy and implement these under a collaborative partnership-based decision-making process. These plans and strategies are subject to performance indicators and other controls imposed by the federal government.

This collaborative regional approach involves a style of governance that seeks wide ranging 'partnerships' between landholders (including Indigenous Australians), regional communities, industry, local, state and territory, and Commonwealth governments, and the wider community. Power (in terms of priority setting and how to achieve those priorities, and programme delivery) is exercised through multi-stakeholder participation in decision making (including local land managers, local communities, NGOs, and other ground-level stakeholders), coupled with monitoring, evaluation, and oversight by the regional bodies by themselves, by state-Commonwealth steering committees, the NRM Ministerial Council, and (through the relevant ministers) the state and federal government itself.[29] There is an emphasis on 'joined-up' institutional arrangements, networks, and knowledge exchange.

---

29 National Natural Resource Management Task Force (NNRMTF), *Managing Natural Resources in Rural Australia for a Sustainable Future: A Discussion Paper for Developing a National Policy* (1999).

Because the regional bodies receive substantial public funding there are (understandable) fears that the funds will be either misspent – or will disappear without trace.[30] Accordingly, strict accountability mechanisms have been established including the accreditation of regional plans (process and short-, medium- and long-term performance targets), partnership agreements, quarterly financial reporting, six-monthly milestone reports on activities, and reporting on developments annually such as progress towards targets.

This experiment is similar in its general contours to forms of new collaborative environmental governance that have emerged in a number of other places. In New Zealand, they are provided for under the Resource Management Act 1991, which locates decision making within regional organizations.[31] In the United States, they can be found in Habitat Conservation Plans under the Endangered Species Act and in the Chesapeake Bay and San Francisco Bay Delta Programs.[32] Within the European Union, new collaborative environmental governance is expressed in increased flexibility in the setting of Community norms, accompanied by a 'proceduralization' of Community law, increasingly open-ended environmental standards, and an increased role of a range of stakeholders in decision-making processes.[33]

Central to the architecture of the new regional NRM is recognition that different regions/ecosystems raise very different environmental challenges, that NRM in each of these regions involves multiple stakeholders, and that the resources, capacities, and institutions necessary to address the NRM challenges can themselves vary significantly. Accordingly, provision is made to enable each region to develop its own mechanisms for addressing NRM challenges within parameters set nationally, thereby combining 'the advantages of decentralized local experimentation with those of centralized coordination'.[34] Like the Open Method of Coordination (OMC) in the European Union, it is a means of reconciling the pursuit of common

---

30 G. Lawrence, 'Promoting Sustainable Development: The Question of Governance' in *New Directions in the Sociology of Global Development: Research in Rural Sociology and Development, Volume 11,* eds. F.H. Buttel and P. McMichael (2005) 145–74.
31 K. Bosselmann and D. Grinlinton (eds.), *Environmental Law for a Sustainable Society* (2002).
32 Karkkainen, op. cit., n. 7; and J. Freeman and D. Farber 'Modular Environmental Regulation' (2005) 54 *Duke Law J.* 795–912.
33 J. Scott and D. Trubek, 'Mind the Gap: Law and New Approaches to Governance in the European Union' (2002) 8 *European Law J.* 1–18; and J. Scott and J. Holder, 'Law and Environmental Governance in the European Union' in de Búrca and Scott, op. cit., n. 1.
34 C. Sabel and J. Zeitlin, 'Learning from Difference: The New Architecture of Experimentalist Governance in the European Union' (2006) 27 (paper prepared for presentation at the ARENA seminar, Center for European Studies, University of Oslo).

objectives while respecting the need for diversity at lower levels, and of fostering collective learning 'on the ground' in a manner that is arguably a prerequisite for the advancement of sustainable policies.[35]

This approach assumes that the state has only very limited ability to achieve its NRM objectives directly and that only by enlisting non-state actors with local capacities and local knowledge are substantial gains likely to be achieved. As Sabel and Zeitlin, describing the OMC, put it, the state proposed an exchange:

> in return for their promise to bargain with one another fairly and in a public-regarding way, the relevant parties are endowed with a semi-constitutional authority to speak on behalf of their members and the assurance that their agreements will be backed by the authority of the state, provided only that they respect the conditions of the founding bargain itself. Parties to such agreements are thus reasonably said to be 'bargaining in the shadow of the state'.[36]

Such an arrangement involves a combination of government and non-government actors, multi-party, multi-level, and multi-faceted, and in which the federal government role is primarily coordination and facilitation of regional decision making by these multiple actors and interests. However, while the architecture of the new regional NRM appears at first sight to be designed to operate as a grassroots democracy, in fact it is structured so that the Commonwealth has such tight control over funding that, as in a number of other new governance experiments: 'should there be mismanagement or policy failure, public authorities may take on the regulatory functions'[37] or at the very least, replace an existing NRM body with a new one. As Whelan and Oliver point out:

> while this may be understandable from an accountability viewpoint, this power prevents partnership relationships between these levels of government and the [regional body] in terms of sharing power and responsibility.[38]

In democratic terms, the architecture of the new regional NRM is a hybrid, with formal democratic accountability at the top level (the population holding the Commonwealth government accountable through the electoral system) and a measure of deliberative democracy at the regional level. From this it might appear that, akin to broader trends towards democratic decentralization of NRM,[39] regional NRM seeks to empower communities

35 J. Dryzek, *The Politics of the Earth: Environmental Discourses* (1997).
36 Sabel and Zeitlin, op. cit., n. 34, p. 40.
37 A. Heritier, 'New Modes of Governance in Europe: Policy Making without Legislating?' in *Common Goods – Reinventing European and International Governance, Governance in Europe*, ed. A. Heritier (2002) 194.
38 J. Whelan and P. Oliver, 'Regional Community-Based Planning: the Challenge of Collaborative Environmental Governance' (2005) 12 *Australasian J. of Environmental Management* 126–35, at 133.
39 J.C. Ribot, *Democratic Decentralization of Natural Resources: Institutionalizing Popular Participation.* (2002), available at <http://pdf.wri.org/ddnr_full_revised.pdf>.

and offer more democratic governance,[40] especially through often elaborate attempts (which vary from state to state) to ensure majority community membership and that all key stakeholders are represented on the new bodies.[41] However, the apparent democratic credentials of regional NRM are undermined to the extent that the views of the regional community and the outcomes of extensive consultations can be ignored should the Commonwealth government sufficiently disagree with them.

Again, in terms of power sharing between public and private actors, on closer examination the extent of genuine devolution of power to local level under the new architecture is far less than it might first appear. Given the substantial constraints the Commonwealth can and does impose, and its capacity to 'pull the rug' from under the entire enterprise by withdrawing its funding, what is left is a devolution of responsibility, rather than of power. As Lawrence points out:

> some NRM groups devise regional plans and priorities only to be told by central government that these are not the main concerns at the federal level. Powerlessness – rather than community capacity – is fostered in such circumstances.[42]

Thus the relationship in terms of power sharing and policy development brings up some familiar neo-liberal themes – there is still substantial steering on the part of the states, albeit rather more rowing on the part of regional bodies.

Finally, in terms of regulatory architecture, it should be noted that the formal establishment of (or enhancement of existing) regional bodies introduces what is, in effect, a fourth sphere of governance located at the ecosystem/catchment level (because effective solutions must cut across ecologically arbitrary political boundaries) – cutting across existing federal, state, and local spheres of governance.

III. DISCUSSION

After the heydays of command-and-control regulation and the swing to markets, property rights and voluntarism, it is arguable that environmental regulation, or more broadly governance (since the state no longer has a monopoly on decision-making) may be approaching a new phase. What this new phase might involve, and what its architecture might look like, has been explored above through the vehicle of the three case studies. All three of these initiatives were developed under the rubric of 'collaborative governance' and have sought to engage non-state agents and agencies, but in rather different ways.

40 A. Fung and E. Wright (eds.), *Deepening Democracy* (2003).
41 Lawrence, op. cit., n. 30.
42 id.

158

These three experiments raise a number of important questions from the perspective of the new environmental governance, for practice as much as for theory. Space precludes exploration of all such questions and the following discussion will be confined to the relationship between these initiatives and the role of the state: what sorts of configurations and architectures work and which don't and why? What is the relationship between these initiatives and state law and to what extent is it essential for the state to fulfil certain functions if there new governance is to succeed? Can the state be effectively 'decentred', becoming simply one of a number of actors involved in governance but no longer privileged in terms of power and influence?[43] These questions will be explored below, with the caution that the answers are necessarily provisional, given the limitations of the case study approach.

It is important to recognize that the three cases vary considerably in their degree of environmental complexity, their scale, and the number of stakeholders engaged in them, and these factors in themselves may have important implications for the role of the state. EIPs involve a single large enterprise whose activities are relatively easily monitored, a single regulator, a few individuals representing (or acting as advocates for) the local community, and possibly a representative from local government. NEIPs, in contrast, involve a much larger group both of enterprises, individuals, and community, state, and local government representatives. They are, however, spatially contained (to the 'neighbourhood') and usually examine only a limited number of issues. Regional bodies addressing NRM problems involve an even broader range of stakeholders, multiple levels of government, a broader geographical scale, and a wide range of complex (some would say intractable) environment challenges.

Unsurprisingly, relatively simple problems involving a small number of actors at a single location are easier to address via direct state intervention than more diffuse problems involving multiple actors and on a broad scale. It may be no coincidence that while the state retains considerable direct involvement and a substantial degree of command-and-control regulation as regards the first issue, it has not attempted to do so with regard to the second or third. That is, the need for and extent of any shift from hierarchy to heterarchy may be directly related to the nature and complexity of the environmental challenge.

The fact that the state played very different roles in the three cases, and that they have varying degrees of success, is suggestive of a number of other lessons concerning state intervention.

In the case of the EIPs, the Victorian EPA was an active participant in three ways. First, it defined the mechanism through which collaborative

---

43 See, generally, A. Mol, 'Bringing the Environmental State Back In: Partnerships in Perspective' in *Partnerships, Governance and Sustainable Development*, eds. P. Glasbergen, F. Biermann, and A. Mol (2007).

159

governance could take place (that is, the structural and functional definition of a CLC, and the size and nature of participating companies). Second, it provided a strong incentive for companies to participate in the programme, either compelling them to do so, engaging in a form of arm twisting that gave them very little choice (the alternative being, as one VEPA inspector put it, to 'have regulators crawling all over you like a rash') or providing an incentive to participation through regulatory relief. Third, it provided a regulatory underpinning that could be invoked in the event of failure (which was assessed on a regular basis by Victorian EPA officials). In short, the state retained a very high degree of discretionary intervention and direct control.

EIPs have been a considerable success. Not least, they have empowered local communities directly, increased pressure on companies to improve their environmental performance and, through structured dialogue, greatly improved relationships between communities, enterprises, and the EPA. In so doing, they have improved environmental outcomes on issues of community concern, increased the level of trust between communities and companies, and created a more predictable investment environment. While the success of this approach in dealing with environmental laggards has been more qualified than in dealing with leaders (our research suggests that the changes were less deeply embedded), even here the evidence indicates a substantial improvement on the status quo.[44]

However, none of these goals would likely have been achieved without the continuing role of the state as direct regulator, willing to invoke command-and-control mechanisms to the extent that companies failed to engage directly with community representatives, to develop negotiated environmental improvement plans and to meet the targets they had committed themselves to. That is, an underpinning of conventional regulation was an essential component of the EIP, and communities would have been neither consulted nor empowered in the absence of EPA oversight and statutory support. Indeed, so important was direct EPA oversight that there is very little evidence that EIPs have provided any of the regulatory resource savings that the EPA had initially hoped for.

In stark contrast, state intervention in the NEIP programme was largely confined to the initial definitional phase – assisting in the development of a NEIP agreement and providing some initial seed funding for a series of pilot NEIP projects. Participation in a NEIP was intended to be purely voluntary and neither sanctions nor incentives were provided to encourage such participation. Further, although NEIP plans are gazetted as legal documents, with the associated legally binding nature that implies, and although those who elected to sign them would be in breach of contract if they failed to honour their undertakings, the only penalty likely to follow was the informal disapproval of other participants.

44 Gunningham and Sinclair, op. cit., n. 5, ch. 8.

Was it optimistic to imagine that multiple actors with widely differing interests and aspirations and no single focus, whose activities caused multiple environmental problems, would come together and agree to be bound by common goals? The substantial failure of the early NEIPs (none of which have achieved significant environmental improvements) suggests it was. Gunningham, Holley, and Shearing's research concludes that the primary reason for this failure is NEIP's reliance upon voluntary collaboration.[45] Certainly NEIP has been successful in facilitating partners from industry, government, and non-government stakeholders to come together for the first time to take action to address a significant environmental issue at neighbourhood level. Similarly, the negotiation inherent in the collaborative process has facilitated partners to better understand the interests of others, and to develop an integrated vision and a shared agenda to an extent that would not otherwise have been possible. However, because NEIP lack the sanctions, leverage or incentives successfully to engage a range of key stakeholders to collaborate in the process, the early NEIPs have fallen far short of their environmental objectives. Although some informal arm twisting or shaming could be used to get buy-in from some reluctant partners, by and large this has proved insufficient to persuade key polluters, like small and medium-sized enterprises, to engage in the process in any meaningful way, far less reduce their pollution. Moreover, even where industry, businesses, and other parties have agreed to collaborate, NEIP has apparently had insufficient 'clout' to persuade them to take positive follow-up action.

This outcome should come as no surprise. The history of voluntarism would suggest that where the private interests of polluters in maintaining profitability and the public interest in protecting the environment do not substantially coincide, then (unless there are countervailing economic or social pressures) pure voluntarism will be largely ineffective in changing behaviour. This is hardly a new point[46] but unless and until it is grasped, policymakers will continue to develop initiatives, such as NEIP, which have little potential for anything beyond token or symbolic gains.

Regulatory redesign that was mindful of these flaws in the current NEIP might be capable of overcoming at least some of them. Where large industry is a significant component of the environmental problem, one obvious option would be for the regulator to use 'the stick' and impose conditions requiring licensed enterprises to participate in the NEIP process, and to incorporate NEIP objectives into individual licence conditions.[47] And as the experience with Habitat Conservation Plans in the United States has shown, penalty

---

45 Gunningham et al., op. cit., n. 13.
46 N. Gunningham and J. Rees, 'Industry Self Regulation' (1997) 19 *Law and Policy* 363–414.
47 B. Karkkainen, 'Adaptive Ecosystem Management and Regulatory Penalty Defaults: Toward a Bounded Pragmatism' (2003) 97 *Minnesota Law Rev.* 943–98.

default rules can often operate effectively to induce key problem stake-holders to cooperate with other more willing partners. In this vein, the environmental regulator could seek to introduce a rule that imposed tough conditions (in terms of inspections and the imposition of administrative notices and other formal sanctions for breach of pollution legislation) on individual enterprises, which could be avoided if the industry 'voluntarily' participated in NEIP in accordance with specified conditions.[48] Another strategy for better engaging and harnessing both small and medium-sized enterprises and industry stakeholders to collaborate in NEIP would be for the environmental regulator to provide financial incentives to encourage participation.

However, what is common to all the above options is that they would require substantial changes to the NEIP's basic architecture. While it is conceivable that this could come from third parties (for example, social licence pressures and shaming might be sufficient to persuade large, reputation-sensitive industry to participate), in very large part it would seem that the state is either the best or the only player capable of providing such intervention. In short, heterarchy, at least in the case of NEIP, can only succeed in the shadow of hierarchy.

In the case of regional NRM, the federal government has played two key roles. First, it established criteria that regional bodies must abide by in their formation and operation. In the language of regulatory standards, these are more performance and process based than prescriptive in that they describe what is to be achieved but leave individual regional bodies with substantial latitude as to how they structure their particular operations, or they set out various procedures that must be followed (for example, in terms of consultation). Second, they provide a powerful motivator for the formation of, and therefore participation in, regional bodies through the offer of substantial sums of money, which can be withdrawn in the event that NRM performance is deemed to be unsatisfactory.

An evaluation of the new regional governance is more difficult since these initiatives are still in their early stages and have not yet been subject to detailed evaluation. In any event, since they are designed to facilitate considerable experimentation at regional level, different approaches are likely to yield different outcomes. Amongst the questions yet to be answered are to what extent this new networked and decentralized approach will bring about a genuine new diffusion of labour between governments, industry, NGOs, and others, or whether the limits of voluntarism, the burn-out of volunteers, and the disparity of resources and power of different interest groups will substantially undermine these aspirations.

Certainly the new regional NRM is much more pluralistic and deliberative than previous forms of NRM governance but, given the extent to which

48 id., pp. 969–70.

regional bodies lack autonomy and ultimately power, one might argue that they are primarily a means of incorporating a broader range of stockholders into the existing political establishment without threatening the status quo,[49] which can be maintained through the Commonwealth's control of financial resources.

And it may even be that rather than identifying, mobilizing, and coordinating local, diverse, and dispersed knowledges and capacities, the regional bodies (or at least some of them) will simply become delivery vehicles for government initiatives. For example, some of the new regional bodies have contracted out the consultation, planning, and prioritization phase to independent consultants, which is hardly in keeping with the spirit of deliberative governance. Further, if participation is premised on an increasing level of accountability to central governments, then regional bodies may 'evolve into bureaucracies, undermining both their potential and their original purpose'.[50]

Certainly the state continues to play major roles and these include that of kick-starting the regional initiatives, which often involve substantial start-up costs and other initial barriers to their adoption. Another is reducing risk, given that one of the difficulties in developing new governance initiatives is the risk involved in moving from one system of production (for example, intensive pesticide use) to another (for example, integrated pest management). Government may have a short-term role in reducing these risks if the private insurance market fails to do so. Part of the funding under the new regional governance initiative may be used for precisely this purpose.

IV. CONCLUSION

From the above it would seem that where the state does devolve decision making to the local level, such devolution has a greater degree of success if the state retains particular roles, but this begs the questions: which roles and in which circumstances? Based on the experiences of the three case studies, there are, at a minimum, three clear roles for the state: definitional guidance, participatory incentives, and enforcement capability.

Definitional guidance – this refers to the state describing and defining the nature of the collaborative governance arrangement. These might include, for example, what issues are to be addressed, who is able to participate, what are the geographical boundaries, what is its legal nature, what performance

---

49 M. Ottaway, 'Corporatism Goes Global: International Organizations, Non-governmental Organization Networks, and Transnational Business' (2001) 7 *Global Governance* 265–92.
50 T. Wallington and G. Lawrence, 'Making Democracy Matter: Responsibility and Effective Environmental Governance in Regional Australia' (2008) 24 *J. of Rural Studies* 277–90.

outcomes are expected, what funding arrangements are to be established, what is the operational relationship to other existing institutional structures. As we can see from a limited sample of three case studies, this definitional guidance role can be interpreted widely, for example, narrow and pre-scriptive (in the case of EIP), or expansive and flexible (in the case of NRM). Irrespective of the particular form it takes, however, it is difficult to imagine collaborative governance operating in the complete absence of a government providing some level of definitional guidance.

Participatory incentives – this refers to the state providing incentives, which may be positive (in the form of various inducements) or negative (in the form of punitive sanctions), for targeted actors, be they companies, communities, individuals or NGOs, to participate in the particular form of collaborative governance being established. As seen from the three case studies, these can be take many forms, for example, in the case of EIP, the state legally mandated some companies to participate (that is, compulsion) and offered others a voluntary route through the incentive of greater regulatory flexibility and fewer inspections. In the case of NRM, there is a powerful incentive to participate in the form of access to very substantial funds and resources. In the one case study where there was not a clear and obvious state role in providing participatory incentives (NEIP), this may have been one of the key factors undermining its eventual success.

Enforcement capability – this refers to the state providing an enforcement role in ensuring that collaborative governance arrangements fulfill their obligations. Such a role may apply to individual participants in the colla-borative governance arrangements, or to collaborative governing entity as a whole. Either way, this entails the presence of performance indicators or criteria against which success or otherwise can be judged. In the case of a body as a whole, these will likely be predetermined by the state itself. In the case of individual participations, it is likely that the collaborative governing entity in the course of its operations has established obligations, targets or performance objectives on the part of various participants; such criteria will necessarily be built into any agreements established by the collaborative governance body and subsequently referred to the state for, in the first instance, establishment approval, and subsequently, after a defined period, in terms of a formal performance evaluation.

Beyond the above, a number of other insights may be gleaned. Arguably, there is far less need for the state to play an active role in governance where the actors at local level have essentially common interests – what are classically described as 'win-win' outcomes.[51] However, agricultural pro-ducers, NGOs, and others will not necessarily organize themselves success-fully even when doing so might provide win-win outcomes. Conservatism, lack of awareness of the opportunities, and practical barriers such as the

51 F. L. Reinhardt, *Down To Earth: Applying Business Principles to Environmental Management* (2000).

absence of mechanisms for off-setting risk may all militate against change. In the absence of external intervention and coordination, many of the potential opportunities for constructive, positive outcomes may never be realized.

Thus in many (though certainly not all) contexts, there is an essential policy coordination role for government in encouraging, facilitating, rewarding, and shaping such outcomes (at least unless some other actor is ready, willing, and able to take on this role, and usually they are not). That is, at the same time as the state may be retreating from many of its traditional regulatory functions and from hierarchical control, opportunities arise for it to forge a new role, coordinating private institutions and harnessing actors and resources in furtherance of public policy.

But in the far more common situation where win-wins are few and far between (as indeed in all three of the case studies), then it is arguable that the state must take on more interventionist roles if new environmental govern-ance initiatives are to succeed. In the case of EIPs, it was only because the EPA was willing to threaten regulatory action that companies were willing to engage in a genuine dialogue with local community advocates, and to act on their agreements. In the case of NEIP it was the absence of any government carrots or sticks (coupled with inadequate resources) and lack of any credible inducements to polluters to join, that doomed this initiative to failure. In the case of the new regional NRM, it is the substantial financial resources provided by the Commonwealth government that is the main driver of these initiatives, and the threat of withdrawing such funding is the main sanction that induces participants to meet Commonwealth-prescribed performance indicators. In short, the effectiveness of new modes of environmental goverance still seems closely linked to hierarchy, and it seems doubtful whether such initiatives can achieve their policy goals except with an underpinning of state intervention, either through incentives or the threat of sanctions.

All this suggests that the shift to new governance is not a matter of substituting new mechanisms for the state but, rather, for a hybrid approach which involves a shift from a situation where the state takes broad governance responsibilities (in Osborne and Gaebler's terms, for both steering and rowing) to one where states still plays important but different roles. But commonly, while it does involve some governance functions traditionally fulfilled by the state being adopted by other groups (for example, civil society and business) and in non-state actors taking on a much larger 'hands-on' role in environmental governance, nevertheless the state continues to play important roles, directly intervening (at least when things go wrong) as well as coordinating, facilitating, and steering. As we have seen, many of these roles are absolutely central to the success of new governance initiatives and it seems doubtful, at least from these case studies, whether the state can now be regarded as simply one amongst a number of other actors, all of whom might be analysed 'in more or less similar ways in terms of power, interests, responsibilities, accountabilities and resources'.[52]

This is not to suggest that the state must always play these roles. Indeed, Gunningham, Kagan, and Thornton's past research[53] suggests that in certain circumstances social licence pressures generated by civil society can fulfil a similar function to the state and indeed can induce business enterprises to go beyond compliance. But even here, corporate behaviour is best explained by interactions between regulatory, social, and economic licences rather than by social licence pressures operating in isolation. For example, government can play important roles in compensating for asymmetry of information and power by structuring mechanisms so as to ensure that necessary information is available (as in EIPs) and by otherwise empowering NGOs and civil society, thereby ensuring that collaborative governance initiatives take place on a less unequal footing. And in the absence of such pressures (which are variable at best), recourse to the state may be the only viable mechanism to ensure policy outcomes.

52 Mol, op. cit., n. 43, p. 230.
53 N. Gunningham, R. Kagan, and D. Thornton, *Shades of Green: Business, Regulation, and Environment* (2003).